HAY FESTIVAL

boxoffice@hayfestival.org
tel: +44 (0)1497 822 629
www.hayfestival.org

Event: **Bill Kissane**

Please quote your order no if you need to contact us

Cust Ref/Order: **13485422/501530/1**

Sale Date/Time: 31 May 2016 00:56

Event No: 261

Date: **1 June**

Time: * **11:30am**

Venue: * **Telegraph Stage**

(*Times or venues may occasionally have to be changed after tickets are issued)

Ticket price: £ 7.00

Customer: Valerie Swain

Details are correct at time of going to press. We reserve the right to change programmes and artists if circumstances dictate.

Tickets cannot be accepted for refund or resale. Note: The management reserves the right to refuse admission.

Hay Festival of Literature & the Arts Ltd. Company no: 2258780. Registered office: The Drill Hall, 25 Lion Street, Hay-on-Wye HR3 5AD, UK. VAT no: GB 826 3209 39

NATIONS TORN ASUNDER

BILL KISSANE

NATIONS TORN ASUNDER

The Challenge of Civil War

To Valerie,

Bill Kissane

1 | 6 | 2016

OXFORD
UNIVERSITY PRESS

OXFORD
UNIVERSITY PRESS

Great Clarendon Street, Oxford, OX2 6DP,
United Kingdom

Oxford University Press is a department of the University of Oxford.
It furthers the University's objective of excellence in research, scholarship,
and education by publishing worldwide. Oxford is a registered trade mark of
Oxford University Press in the UK and in certain other countries

© Bill Kissane 2016

The moral rights of the author have been asserted

First Edition published in 2016
Impression: 1

Published in the United States of America by Oxford University Press
198 Madison Avenue, New York, NY 10016, United States of America

British Library Cataloguing in Publication Data
Data available

Library of Congress Control Number: 2015944365

ISBN 978-0-19-960287-2

Printed in Great Britain by
Clays Ltd, St Ives plc

ACKNOWLEDGEMENTS

This book has been some time in the making, and the debts accumulated have accordingly grown. I want to mention at the outset two research assistants, Meor Alif Azalan and Marta Wojcie-chowska who did invaluable work for this project, while Hamid Seyedsayamdost provided a translation of the 'Bürgerkrieg' sections of the *Geschichtliche Grundbegriffe*. I am also in debt to Matthew Cotton at OUP, first for sticking with the project and, secondly, for providing expert editorial assistance throughout. Likewise I must mention the internal reviewers at OUP. Early drafts were completed in 2012 while I was a visiting Fellow at the National Center for the Humanities, North Carolina, and at the Nanovic Institute for European Studies at the University of Notre Dame. I am grateful to Geoffrey Harpman, Kent Mullikin, James McAdam, Monica Caro, Sharon Konopka, and Lois Whittington for making these visits possible. The last draft was completed when I was a Research Fellow at *ZIF: Zentrum für interdiszi-plinare Forschung* at the University of Bielefeld in 2014. Thanks go to my then Head of Department, Simon Hix, for making this visit possible. I would also like to mention Samer Abdelnour, Mark Boden, Richard English, Aaron Glasserman, Angela Hall, Daphne Halikiopolou, Mirjam Künkler, Denisa Kostovicova, Jim Hughes, Hanna Lerner, John Madeley, Alison McKechnie, Michael Middeke, Paul Mitchell, Gary Murphy, Dann Nassemullah, Nick Sitter, Sarah Payne, Kálmán Posza, and Shylashri Shanker. My knowledge of this area has been greatly stimulated by a number of conferences I participated in: 'Beyond Classical Key Con-cepts', Compultense University Madrid 5 December 2008; 'Communi-ties in Conflict: Civil Wars and their Legacies', 4 September 2009; 'The 18th Annual ASN World Convention', Columbia University 18

December 2012; 'The ASEN Annual Conference', London School of Economics April 2013; and 'Civil War and the Statebuilding Challenge', University of Birmingham 17/18 September 2012. I must express my thanks to Mrs Anna Londou, Athens, for her generous permission to use the lines from the Greek poet George Seferis in the epigraph for this book. Finally, I have been teaching a course on civil wars at the LSE since 2006; this consistent engagement with high-quality students has sharpened my ideas. The views expressed remain mine alone.

CONTENTS

LIST OF MAPS

Man frays easily in wars;
Man is soft, a sheaf of grass,
Lips and fingers that hunger for a white breast
Eyes that half close in the radiance of day
And feet that would run, not matter how tired,
at the slightest call of profit.

George Seferis, from 'Logbook 11', *Complete Poems*, ed.
and trans. Edmund Kelley and Philip Sherrard
(London: Anvil, 1995), p. 155.

I have never been happy with the word 'modernity'. Of course, I feel that what is happening in the world today is something unique and singular. As soon, however, as we give it the label of 'modernity', we inscribe it in a certain historical system of evolution or progress (a notion derived from Enlightenment rationalism) which tends to blind us to the fact that what confronts us today is also something ancient and hidden in history. I believe that what 'happens' in our contemporary world and strikes us as particularly new has in fact an essential connection with something extremely old which has been covered over (archi-dissimulé). So that the new is not so much that which occurs for the first time but that 'very ancient' dimension which recurs in the 'very modern'.

Jacques Derrida. Interview with Richard Kearney Paris 1981, from
Richard Kearney, *Dialogues with contemporary Continental Thinkers:
The Phenomenological Heritage* (Manchester: Manchester
University Press, 1984, p. 112).

1

INTRODUCTION

It would be a source of some disillusionment were those who saw in the collapse of communism an end to world history to look back on the vista of human conflict that has unfolded since then. History seems rather to have reasserted itself in the form of endless civil wars, ethnic conflict, genocide, democratic revolutions, state collapse, and terrorist campaigns, many lasting decades. The end of the Cold War showed once again liberation finding its own negation in internal war. This had been true of classic European revolutions, it was the case in many new states after decolonization, and so it has been with the end of communism. Since 1989 the world has become more intercon-nected, clear-cut wars between states remain rare, and the world seems tormented by no universal differences of principle. And this self-same context is giving rise to more and more civil wars.

Civil war is an apt metaphor for a divisive tendency in human beings, which in the Afghanistans, Iraqs, and Mexicos of this world continues to give rise to new forms of warfare. This book takes this old concept—civil war—and applies it to the crisis of which these contemporary conflicts form part. Although gestating since the 1940s, its full extent only became apparent after the 1980s, when the lifting of the veil provided by the Cold War revealed the sheer number and variety of internal conflicts, some accumulating, literally, for decades. This crisis, no less serious than that posed by AIDS, global warming, or population explosion, has persisted through several phases; decol-onization, the Cold War, globalization in the 1990s, and more recently, the War on Terror and the Arab Spring. The years between 1990 and 1994 provided its last peak, but the civil wars now raging in the Central African Republic, South Sudan, Syria, and now Ukraine, have given it fresh momentum.

Scholarly interest in civil war now eclipses that in both revolution and conventional inter-state war. What does this scholarship tell us about these waves of civil war? This book summarizes and evaluates the literature which has emerged over the past two decades, for readers whose knowledge up to now has been confined to a few big historical conflicts, such as the Spanish civil war. It discusses what this literature has to say about the patterns, causes, and consequences of civil war; what the possible remedies are; and what these conflicts tell us about the age-old problem of human divisiveness. The ultimate aim of this body of work may be to guide action. Civil wars are part of a family of problems—crime, ethnic conflict, nuclear proliferation—for which we must hope solutions can be found. If their dramatic increase since 1945 can be explained by contextual factors—which are perforce temporary—civil wars could disappear with more economic develop-ment, more democracy, or better regional security. Yet solutions are not immediately apparent. Short of taking sides militarily, what can outsiders do to prevent the disintegration of Syria? In January 2014, there were reports of 1,000 deaths, in just one month, due to infight-ing among the opposition alone in northern Syria (*Zaman*, 16 January 2014). Civil wars carry with them the shade of mortality. As with a terminal illness, the possible death of a political community could lead one, not towards action, but to simply reflect on the mortality of all societies. The conclusion may be that such wars are not the product of a reversible set of conditions, but, at bottom, the expression of some-thing in human nature.

Not thinking about civil war

Notwithstanding its very dramatic recent history, the topic of civil war is very old. To survive and evolve, human beings have needed to cooperate, but every form of societal cooperation they have devised has given rise to civil wars. No regime form—from the Greek city states, to the Roman Empire, to the nation states today, has been immune. By posing the ultimate question of what holds societies together, civil wars raise the stakes of conflict in a way that is not true for international wars. As Thucydides observed of Corcyra (present-day Corfu) during the Peloponnesian wars, by relaxing legal and moral constraints, civil war encourages people to pursue only their self-interest (1972: 236–45). Yet since this pursuit also weakens all that which holds society together, no amount of individual latitude can compensate for the state of fearfulness and uncertainty people are thrown into. The outcome is collectively irrational for the society.

It is therefore a surprise, and an omission worthy of contemplation, that the topic has largely been ignored by political philosophy. There has been, in the history of political thought, no systematic treatise on civil war to compare with Edmund Burke's *Reflections on the Revolution in France* (1969 [1790]) or Immanuel Kant's *Perpetual Peace* (2007 [1795]). Avoiding civil war seems to have been true for the academy, as much as for states. There are fragmentary discussions of 'stasis' in the Greek classics, and civil war looms large in all the famous accounts of the decline of the Roman Empire in the first century BC. Yet there is little in the way of systematic analysis. The tendency has been to consider civil war a residual form of conflict; as if it should be kept in the dark. Karl Marx's (1971 [1871]) classic analysis of the Paris Commune of 1870 was assimilated into his general theory of revolution, for to Marx, revolution, not civil war, was to be the driver of future world history.

If philosophy began only because of division (Hegel in Beiser 2005: 47), what explains the neglect of civil war? One reason is the greater interest in other forms of war. Revolution is indelibly linked to the idea of progress, while fighting for one's country against another state is generally accepted as an expression of patriotism. Both progress and patriotism seem to be ruled out for a form of conflict that implies conflicts of great violence and brutality. In higher education, before the 1990s most undergraduate course convenors also saw revolution as the conflict worthy of study. This applied especially to conflicts—like the French Revolution—which constituted breakthroughs in some way. In his (1988) study of Enlightenment thinking before and after the French Revolution the German historian Koselleck suggests that those who had the greatest hopes invested in the future of mankind were precisely those who failed to see the coming spectre of civil war. Indeed, ever since the European Enlightenment revolution has been welcomed by 'progressive' intellectuals, while civil war was used only to describe the violence and extremism generated by the revolutionary process (González Calleja 2013: 19).

The distinction between the two forms of conflict is not watertight. In Marxist theory the proletariat was to be the hard nucleus of revolution; in practice, in Russia, China, and further afield, civil war came to constitute the hard nucleus of revolution. In Andreï Makine's collection of short stories, *Brief Loves that Live Forever*, Alexandra Guerdt appears as an impoverished elderly woman living alone in the Russian village of Perevoz (Makine 2013: 49–70). The obscurity of village life was her final destination after a youth spent in the maelstrom of the Russian Revolution. For Guerdt had been very close to Lenin, another Russian revolutionary leader, in his youth. Since she had spent time with him in exile in Switzerland and France, it surprised people that 'the woman who knew Lenin', and had worked on his secretariat during the civil war, refused to speak about the past. The reason was that one day during the civil war which began in 1918, she had read a telegram Lenin had just dictated to be sent to a political commissar in a town resisting Bolshevik authority. In the letter Lenin simply told the commissar to kill '100–1,000' people as an example. The dash between the two figures destroyed her belief in the revolution. It represented the hard nucleus of civil war.

The scholarly neglect of civil war could also be an instance of the general human tendency towards such repression of unpleasant realities. The philosopher Thomas Hobbes (1985 [1651]) who witnessed the vicissitudes of the War of the Three Kingdoms, known as the English Civil War, in the 1640s, saw the state's essential functions in this domain as being repressive. Likewise, faced with political violence, Christian teaching also stresses the need for obedience to lawful established authority. In Freudian terms, what comes out in civil war can be compared to any repressed element within the psyche. As with the sexual instinct, perhaps violence is there just under the surface, its possible expression never far away. Whether understood as competition (in Hobbes), sinfulness (in religion), or libido (for psychologists), all three perspectives suggest that what comes out in civil war is something in human nature that ought to be repressed.

Civil war could have been avoided by political philosophers then, because it is a specifically 'unnatural' form of war. The idea returns us to Hobbes' fear of internal war destroying the body politic, as if the state was just the political expression of a human body. Interestingly, Hobbes described his Commonwealth as an 'artificial person' and as a body politic that mimics the human body (1985 [1651]: 81). The frontispiece to the first edition of *Leviathan*, which he helped design, portrays the Commonwealth as a gigantic human form, built out of the bodies of its citizens, with the sovereign as its head (ibid.: 71). The approach has persisted. 'Los Disastres de la Guerra' is a series of 82 sketches on the disaster of war painted by Francisco Goya who had witnessed the Peninsular War between the Spanish and Napoleon's forces between 1808 and 1814. During the war, placing human remains (entire bodies or mangled limbs) on top of trees became a common practice. Plate number 37 'Esto es Peor' ('This is Worse') is reproduced on this book's cover. It shows an enormous half human body on top of a tree. The image of a stretched and mangled torso suggests that the effect of violence and death is to turn this man into something other than human.

Although the resistance to Napoleon, which ended in 1814, was a national struggle, Goya, was a psychological realist and stressed above all the brutality and suffering such wars bring. Since Spain was then entering into what would be more than a century of bloody conflicts, Goya's sketches could also be an image of the future, especially of the 1930s, when the establishment of a Republic tore a complex society into two armed camps, each dedicated to the extirpation of the other (Casanova 2012). Indeed the image of a torso stretched to the extreme did return in a different form in 'Soft Construction with Boiled Beans: Premonitions of Civil War', a painting by another Spaniard, Salvador Dalí, in the 1930s. This shows a torso being stretched, mangled, and disfigured as Spain fell apart as a society that decade. Dalí also suggests that there is something unnatural about a society destroying itself in civil war. Or at least it suggests that this form of war, more than any other, stretches humanity to its limits. When recalling this painting, Dalí made the analogy between civil war, disease, and deformity, all of which produce bodily contortions and distempers:

> When I arrived in Paris I painted a large picture which I entitled *Premonitions of Civil War*. In this picture I showed a vast human body breaking out into monstrous excrescences of arms and legs tearing at one another in a delirium of auto-strangulation. As a background to this architecture of frenzied flesh devoured by a narcissistic and biological cataclysm, I painted a geological landscape, that had been uselessly revolutionized for thousands of years, congealed in its 'normal course'. The soft structure of that great mass of flesh in civil war I embellished with a few boiled beans, for one could not imagine swallowing all that unconscious meat without the presence (however uninspiring) of some mealy and melancholy vegetable. [cited in Kamen 2007: 310]

Finally, civil war could have been avoided in the history of political thought because of its association with fratricide. The Roman historian Lucan began his account (1992 (trans. Braund)) of the civil war between Caesar and Pompey (49–45 BC) with 'Of wars across Emathian plains, worse than civil wars'. 'Worse than civil wars' because Caesar and Pompey were not just fellow citizens, but related by marriage. Frank O'Connor, the Irish short-story writer, remarked that 'We all know that in civil war father is often set against son, and brother against brother, and no doubt from time to time they have killed each other' (O'Connor 2004: 90). Using violence against members of your own society (or here family), requires one to twist and suppress aspects of one's own humanity; the appropriate comparison could be with incest, infanticide, or patricide. The theme of fratricide goes back to the story of Cain and Abel in the book of Genesis. Out of jealousy, one of Adam and Eve's sons, Abel, who farmed his own land, is killed by the other, Cain. Hence in biblical legend the first step human beings took towards the formation of a social grouping, the family, also resulted in fratricide. Today the term civil war in Hebrew is equivalent to war between brothers. 'Civil war' in modern Hebrew is *milchemet ezrachim*, while 'war of brothers' is *milchemet achim*. Both *achim* (brothers) and *milchama* (war) appear in the Bible, but separately.

There must be some intellectual purchase in studying such conflicts. Yet the responses have been defensive. Modern international law itself has its origins in Europe's religious wars of the sixteenth and seventeenth centuries. Once the legal claims of the various sides were attributed to confessional (hence fanatical) positions, the sovereign claims of the Absolutist state became vindicated. The Peace of West-phalia in 1648, which inaugurated the European state system, led to a new body of international law whose primary purpose was to regulate relations between states and suppress the possibility of civil war. This body of law prohibited *bellum intestinum* (internal war) by giving the state a monopoly on the use of force within its borders, and the sole right to declare war externally. When only wars waged by states are deemed legitimate the state becomes the counter-concept to civil war (Koselleck 2005: 47). Later the French Revolution helped establish the nation as a source of unity in society. Once it was seen as indivisible, those who threatened the nation with civil war could be accused of prejudicing its very basis, and efforts at establishing national unity then became ways of suppressing internal divisions that could bring civil war (González Calleja 2013: 18). Since the 1990s the rediscovery of civil war as a scholarly topic has led people to deny contemporary conflicts a civil character, and take refuge in a vision of the world where the universalizing and allegedly pacific trends of global civil society make the concept of civil war anachronistic. This claim is discussed in the next chapter.

These responses show that, rather than building self-doubt into our social and political theories, political thinkers tend to declare such conflicts outside our value system, or to articulate a vision of a world within which civil wars could not occur. In particular, a strong tension exists between the progressive values of the European Enlightenment and a form of human conflict that was seen through the prism of violence and destruction even 3,000 years ago. This is especially so when notions of modernity and progress are built into the self-conceptions of these social orders. Do we not, as with the centenary commemoration of World War I, tend to look back on past violence as if we have somehow evolved beyond that stage? Yet there is no element in the Western value system (be it democracy, rationalism, secularism, or nationalism) that has not led to civil war. The undeniable evidence of human divisiveness these conflicts offer in a world where people pay lip service to human rights, democracy, and peace may eventually force people to relativize the foundations of the political and social orders they think of as being permanent.

The prevalence of civil conflict has been no less strong since the 1990s, when globalization became a popular term. Indeed, it is the strength of this current that explains the emergence for the first time of a new and systematic literature on the topic of civil war since the 1990s. Its main empirical focus is on a period—from 1945 to today—when global convergence and the fragmentation of states were interrelated processes. The sheer number and variety of civil conflicts that have taken place in this period mean that this literature has followed a simple logic of enquiry. First, categories of conflict have to be applied to these conflicts. Only then can one trace their patterns. On the basis of these patterns, generalizations about causes and consequences have been made. The final, perhaps ultimate, question is to learn how societies recover from these conflicts. This logic of enquiry is reflected in the chapter structure of this book; a chapter is devoted to each step in this process (definitions, patterns, causes, consequences and recovery from conflict).

To be sure, people were thinking about civil war before the 1990s. Some societies have gone so far as to construct national myths out of their conflicts: such as Costa Rica, which experienced a short civil war in 1948, and then became Latin America's most stable democracy. States faced with the possibility of absorption into a neighbouring civil war (such as Lebanon today), are always thinking about civil war in some way. Thinking need not be conscious. The fear that the Northern Irish Troubles of 1969–98 could lead to an island-wide civil war undoubtedly shaped the policies of Dublin governments during that period. Indeed, a different reading of the classics could excavate the way unconscious thinking about civil war has taken place among the world's most famous thinkers. What has been missing is the systematic analysis that has emerged only in recent decades. My aim in this book is to summarize this social science debate for an audience who may not be familiar with it, and to evaluate it from a historical perspective. Civil war is both a general phenomenon which can happen to any society, and a historical event experienced by an individual culture. Hence, there should be such a dialogue between a social science perspective, which tries to assess general causes and consequences, and work in history and literature that is a much better guide to the experience of what takes place in different countries. Civil war is a subject with a very long past, and a very explosive recent history. Hence the range of reference to examples in this book, beginning with ancient Greece, is necessarily very wide.

Thinking about civil war in history

Ignored by philosophers, civil war has doubtless obsessed historians. The literature on the American civil war alone amounts to more than 50,000 publications. No synthesis of this work is possible, but some general themes found in the historical literature have reappeared in the recent social science work. Before the European Enlightenment, for which the French Revolution became a creative symbol, civil war was unfailingly seen in catastrophic terms. From the ancient Greeks onwards, the associations were with chaos, disorder, and catastrophe (González Calleja 2013: 14–17). For over 1,800 years, these negative associations provided a thread connecting the Greek historian Thucydides to his first English translator, Thomas Hobbes, in the seventeenth century. Yet these associations are even more prevalent today, as the global media's coverage of the effects of genocide, state collapse, and other human disasters brings them right into our living rooms.

This catastrophic perspective has its roots in an acute sensitivity to the fragile basis of all political communities. For civil war put an end to the Delian League of Greek city states in 404 BC and the Roman Republic in 31 BC: the two great polities of antiquity. Both these great civilizations had to live with the fact that civil war was both the most destructive form of conflict, and at the same time the one most likely to occur (Armitage 2009: 6). Self-doubt can affirm commitments to happiness, justice, or religion. Yet a political order aware of its potential to collapse may find it hard to flourish. On the other hand, the tension between self-doubt and self-confidence has produced political literature of the highest quality. Lucan (AD 39–65) for example wrote of mighty Rome unable to bear herself 'under too much weight' during the civil war between Caesar and Pompey; the dissolution of Rome's basic structure led to 'primeval chaos' (1992: 5).

Fear of factionalism in politics has also been a consistent theme. In *The Republic*, written around 380 BC, Plato contrasted war between Greeks and barbarians—fought no doubt between unequals—with wars within the city states. The former conflicts were natural, and war was the appropriate name for the enmity between Greeks and their enemies. Wars between people who were by nature free, however, were 'unnatural'; these came about when the city states became divided by factions. Indeed, the ancient Greeks included factions and the consequences of factions in their conception of what stasis (meaning 'civil war', 'political standing up', and 'faction') brings. Since then, the themes of faction and public discord have dominated the literature on civil war in smaller sovereign entities, while ideas of sedition and rebellion have been current in larger entities such as empires (Kalyvas 2006: 18). When a society was seen in holistic terms—almost as a natural organism—factionalism was condemned as unnatural, as when (between 170 and 180 BC) the Roman philosopher-emperor Marcus Aurelius (AD 121–80) criticized rebels, schismatics, and those that proved 'a faction to himself' in the Assembly (Aurelius 2003: 56, 123). Aurelius described their activities as 'cutting', 'hacking', and 'destroying'. Hobbes, by contrast, thought factionalism all too natural: the egotistical and selfish nature of human beings leading to 'Emulations, Quarrells, Factions and at Last Warre' in early modern Britain (1985 [1651]: 235). The issue of factionalism took on a fresh contemporary importance with the French Revolution. Far from the problem being one of the whole organism, violent conflict in 1789 was seen as an expression of the distance between two opposed poles in society.

An unflattering contrast with wars between states is another enduring theme in the literature on civil war (Regan 2009: 121). In *Droit de la guerre et de la paix*, published in 1613, the Dutch legal theorist Hugo Grotius broke new ground in comparing wars fought between sovereign entities with an identical status—such as states—with civil wars where parties do not recognize each other's status. The disorderliness and extremism of the latter results from the fact that they are not regulated by well-established procedures, laws, or military doctrines, and tend to be fought with the intention of extirpating the enemy. Colloquially, 'civil war' still suggests an all-out fight to the finish. For example, once the power struggle between the AKP government and the Islamist Gülen movement broke out in Turkey on 17 December 2013, one commentator saw in the censorship, campaigns of defamation, and the purging of public officials from their posts a 'post-revolutionary civil war' within political Islam (Aykol 2013).

The tendency to see such conflicts primarily through the prism of violence also provides a thread connecting pre-Enlightenment fears of civil war with contemporary thinking on conflict. The Jewish historian Josephus's account of the revolt against Roman rule, which began in Palestine in AD 66, depicts a land drifting into anarchy: under the influence of 'false prophets, bandit warlords, communal hatreds, and an unsatisfactory governor'. The historian John Burrow (2009) remarks that if this account is harrowing, 'it is also peculiarly familiar'. For Josephus wrote of 'massacres', 'suicidal intransigence', 'ruthless terrorism', and 'fratricide' between rival groups and their warlords (ibid.: 152, 156). The question has always been whether such wars could be considered political. From Thucydides to those who condemned the role of *le peuple* in the French Revolution; to the (2006) work of the political scientist Stathis Kalyvas on the Greek civil war (1946–9), violence is treated not just as a symptom of a political crisis but as a force that takes on a momentum of its own.

'Conflict recurrence' is a modern concept for another older theme. The Romans tended to see individual civil wars as part of a series of wars: the spectre of civil war, when it arose, would appear in the form of previously remembered conflicts, and was then placed into 'an unfolding and seemingly unending sequence' (Armitage 2009: 6). Conflicts came not as 'a mere sequence' but as a fateful 'concordance' (Aurelius 2003: 47). The historian David Armitage (2009) shows that even in eighteenth-century England, people looked back on the 'English civil war' of the 1640s as an episode in a series of wars. Contrary to what became the Marxian view, they thought that history was being driven forward, not by revolutions, but by a succession of civil wars. Is this perspective obsolete? In parts of Central America, sub-Saharan Africa, parts of South-East Asia, it is peace that is exceptional; the persistence of conflict is the most salient fact on people's horizon of experience. People in these places can appreciate what the historian Lucan was doing when he projected the consequences of Rome's past conflicts into the future, and suggested that the resolution of current crises could require further wars (Armitage 2009: 6).

Some modern European societies incorporated the idea of continuous war into their historical self-understanding. Between the end of the Napoleonic Wars in 1815 and the 1905 revolution in Russia, Europe saw relative domestic peace. Spain was a big exception. During its own age of liberalism (1833–74) it experienced no less than three military coups, a major crisis of the Isabelline Monarchy between 1862 and 1868, and the first Carlist War (1833–40) (Fusi 2012: 277–8). In the latter conflict nearly 150,000 men died, a very high figure considering the much lower Spanish population of around 12.3 million at that time (Payne 2008: 151). The second Carlist War lasted from 1873 to 1876.

Reflecting on this experience of conflict in the 1930s, Spanish intellectuals like Gregorio Marañón considered the whole of Spanish history a continual civil war (Kamen 2007: 403).

What about the role of ambitious and unscrupulous politicians? Every major Roman historian discussed the succession of conflicts which ended the life of the Roman Republic in 31 BC. At their nadir—in the first century BC—nearly a quarter of all adult males between 17 and 46 were under arms (Armitage 2009: 14). Roman historians were very contemporary in pointing the finger at elite ambition, and vividly described the way civil war usually licensed crime and the lust for power. The historian John Burrow discusses Appian, Cassius Dio, and Sallust (2009: 67–179). Appian's subject is the decline of the Republic into political violence, gangsterism, civil war, and chaos. He traced this process to the year 121 BC, after Tiberius and Gaius Gracchus, two of the people's tribunes, were murdered (in 133 and 121 BC respectively) after they had attempted a land redistribution on behalf of the poor. The murders broke the Roman tradition of political moderation; after this moral barrier was broken, violence inevitably escalated into civil war (ibid.: 120). For Sallust, the defeat of Carthage in North Africa (146 BC) removed a badly needed source of restraint in Roman politics: civil strife was the product of peace and prosperity, not poverty (ibid.: 87). If one of the themes which preoccupied these historians was the deterioration of public morality through greed or unlimited ambition, scholars today pose the issue in terms of whether rebel movements feed off 'greed or grievance', and lament the exploitation of social tensions by politicians.

Only much later did the view emerge that civil war might symptomize the birth of something new. The stimulus for this outlook was the experience of modern revolution, the first of which took place in Britain between 1642 and 1688. These revolutions could be condemned in the Roman way: Edward Hyde the Earl of Clarendon attributed the 'Great Rebellion' in Britain to the wilfullness, wickedness, not to say the mischief of particular men (2009: 3–4). Yet the 'rebellion's' claim to be the engine of great changes in state and society could not be dismissed. The nineteenth-century historian Thomas Babington Macaulay encapsulated the modern sociological view when he remarked 'there is a change in society, there must be a change in government' (Burrow 2009: 368). Burrow underscores the symbolic importance of the fact that the execution of Charles I in 1649 was not an act of the barons, but of the House of Commons, which essentially arrogated sovereignty to itself (ibid.: 327). Since then revolution has primarily meant a violent conflict, marking a rupture with the *Ancien Regime*. Whether it be the Russian Revolution of 1917, or the civil wars of the post-colonial world, explanations of why they occur, and of the consequences they bring, tend to be sociological.

The promise of change implied in the modern concept of revolution cast civil war in an even more unfavourable light. An important conceptual change in the way we think about human conflict occurred as a consequence of the Enlightenment. The bloody religious struggles of Europe's sixteenth and seventeenth centuries were seen as civil wars—with terms like 'rebellion', 'insurrection', and 'uprising' used to convey their 'fanatic' qualities. In the eighteenth century, however, 'revolution', in contrast, acquired a meta-historical and philosophical character: the French philosopher Voltaire commented that a revolution had succeeded in England, while other countries got stuck in futile civil wars (Koselleck 2005: 48). While revolution implied progress, civil war, by default, acquired the meaning of 'a senseless circling upon itself, with respect to which Revolution sought to open up a new vista' (ibid.: 49).

The contrast between the concepts is important to note because so much of the recent literature on civil war—notably that on Africa— reinforces this image of societies senselessly circling upon themselves. The association of civil war with catastrophe and total destruction continue. Perhaps no era committed to a view of history as unending progress can really reconcile itself to the permanence of civil war. The famous French *Encyclopédie*, mainly compiled between 1751 and 1772, was a dictionary of thought on the arts, crafts, and sciences that represented the 'best' thought of the European Enlightenment. It contained eight articles treating different aspects of war under the term *guerre*: the term *'guerre civile'* was nowhere to be found. This is even more surprising when we consider that the main editor, Denis Diderot, an opponent of the optimistic Jean Jacques Rousseau, had elsewhere described man as waging a lifelong civil war within himself (Koselleck 1988: 188, 163).

The historical literature on civil war is fragmentary, in the sense that few major historians have made civil war in general the subject of an entire book. These wars have long been seen as appendixes of other conflicts such as wars between states, independence struggles, or parts of wider ideological struggles. The entries in the famous German *Geschichtliche Grundbegriffe* (a historical lexicon of contemporary terms published between 1972 and 1997), form only four pages of the 126-page discussion of revolution (Brunner, Conze, and Koselleck 1972: 653–789). It was only after 1945—a period of so many national liberation wars—that an attempt was made to study civil wars systematically. Yet since the rivalry between the superpowers still dominated the scholarly agenda, theoretical interest in civil war remained 'discontinuous' and 'subordinated' (González Calleja 2013: 13). It took the end of the Cold War to open up a vista for civil war studies in their own right. One source of change was the new interest in civil war shown by economists working on Africa. The growing willingness of the UN to intervene in internal conflicts after 1989 was another. Yet the old survives in the new. Just as historians in antiquity had associated civil war with chaos and disaster, publications like the World Bank's *Breaking the Conflict Trap* (Collier et al. 2003)—which coined the phrase 'development in reverse' for such conflicts—articulate the old standpoint in new language. In both cases a time horizon is incorporated into the conception of what these conflicts actually mean. Since much of the literature discussed in this book originates in development studies, and because this book involves a critical evaluation, the existence of these old associations and powerful continuities ought to be stressed at the outset.

Thinking about civil war in social science

Charles Tilly, the late sociologist, has estimated that since 1914 the world has given rise to at least 250 new wars (Tilly 2002). Hence the scale of the contemporary challenge posed by civil war is enormous. Most have not been wars between states: rather civil war has become the master concept for a bewildering variety of internal conflicts. Various research centres on peace and conflict have assembled large datasets which identify a basic pattern: a very dramatic decline in the incidence of inter-state war has been accompanied by a steady rise in civil wars over the decades since 1945. While the first decades of the Cold War saw the most destructive internal wars, the middle of the 1980s may have produced the greatest number of such wars in human history. Hence the emergence, since the 1990s, of the first systematic study of this form of warfare is no surprise.

The wave shows no sign of abating, despite the very dramatic changes in international relations which have taken place since 1945. After the Peace of Westphalia signed in 1648 the world gradually became dominated, not by religions or empires, but by states. The multipolar era of international relations that lasted until the end of World War II had its origins in this development. Multipolarity has often been considered the most unstable international system (Waltz 1979: 161), but the bipolar system that came with the Cold War actually produced an explosion of domestic wars. Contrary to expectations the process of decolonization—which increased the number of states dramatically—resulted in a decline in conventional inter-state wars and an explosion of civil wars. When the Soviet Union collapsed in 1989, hopes were raised that the dominance of the United States—a new unipolar system—would result in more peace. Neither this change, nor the gradual return to a multipolar system since 2000, has pacified the large parts of the world that began to suffer from civil wars during the Cold War. In short, civil war seemed to require no one international context to flourish. Hence the current belief that the sources of these civil wars lie *within* states—not in relations *between* them.

16

Will this wave of civil wars prove ephemeral? The sociological corollary of our belief in the capacity of human beings to live happy and productive lives is the tendency to see negative states—poverty, injustice, oppression, and wars, indeed any form of primordial disorder—as avoidable and thus preventable, the product of transitional circumstances. The novelist David Malouf traced our belief in a progressive future to the French philosopher the Marquis de Condorcet's 1793 *Sketch for a Historical Picture of the Human Mind* (2011: 41–3). In place of what had been an orthodox view of human history as 'a storehouse of exempla', of characters, events and movements that were fixed in number and constantly repeatable from age to age, Condorcet saw no less than nine stages of human progress, culminating in the French Revolution of 1789. What was new was Condorcet's idea that history might be progressive rather than circular, that an event might have no precedent, and was thus original rather than recurrent. If so, the best guide to the interpretation of this event might be the present and future rather than the past (Malouf 2011: 4).

When it comes to contemporary conflict our minds have also developed an eye for conflict occurrence not *recurrence*; for the investigation into the unusual, the unknown, or the entirely new aspects of wars. The most obvious example is the interest in how technology is changing the conduct of war. Yet past centuries were not mistaken in seeing *civil war* not only as the type of conflict most to be feared, but as the one most likely to reoccur. Indeed the contempory literature rests on a basic paradox. It explores how unmistakenly new things—the Cold War, post-colonial states, globalization, the arms trade, democracy—have caused the recent waves of civil war. Yet it is almost always focusing on conflicts which are recurrent. As historian David Armitage said of seventeenth-century England, in places as far apart as Angola, Columbia, or Northern Ireland civil war becomes a historical and cumulative concept: that is, that whenever the spectre of civil war arises, it does so in forms that recall previous conflicts and that places these conflicts in an unfolding and seemingly unending sequence (2009: 6).

Consider Chechnya. A state of civil war may have existed only during the secessionist wars with Russia beginning in 1994 and ending in 1999. However, it is difficult to say that the conflicts of the 1990s were not part of Chechnya's essentially colonial relationship with Russia, which began in the nineteenth century (Hughes 2007: 8). If they were, Stalin's deportation of Chechens for allegedly collaborating with the Germans, which began in 1944, and their exile to Siberia, was also part of this cycle of conflict.

The question that follows is whether violent conflict is an exceptional part of the human experience. We in the West do see violent conflict as the exception; the period of peace between wars is the norm. When we look elsewhere the problem is that our conceptions of social life can only explain order. Violence, when it occurs, is temporary, incidental to the basic character of social structures and social processes. Its origins are traced to the impact of external events, or to the occurrence of destabilizing social change (Feldman 1964: 111–36). Yet in places like the Sudan the sources of civil war are never far away, and for large parts of Africa, Asia, and Central America today, we need a different image of social systems, different types of explanation. The language the reader will encounter in this book—of 'conflict traps', 'conflict zones', 'intractability', 'crisis states', and 'state weakness'—is a step in that direction.

It is fair to say that the troubles of the post-colonial states make up the largest part of the contemporary challenge posed by civil war. The pattern has been for decolonization to lead to many civil wars, the location for which became generally—though not exclusively—the developing world. Many of the new states were unprepared for independence when decolonization came; few foresaw how enduring their problems would be. For example, the current traumas of Iraq and Syria in the Middle East—states formed after World War I—show that the artificiality of such states can be their undoing, long after they have been formed. Hence when it comes to explaining the causes and consequences of civil war, new explanatory concepts, such as 'state weakness', are intended to convey not just vulnerability to civil war, but a sense of vulnerability over time.

Hence too, the growth of the sophisticated social science literature which has become sufficiently large to justify synthesis and critique in a single volume. What makes it systematic is the range of cases studied, the use of civil war as a general category for these wars, and the way empirical evidence is used to validate or disconfirm causal explanations. Since many social scientists see this wave of civil war not as the product of multiple national histories, but as something *general*, the causes of which transcend national boundaries, civil war is treated in social science as a unified subject. In principle, in social science no case should be treated as more important than another; the geographical range of this literature is consequently wide. This is because what links conflicts to other conflicts—Sierra Leone to Ivory Coast for example—is more important than what separates them. Sierra Leone may be far removed geographically from major power centres, and it may be small in size, but it might still explain something about the location of such wars in poor countries, or about the problems of West Africa generally.

In terms of individual cases most students of civil war probably have at the forefront of their consciousness dramatic conflicts such as the Chinese civil war, the Russian Revolution, or the Spanish civil war which left their mark on the international relations of their era. In contrast, the cases most discussed in this book—Algeria, Angola, Mozambique, Turkey, and Yugoslavia—are often seen as 'peripheral' in some way. Yet they illustrate general themes: the connection between decolonization and conflict, problems of state collapse, humanitarian disaster, and sometimes ethnic cleansing and the mass violations of human rights. Each case stands out for different reasons. What was shocking in Mozambique was how quickly the common front against the Portuguese Empire gave way—after independence in 1975—to a civil war leaving over 900,000 fatalities. In Turkey what is notable is how the pattern of state- and nation-building—which has generally been a success—produced the strongest counter-mobilization in the south-east of the country, a region now being sucked into the turmoil of neighbouring Iraq and Syria. The eruption of civil conflict in Algeria in 1992 raises the question of whether a state which was once a model for the Arab world had really succeeded in defining its identity in the three decades that had elapsed since the end of French rule in 1962. The same question could be asked of the Federal Socialist Republic of Yugoslavia, which stands out for the rapidity with which relations between different ethnic groups deteriorated once the communist system collapsed in 1989. Angola is a classic case of conflict recurrence: its civil war went through three phases; (1975–91, 1992–4, and 1998–2002), linked by very fragile periods of peace. For further reading, bibliographic essays on these cases can be found elsewhere (Gunter 2012 on Turkey, Naylor 2012 on Algeria, van Hook 2013 on Yugoslavia, and Pitcher and Machava 2013 on Angola and Mozambique).

The recent proliferation of such wars has created a major policy challenge in four ways. (1) Since the economic gap between different regions of the world has increased because of such wars, a developmental challenge exists. (2) For most of the past 30 years large states have not been the main threat to international security. As civil war-prone states became potential sources of international terrorism, especially after 9/11, a security challenge has also emerged. (3) The media reportage of conflicts in places such as Rwanda, Syria, and Yugoslavia has also brought home the link between civil war and humanitarian disaster, in a way that past means of communication could not do. Hence the humanitarian challenge. As a consequence, peacemaking has come back to the heart of foreign policy, in a way that it was not during the Cold War. The change is reflected by the fact that most political science departments now teach courses on 'conflict mediation', 'crisis management', 'post-conflict reconstruction' and 'peace building'. (4) Finally, there is a less acknowledged paradigm challenge. Up to 1989 it was possible to assimilate many of the world's conflicts into a universal paradigm of class war, ideological conflict, revolution, or anti-colonial struggle. This is no longer the case. For example, the drug wars now raging in Mexico are taking place in a country once home to a classic modernizing revolution. They have resulted in an estimated 75,000 deaths since 2008. If this is a new form of war, there is a fourth challenge: one of interpretation and meaning. Such wars stretch some traditional conceptions of war and peace. The next chapter considers whether the very concept of civil war makes sense in a world of increasing globalization.

These policy challenges have also made more urgent the scientific search for general causes of civil war. Much of this work has been done by political scientists; they study a large number of cases statistically, in order to test popular explanations for why civil wars occur, such as the link with poverty. Since this work assumes that something systemic has been going on, the focus has been on factors with general explanatory significance. A recent handbook on civil war and fragile states considers security, poverty, ethnicity, equality, climate change, and natural resources to be factors of this kind (Brown and Langer 2012). The assumption is that a factor, such as ethnic diversity, is only causal if it has the general capacity to trigger an event. This approach is useful when one considers whether a theory can be applied further: to help us identify a pattern on the basis of which we expect something to follow. In contrast, a historian will assume that what caused a civil war has been affected by what went before. An example is a quote from Simon Schama (2002) by a Royalist in England in the 1640s lamenting that they had arrived at the civil war situation borne along by a succession of waves.

Yet this does not mean that history is relevant only to the study of individual cases, since a very specific historical context has produced this wave of relentless internal wars. Even if we exclude anti-colonial struggles against outside powers, one estimate (Holsti 1996: 22) is that the period between 1945 and 1995 gave rise to at least 126 internal wars. The crucial context is post-colonial. Indeed, all the worst conflicts which have caught the European media's attention in the last 30 years—Iraq, Palestine/Israel, Syria, and Yugoslavia—are the consequences of the collapse of one empire, the Ottoman. This wave of conflict was not the result of a multitude of conflicts developing completely independently from each other. The fact that so many of them happened at the same time means we must identify what the historical factors unique to this period were, or identify some older factors which grew in importance in that period. Both questions require historical answers.

Two well-established explanatory paradigms will be considered. In the nineteenth century 'naturalists' saw war as the natural expression of mankind's dark side, of the conflict potential in our inherent biologically and culturally competitive traits, while 'situationalists' preferred to explain trends in warfare as reflecting very specific, usually exceptional contexts (Hall and Malešević 2013: 2). The situationalist will ask what it was that made the post-colonial context so explosive: the arms trade, the Cold War, weak and fragile states, radical ideologies, or population growth? In contrast, naturalists would argue that since factors bequeathed to us by evolution, such as differences over inherited culture and the struggle for scarce resources, are constant, the creation of new states was the occasion rather than the cause of these civil wars. Put differently, the post-colonial context only mattered by creating so many new states for people to fight over. The conclusion to this book will ask what the recent literature tells us about this debate.

In its course, the reader will become aware of the huge difficulty of creating a unified body of social science knowledge about a form of conflict which has happened at every point in history, in every part of the world, and for all sorts of reasons. One could make a comparison with psychology, where the unifying potential of evolutionary neuroscience sits uneasily with a discipline which is no more than a loose federation of techniques and inquiries (Smith 2013: 13). Questions about the scientific enterprise that is psychology also apply to the study of civil war. If a discipline is characterized by its method, should we consider scientific only those studies of civil war informed by social scientific practices? Was Thucydides' focus on the moral distemper occasioned by stasis in ancient Greece not scientific? Are there, in any case, clear boundaries between social science and the humanities here? Is the Oedipus myth in Greek legend not about patricide, and Shakespeare's *The Tempest* not about reconciliation? Perhaps Dalí's dramatic painting 'Soft Beans' is the last word on Spain's torment of the 1930s.

The final question is whether the subject is itself universal. Can the very term 'civil war' be applied to societies like China, which placed little value on the civic sphere as understood in the West? Or to the Arab world, where the Western and secular concept of citizen was a recent import into Arabic? Are the conflicts taking place in Central Africa really civil wars? Or does the concept not imply something about the level of state development? The topic has its own challenge of hermeneutics and meaning. This challenge matters because of the existence of a scholarly division of labour, in which local scholars supply the data, but the theories that are applied to their experience come from prestigious Western centres of research. This may be the price of treating civil war systematically. Yet it raises the question of whether, if the division of labour were south–north, involving theoretical work also by those close to the conflicts, this would mean the end of a scientific research programme in the conventional sense.

The conclusion to each chapter will reflect on three things that have been necessary to create a unified research programme in this field. The first issue is how to define civil war. An inevitable consequence of studying civil war as a general phenomenon has been to use a fairly minimalist definition. This allows for comparison of so many different cases. Yet the question of whether we have been seeing a lot of one thing, which we call civil war, or a proliferation of different kinds of conflicts, remains. The second issue is the place of the state in explanations for why there are civil wars. Linguists argue that were one to look at the world's languages from outer space there would only be one language: the different languages would seem mere dialects. Were someone from outer space to look at a *political* map of the world, the state would appear to be the organizing principle. We can no more think about world politics without states, than we could speak languages without grammar. The question is whether these states are sufficiently similar the world over to make the state central to general explanations of why civil wars occur. In a world of 'weak', 'failing', or 'collapsing' states, would comparisons with conflicts which happened before the advent of the modern state be better? Finally, what does the literature tell us about human divisiveness, the tendency for human beings to divide into ever-smaller political communities. This topic obsessed theologians in the past, but civil war has now become its most violent manifestation. Syria and Ukraine, relatively stable until recently, are good examples of its underlying force. Does the current literature tell us something new about this tendency, or does it rely on older conceptions of human nature (whether found in William James, Thomas Hobbes, or Thucydides) in order to explain why, when so many states were created, a multitude of civil wars followed? Each chapter will end with a reflection on what its subject matter has told us about these issues. The epilogue brings together my conclusions on all three.

2

CIVIL WAR IN HISTORY

The poet Ezra Pound once reflected that 'only emotion endures' (2005: 261). We can feel the same emotion about fresh journeys as 'those that launched a thousand ships' in times gone by, despite our different values, modes of travel, and intellectual traditions. There are many ways of thinking about civil war. Yet one endures. Civil war is always negative: it inflicts a deep wound on a society's sense of itself, and this wound remains the most sensitive part of the body politic for at least a generation. This chapter summarizes the ways people have defined the experience of civil war since antiquity. It asks what it is they tell us about civil war that has created such enduring emotions.

Words for civil war

So negative are the connotations of civil war that euphemisms like 'crisis', 'emergency', or 'troubles' are often preferred. When the term 'civil war' is used, the concept stands almost as a metaphor for conflicts of great violence and brutality. The Iraqi conflict is a case in point. In the beginning, the words 'occupation', 'terrorism', or 'insurgency' were used. However, a key turning-point was the bombing of the Al Askari Mosque, a Shi'a shrine in Samarra, on 22 February 2006. Following this, the rate of civilian casualties roughly doubled over the next year, to almost 3,000 deaths a month by July 2007. For many the attack signalled the beginning of 'a brutal civil war' centred in Baghdad, between Sunni and Shi'a Muslims. In other words, when the conflict became worse, the term 'civil war' began to be applied to it.

The question of what makes civil wars self-evidently worse than other forms of conflict has general implications. Two American political scientists referred to frequently in this book, James Fearon and David Laitin, counted as many as 127 major civil wars occurring from 1945 through the year 1999 (2003: 75). They considered three-quarters of these insurgencies. While arguing that the same conditions which give rise to insurgencies also lead to civil war, they do not tell us how we can distinguish between insurgencies and civil wars. In 2009 the US Bureau of Political-Military Affairs published an online guide to counter-insurgency, in which insurgent warfare was said to involve 'the organised use of subversion and violence to seize, nullify, or challenge political control of a region...through the use of force, propaganda, subversion and political mobilization' (2009: 6). Yet civil wars are conflicts that extend beyond specific regions to the whole society, and in which the use of force is primarily directed towards one aim: the achievement of state power. Not all insurgencies meet these criteria.

The task of definition is not made easier by the fact that civil wars have occurred throughout human history, in all sorts of places, for all sorts of reasons. Were we to consider just Spain, Juan Pablo Fusi's *Historia Mínima de España* lists many wars of conquest and reconquest, several wars of dynastic succession, civil wars within specific regions (such as Castile), two Carlist wars in the nineteenth century, and many military *pronunciamientos*, before the Spanish civil war fought between 1936 and 1939 (Fusi 2012: 271–91). Is there one concept linking these conflicts, one which could also link them to the many wars which took place within the Greek city states, those that led to the dissolution of the late Roman Republic, the fanatical religious wars of sixteenth-century Europe, or the sectarian killing in today's Baghdad? Is there something other than violence and brutality that links them? If not, all we are left with is civil war as a metaphor for this violence.

Civil war has been defined, economically and influentially, in terms of some basic elements, such as the existence of two sides fighting for control of government in a recognized territory (Singer and Small

1982: 205–6). A threshold of casualties—usually a thousand deaths—can also be added to exclude less destructive conflicts from genuine civil wars. The problem is that such definitions 'lump' together conflicts—such as insurgencies and revolution—that are essentially dissimilar, while a good definition should establish clear analytical boundaries between different types of conflict. In this respect social scientists tend to be 'lumpers' rather than 'splitters'. By this I mean they group together as many conflicts as possible in order to make valid generalizations. This exercise may help us trace broad patterns of conflict, but runs into the problem that civil war may be a distinctive, rarer type of conflict.

Historians are more likely to stress the specificity of individual conflicts. The *Diccionario político y social del siglo XX español* contains a whole chapter on how the Spanish civil war of the 1930s has been conceptualized by the protagonists and their followers, ranging from 'a crusade of national liberation' to 'a national revolutionary war' (Fuentes 2008: 609–17). Conceptions of conflict matter politically once the main protagonists become aware of the practical consequence of any definition of the situation. Hence consensus on any name is unlikely. The acceptance of the term civil war (*guerra civil*) in the 1970s actually represented a cooling down of the Spanish debate and an openness to some form of reconciliation during Spain's transition to democracy (ibid.: 616–17). Comparing the older historical conceptions could tell us much about the experience of conflict. Yet since they are morally loaded, they bring us no closer to saying why the Spanish conflict was a civil war, and what it was that links it to other civil wars.

We need a specific type of concept for such a purpose. The German historian Reinhart Koselleck discussed three different types of concept that were applied to the experience of revolution in Europe. The first were concepts which cover past experiences, more or less similar to what we mean by those terms today, but which have been conceptualized in the past by a set of terms different to those which we use today. He gave *tumultus, seditio,* and *rebellion* as examples. This group of concepts has in common the definition of such events as political acts of violence—a definition formulated from above by those in power, to denote acts of subversion from those under their rule. Terrorism is the contemporary example par excellence. Secondly, there were classifications from an apparently neutral perspective—*Discordia, bellum civile, Bürgerkrieg*. The neutrality of the second group consists in saying what a conflict is compared to other forms of conflict. In the Roman concept of 'civil war'/*bellum civile* this is achieved by classifying a conflict simply in terms of the enemy being fought (the civilians). Thirdly, there were concepts which classify uprisings in terms of their respective claims to legitimacy, and which are justified in terms of actions taken by those below against their rulers (tyranny, despotism and, after 1789, dictatorship) (Richter 1995: 42–3). The third group conveys the sense of legitimacy which concepts can endow on those challenging rulers, as with most modern conceptions of revolutions.

We require neutral (or scientific) concepts of the second type to help us stand outside a conflict. Suppose you were observing a bonfire. You would be able to see the flames, and feel the heat. In this sense your thought and experience are the same. Yet when you ask a question like what would happen if the wind changed direction, such a question is prompted by thought. Thought requires concepts more than direct experience. You are able to experience a bonfire without a concept, but you are not able to think about it (*New Scientist* 21 September 2013). Likewise, neutral concepts allow us to think about civil wars, to step out of individual experiences, and to ask 'what they are like compared to other conflicts?' This would not be possible were we to consider only the concepts used by the actors themselves.

This chapter compares three conceptions of civil war, taken from periods in which significant shifts in perspective took place: the period before the French Revolution, the period of the Cold War, and the globalized world today. The term 'civil war' has been used since Roman times, 'internal war' began to be used for a variety of wars in the 1960s, while the 'new wars' concept was developed in response to the way globalization was creating new forms of conflict. This chapter will discuss these concepts in that order. Each is neutral in the sense that they have been formulated for the purpose of classifying wars, and helping comparison. All three enable us to ask 'what is it like' questions about experience, and to compare civil war to other forms of war. Yet although each concept reflects a given time and place, it does not follow that because these concepts interpret the horizon of experience differently comparison between them cannot help organize our knowledge. My comparison of them is faithful to the Spanish philosopher José Ortega y Gasset's understanding of 'perspectivism': that all historical epochs participate in and contribute an element of truth to reality. Individual perspectives are 'definite points of view directed upon the universe' (Ortega y Gasset 2007), and can add to our knowledge about what it is that has endured about civil war.

Some historical concepts which are very specific (the Palestinian *nakbha*, the Jewish *shoa*, or the Spanish *reconquista*) also have negative connotations. Yet these do not help us with comparative questions; they assume a singular experience. Luckily, there are concepts that we can take from history that have not been so abstract, nor so rooted in a specific time or place, that they cannot be applied to other situations (Richter 1995: 43). The ancient Greek concept of stasis is one. Meaning 'political standing up', this concept—rooted in the Greek tradition of democratic politics in the city states—suggests both the objective character of conflict (what is it like) and its negative connotations (faction and the consequences of faction). The discussion that follows will show that the three adjectives (civil, internal, and new), are also key, both to the objective character of these conflicts and to their negative connotations. Indeed, despite the many conflicts covered by them, the immense variety in experience they have given rise to, some negative associations have endured since antiquity. It is these very associations that will enable us to grasp why the Iraqi conflict has become a civil war.

Civil war

When the Greek poet George Seferis made his banquet speech at the Nobel prize-giving ceremony at Stockholm City Hall on 10 December

1963, he referred to what was enduring about the Greek tradition (Seferis 2014). Seferis could see an enormous difference between the discoveries of ancient and modern science, but between classical and modern Greek drama no such gap existed. Could this be true also for our understanding of civil war? Are the methods of the contemporary world so sophisticated, and their discoveries such that the thought of the Greeks is only of antiquarian interest? Alternatively, were their insights into stasis so penetrating that the task left to us is one only of validation and refinement?

The ancient Greeks did not invent the term civil war; the adjective 'civil' did not exist in their city states. Yet their internal wars were both frequent and feared. Stasis was a condition closely connected to their tradition of democratic politics, and the form of conflict most likely to bring self-destruction to the *polis*. The most vivid account is Thucydides' presentation of stasis in the Greek *polis* of Corcyra (modern-day Corfu) in his *History of the Pelopponesian Wars*, which broke out in 431 BC. Corcyra was the first example of a type of conflict which then became common in the Greek world as the wider conflict between Athens and the Delian League went on. Its spark was the decision to murder those who supported a defensive treaty with Athens, hence raising the very contemporary question of whether internal war was the natural consequence of war between states (Manicas 1982: 685).

Stasis, which had affected all of Greece, was finally to reach Athens in 411 and 404 BC. The city was then ruined by its internal divisions. In many ways stasis has never disappeared from reflection about the rise and fall of nations. The two opposite ideas of concord and stasis are the starting point for a whole series of texts in Greek and Latin (de Romilly 1991: 55). It is appropriate to extend these themes to our own age. For a start the decentralized Greek world was also one where city states could rise and fall, and where death, dispossession, or forced exile awaited the losers. Greek concerns were contemporary in the additional sense that vulnerability to stasis was seen as a problem of a polity: the *polis* was egalitarian in its ethos, but lacked a professional standing army which could keep the effects of political competition in check (Manicas 1982: 688). Hence the analogy with contemporary worries about the effects of regime change on weak or fragile states. Such conflicts were usually the product of unrestrained political ambition and greed. Perhaps it was the special life of the Greek world—'its politics, its fierce pride in autonomy, and, within its own boundaries, its open character—which permitted and indeed encouraged stasis' (ibid.: 680).

It was left to the Romans to coin the term 'civil war'. This term (*bellum civile*, derived from *cīvilīs* in Latin) has since been applied to the death throes of their own Republic, to some major revolutions (like the Russian in 1917), and to the ongoing conflicts in Afghanistan, the Congo, and the Middle East. The neutrality of the concept reflects the classic Roman way of classifying conflict in terms of the enemy being fought. The *Chambers Dictionary* defines civil war simply as a war 'between citizens of the same state' (1993: 315). Of the many reasons why the concept remains influential, one is that citizen involvement in conflict—from the people's revolutions in communist Europe, to the Maoist struggle in Nepal, to the Arab Spring—has never ceased. 'Civil' can pertain to the community, ordinary life, or individual citizens. It denotes a sphere, free from military and ecclesiastical authority, where civil values and citizenships can flourish. The irony is that it is precisely within this autonomous sphere that the worst conflicts take place.

Does the Roman concept tell us anything new about why these conflicts have had such negative associations? The first thing is that when one's fellow citizens become the enemy—when there might be no fixed battle-lines—escape from the theatre of war is much harder. Secondly, if the fight is between fellow citizens, the threat of violence comes not from afar, as in an inter-state war, but from up close. Neighbours become enemies, families are divided, and each nation becomes, potentially, a nation of enemies. Both these apprehensions have endured. The French philosopher Jean Jacques Rousseau commented that everyone becomes enemies during civil wars, alternatively persecuted and persecuting, each on top of everyone and everyone on top of each (Koselleck 1988: 28). Both fears point to the conclusion that because we are so close to our fellow citizens, civil war divisions especially come to dominate every aspect of society. When there are no battle-lines to retreat to, no safe place to go, both sides might feel it is safer to carry on fighting rather than face retributive slaughter (*The Economist* November 1913). Thus the Roman conception is of an 'all-out' form of violent conflict. Civil wars, unlike wars between states, are typically fought to the bitter end.

The Roman fear of civil war had another root. A succession of civil wars led to the replacement of the Roman Republic with the Empire in the first century BC. These were conflicts that involved mobilizing the citizens themselves for the purpose of getting control of the state. They placed civilians at the head of armies, with soldiers leaving their posts and forming civilian armies, thus shattering the separation of civilian and military authority on which the Republic rested. Hence civil war was feared because it disturbed the sense of hierarchy on which the Republic was based (Armitage 2009: 4). The ancient Greeks had also thought in terms of hierarchies. The occurrence of stasis undermined the cherished view they had of the *polis*; of the city as a place where only citizens made decisions according to constitutional rules. Stasis allowed both slaves and women—the 'hidden Greece'—to emerge into the light of day as combatants, and thus to soil this image of the *polis* (Loraux 2006: 42). The idea of the social order being turned on its head was shared by Thomas Hobbes, who experienced the succession of conflicts that took place in Britain and Ireland in the middle of the seventeenth century. Famously, Hobbes argued that civil war returned people to a state of nature. The very concept of a civil war was to him an oxymoron: such wars actually returned people to a pre-civil state and destroyed civil society (Armitage 2009: 10).

Civilité could also be used as part of the distinction between public and private—another boundary which collapses with civil war. The seventeenth-century Dutch legal theorist Grotius distinguished between public, private, and mixed wars, the latter occurring most when the public authority is on one side with private persons on the other (Armitage 2009: 9). A civil war becomes worse when these categories collapse, making it unclear who the lawful authority is. Political scientist Stathis Kalyvas's *The Logic of Violence in Civil War* (2006) is a study of the way private violence flourished during the Greek civil war of the 1940s. The conflict began during the closing stages of World War II; it concluded with the defeat of the left in 1949. Thus it was decisive in terms of keeping Greece out of the Soviet bloc. The war was traditionally seen as a left–right conflict, but Kalyvas focuses specifically on the violence against civilians in the Argolid region of the southern Peloponnese peninsula to show that behind the veil of a left–right conflict was the logic of territorial control and of private violence. Since it is at the local level that social hierarchies are most visible and intricate, their collapse provides an opportunity to settle scores that is not available during peacetime.

The German sociologist Norbert Elias argued that the very concept of *civilité* came into existence as part of an effort to suppress the spontaneity and destruction of human affairs (Richter 1995: 103–5). To him (1969, 1982) we owe the view of the modern civilizing process as one that involves the construction of clear political *and* social hierarchies, which are intended to eliminate or suppress the potential for disorder in society. Since these social hierarchies collapse during civil war, one fear of civil war is that of a society becoming turned on its head. The Finnish civil war, which took place in the first months of 1918, was the first major civil war of twentieth-century Europe. For many it involved a leftist attempt to seize power in the wake of the Bolshevik revolution which had taken place in October the previous year. The concept of revolution had been translated into Finnish only in 1845. The new concept *Vallankumous* suggested 'the turning upside down of state power', or 'the overthrow of the state power'. The image appealed in a very rural society, and corresponded with the peasant vision of a complete exchange of the positions between the powerful and the powerless. When it came, civil war was understood by many of the poor in quasi-religious terms: as the coming of an empire of justice and righteousness. To respectable society however,

Vallankumous suggested only anarchy; they experienced the events of 1917 and 1918 as a profound shock (Alapuro 2003: 519–68). What took place in the first half of 1918 was fratricidal war, resulting in more than 35,000 casualties, most of whom died as a result of the Red and White Terrors, or because of conditions in the White prison camps.

What the Roman, English, Greek, and Finnish examples suggest is that the negative associations of civil war which have endured have a lot to do with the fear of boundaries becoming violently overturned during such conflicts. The historian David Cressy noted that when the bonds uniting English society began to unravel in 1642, the concept of revolution acquired a new meaning (2006: 18–19). As in Finland much later, English writers now used the term metaphorically, to signify a sudden and dramatic change, or a significant and abrupt turnover in the politics and religion of the state. Changes in the way language was used were indices of the social fabric unravelling. Sectarian preaching, and widespread attacks on the common (Anglican) prayer book, were examples of this unravelling in what was then a very religious society. Although the context would change greatly in the modern era, this fear of the social fabric unravelling remains a central concern in most civil wars.

Nonetheless, much did change over the centuries in the understanding of what constituted civil war. In the Roman world, what first set civil war apart from other conflicts was the concept of citizenship. Indeed, as late as eighteenth-century Germany, the concept of *Bürgerkrieg* ('war of the Burgers' or citizens), suggested a form of conflict taking place within a society of fixed social orders. The Roman concept of citizenship was also promoted by the French Revolution, but the French conflict would extend the range of participants in all wars to the people as a whole, or 'the nation'. In contrast to antiquity, where civil war was seen as the outcome of factional divisions, after 1789 political claims were now made in the name of a people, nation, or class; potentially universal categories. Civil war ceased to be defined as a war among citizens, but became a war of a part of a nation against another.

Hitherto, the use of specialized political language had been the preserve of the nobility, the lawyers, and scholars. As the older system of stratification dissolved, the bourgeoisie, and then the working class, learnt to manipulate language, and intense stuggles over how to categorize conflicts in a changing and more technological age emerged (Koselleck 2004: 252). Koselleck argued that during the French Revolution 'control over language became more urgent as the number of men whom it comprehended increased' (ibid.). Not only did concepts have a more universal application, more people were affected by how they were used. As the German philosopher and political theorist Carl Schmitt warned, when it comes to words such as state, republic, society, class, as well as sovereignty, we need to know exactly who is to be 'affected, combated, refuted, or negated by such a term' (Schmitt 1996: 31). Unsurprisingly, since the next two centuries were an age of mass politics, 'people's war' became used for civil war in some languages, such as Arabic (*harb ahliyya*) which was late incorporating the term citizen into its vocabulary. In Finland the use of people's war (*kansalaissota*) for the 1918 conflict was intended to convey the sense of this conflict being a common tragedy for the Finnish people. In Britain, the use of 'people's war' for World War II signified the huge degree and variety of popular involvement in the British war effort.

These conceptual changes clearly reflected the growth of modern technology, which made both the organization of violence and ideological propaganda effective on a mass scale (Mališević 2010: 5–11). Indeed the structural transformation of European societies in the nineteenth century has had important consequences for the way we think about conflict within societies. The modernization of Europe resulted in the diminishing of the power of intermediary structures (such as guilds, corporations, churches) between the individual and society, which resulted in a clear articulation of 'state' and 'civil society' as two opposite poles in political life (Breuilly 1996: 164). As a result, one traditional conception of civil war, as a war within or between fixed social orders, as in *Bürgerkrieg*, could no longer occur. Rather, nationalism became the integrative ideology that connected these poles, turning the individual into a citizen who was also part of a collective enterprise (Breuilly 1996: 164–6). This ideology made state and nation, not necessarily citizen, the key concepts in civil war. Indeed, in the twentieth century we increasingly saw a close correspondence between the language used to describe conflict within states and that used to describe conflict between states. The terms nation, people, and state become ubiquitous.

The French Revolution which began in 1789 showed how the effort to deny one's opponents citizenship by excluding them from the modern nation could create the permanent conditions for civil war or political oppression (Koselleck 2005: 56). The earlier religious wars in Europe found a modern echo, because 'the fervour that arises during the course of a revolution, merely as a by-product of the struggle of the parties, is of such a furious kind that it can destroy everything that is good' (Brunner, Conze, and Koselleck 1972: 778–80, 726–7). Indeed for most of the period since 1789, civil war has been indelibly associated with the worst consequences of the revolutionary process: radicalization, total hostility between enemies, and the brutalization of political and legal procedures (González Calleja 2013: 19). It was only very late in the twentieth century that social science would develop a concept, 'internal war', potentially free of these negative associations. Yet during the Cold War and after, the tendency towards the absolute criminalization of the enemy showed no sign of abating, and has marked genocidal conflict in places as far apart as Cambodia, Russia, and Rwanda (González Calleja 2013: 18). Despite the defeat of communism in 1989, this way of seeing civil war, as the nasty underbelly of revolution, still endures.

Internal war

The term 'internal war' began to be used by political scientists in the 1960s. Its champion, the political scientist Harry Eckstein (1965), thought internal war a generic concept, with civil wars, massacres, revolutions, etc., mere species of it. This concept thus had the advantage of not excluding conflicts which were not classical civil wars or revolutions. Eckstein's ultimate purpose was to make comparison between many cases, and thus generalization, possible. The concept was very inclusive in the sense of recognizing different subtypes of internal war (revolution, civil war, revolt, rebellion, uprising, guerrilla war, insurgency, *jacquerie*, coup d'état, terrorism, insurrection). It is also neutral in its suggestion that civil war is just an internal variant of war in general. Eckstein's approach has also been very influential in social science. Most large datasets on civil war distinguish between wars that are between states and internal or 'intra-state' wars. This distinction has helped scholars identify a striking pattern in the history of human conflict which emerged during the Cold War: while they see only 25 inter-state wars happening between 1945 and 1999, Fearon and Laitin (2003) count a total of 127 internal wars.

The 'internal war' conception was very appropriate to a world where decolonization had created more than 130 new states, and where the nuclear stand-off during the Cold War gave rise to an international environment in which wars had to be kept internal. The growing use of the concept also reflected the fact that territorially concentrated insurgencies against the state were becoming more frequent. To reiterate, Fearon and Laitin (2003) had estimated that three-quarters of the 127 conflicts they studied between 1945 and 1999 were armed conflicts of this kind—that is, mostly insurgencies. In 1949 the Geneva Convention tried to specify the conditions which would allow a conflict to be classified as 'an armed conflict without an international character'. These include the existence of a rebel group in control of territory within a state, its possession of de facto authority over this area, and the military threat it posed to the authorities (González Calleja 2013: 21).

As a political scientist, Eckstein's main interest was in how different forms of conflict morphed into one another, a protean quality of internal wars which could not be investigated by classifying the nature of conflicts in advance. Most importantly, not all internal wars become civil wars. The *International Encyclopedia of the Social Sciences* (Sills ed. 1968) described a 'spontaneous' type of internal war—where violence occurs without much leadership and planning—mainly in societies with no tradition of stable institutions anyway. The more common 'planned' type, however, where channels for the settling of grievances are blocked, involves an attempt at seizing power violently, involving a guerrilla group and an organized campaign (Sills 1968: 499). Either type *could* escalate into civil war, but there are many forms of internal wars—major strikes, demonstrations, guerrilla warfare, rebellions, coups, insurgencies, or terrorist campaigns—which do not become civil wars.

The use of the concept of 'internal war' also reflected a shift in the geographic focus of war studies, east and south, during the Cold War. While state and nation have become universal political concepts, the adjective 'civil' had been given a privileged position only in the political thought of the Western world. The concept of a war fought among citizens made less sense in the Arab world, for example: before 1945 classical Arabic lacked an equivalent secularized concept for 'citizen'. Most wars in the twentieth century took the form of rural insurgencies and wars of national liberation; the classic symptom of 'a weak state' remains its inability to guarantee security in all its rural regions. Consider the last decades of the Ottoman Empire (1900–23), when the transformation of a culturally diverse population with strong intermediary institutions—such as churches and religious brotherhoods—into a series of separate nations, reflected the strength of religious and ethnic divisions in the face of weak civic ties. The Balkan Wars of 1912 and 1913 and the Turkish War of Independence (1919–23), were international, ethnic, genocidal, religious, and paramilitary conflicts, all at the same time (Mazower 2001). Did such unfamiliar contexts not require new concepts? In modern Chinese (*nei zhan*/内战), Persian (*jang dakhali*), Turkish (*iç savaş*), and indeed Finnish (*sisällissota*), the literal translation for civil war is internal war.

Yet the idea that the essence of civil war had something to do with the fact that these are primarily internal conflicts goes back a long time. Koselleck also related the Greek fear of stasis to their belief that the Hellenes were a distinct species that could degenerate with increasing contact with the barbarians around them (2005: 162). Plato argued, provocatively, that while war with the barbarians was natural, stasis—an internal war among Greeks; indeed, among brothers—was pathological. Moreover, conflicts among Greeks should be mild and conducted with minimal force, while those against the barbarians should aim at total annihilation (Plato 2012: 188–9). This way of thinking about war contributed to the creation of a 'political interior' that shielded Greece from the outside world (Koselleck 2005: 162). Yet the shield did not prevent many ferocious internal wars occurring behind it.

The contrast the Greeks were fond of making raises the question of what—if not citizenship involvement—defines the quality of being internal. Internal wars could take place within a politically organized community recognized as a state by the international community, or within a community held together by social mores or customs. Alternatively, they could be conflicts 'within a society' that usually resulted from an attempt to seize power and the symbols of legitimacy by extra-legal means (Eckstein 1965: 165; Sills 1968). For the Italian historian Ranzato (1994) '"internal war" takes place within a state or a city—among citizens of the same state or city—as opposed to an external war that is fought between sovereign states'. The International Relations scholar Michael Brown sees internal wars as conflicts whose origins are *primarily* due to domestic rather than international factors, and in which violence takes place *primarily* within the boundaries of a single state (1996: 1).

The crucial difference with an inter-state war is that during an internal war a struggle for the control of the state takes place. The rival legitimacy claims that internal war gives rise to are not an inescapable element of wars between states. To the German sociologist Max Weber we owe the conception of the modern state as an organization that *legitimately* monopolizes the means of coercion over a given *territory*. Weber made the activity of legitimation—as distinct from the ascribed quality of legitimacy (such as Divine Right or democracy)—a defining characteristic of government, and one whose style and substance varied with the formal and substantive nature of the regime (Barker 2001: 13). This activity of legitimation is vital to internal conflict whether the internal war happens in monarchical systems (England in the 1640s), democratic ones (Finland in 1918), or those where the divisions are primarily cultural (Rwanda in the 1990s). Kalevi Holsti, an International Relations scholar, makes a useful distinction between what he terms 'horizontal' and 'vertical' legitimacy (1996: 82–99). 'Horizontal legitimacy' refers to the societal base of the state, the sense of community on which the state rests, while 'vertical legitimacy' comes down to whether the system of rule is supported by the population: whether it is 'legitimate'.

The two decisive aspects of most internal wars—a divided territory and the struggle for legitimacy—are also Weberian themes. A state that does not control its territory will find its legitimacy seriously challenged, but a challenge to the state which is not territorially based will find it hard to sustain itself. One consequence is that many internal wars are fought as if they were wars between states controlling different territories. The Confederate challenge to the United States between 1861 and 1865 led to an internal war that was fought as if it was also an international war. On both sides, the mobilization was of a comparable scale to any of America's international wars. Believing that the Federal Government did not have the legitimate authority to change their slave laws, the South used its territory to accomplish a massive mobilization of manpower against the Union. Those who defended the Union were not prepared to tolerate the existence of two governments under one constitution, and wanted to save the Union and its right to govern all the states which had formed the United States in 1776 (McPherson 1988).

The importance of the struggle for legitimacy makes internal war something much more than a domestic variant of war in general. The legal theorist Grotius criticized the Roman author Cicero's definition of war as 'contending by force', because war was not a 'contest' but

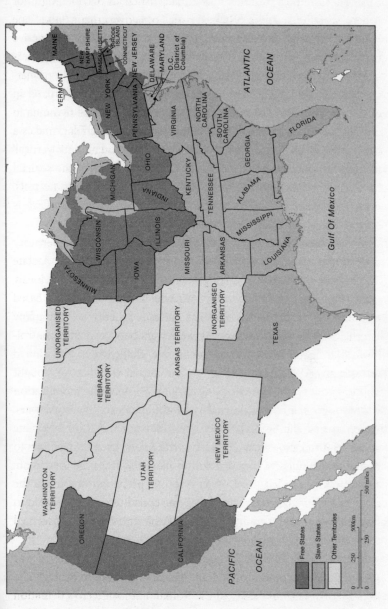

Map 1 Free states and slave states: the territorial basis of the American civil war, as at 1860

Free States

Slave States

Other Territories

0   250   500km

0   250   500 miles

more of a 'condition' (Brunner, Conze, and Koselleck 1972: 701). In the modern 'condition' the struggle for legitimacy and for control of territory are factors of overwhelming importance. Perhaps the struggle for legitimacy should be considered *the* defining aspect of internal wars; in conventional inter-state wars the status of the opposed states is usually uncontested. This struggle is also decisive in the aftermaths. After international wars troops eventually return to their own countries. After civil war the problem of coexistence in one territory means that a new basis for legitimacy must be found. This is no easy task. During civil war a simplification of the national past occurs, one that obliterates nuance in favour of a dichotomous reading of national values, thus leading to polarization. At the same time, since nationhood is deeply subjective, these arguments over its essence have the character of a 'hot family feud', and make civil wars more embittered than war against a foreign oppressor would be (Hutchinson 2005: 101).

Arguably Carl Schmitt, precisely because he feared inter-state war becoming internalized, was an early theorist of 'internal war'. He thought that the primary purpose of any state was to prevent the absolute enmity of international conflict becoming reproduced at the domestic level. War he defined as 'armed combat between organized political entities', civil war as 'armed conflict within an organized unit' (Schmitt 1996: 32). Schmitt argued that the 'friend–enemy' distinctions that are true of all political conflict, reach their worst level of intensity in wars within states. Why so? First he feared that one consequence of internal war would be 'the dissolution of the state as an organised political entity' (ibid.: 47). Secondly, only the state was really free to define its internal enemies. During the social and ideological conflicts of the late nineteenth century, he noted that only the state (not parties or the church) was prepared to engage in civil war (ibid.: 43). A war could be fought, like a duel, with the application of some agreed method of adjudication and reward. Once it becomes clear which side has prevailed militarily, the application of this method settles the conflict. This often happens in wars between states. Yet when the state has defined one side to be outside its own political community, a conflict may turn into a war of hatred and revenge.

Since it sees the modern state as the framework for war—as for political competition—the concept of an internal war is neutral in the sense that violent conflict is not seen as abnormal. This very neutrality can be an attractive feature of the concept. The Finnish civil war of 1918 had been described by the victors as a *vapaussota*/war of liberation, and by the left as either a *luokkasota*/class war, or *kansallaissota*/people's war (Alapuro 2002: 172). Despite the lack of common ground at first, the term *sisällissota*/internal war eventually found its way into academic discussion and indeed school text-books. Perhaps the scientific objectivity of 'internal war' rests ultimately on the fact that it was not (cannot be?) a term used by the actors themselves. The shift in Finland occurred at a time (in the 1960s) when the conflict in 1918 was beginning to be seen as a common national tragedy for the Finnish people. Another attraction is that the concept of an internal war could facilitate comparisons with other conflicts.

The stress on legitimacy is also consistent with the view of civil war as the continuation of politics by other means. The parallel is with ancient Greece where stasis was an unavoidable feature of democratic politics. Stasis suggested two consequences—polarization (between factions) and fragmentation (the consequence of factions)—that are present in the concept of an internal war too. This is because the struggle for legitimacy can also escalate to the point that normal politics becomes impossible. 'Internal war' also implies an internal struggle for legitimacy which observes no limits. The American sociologist Talcott Parsons suggested a simple thought-experiment. In a society held together by shared norms, two-party competition will be restrained. When defeated, the losers will show restraint in demanding the fulfilment of their wishes, or accept that the realization of these wishes must be delayed. And the victors will show restraint in their use of the coercive capacity of the state. In contrast, the absence of such restraint on both sides means that the losers will not see any future for themselves, and the state (not just the government) will be unable to satisfy everyone's demands (Parsons 1964: 66–9). The polarization which follows can then lead to violence.

Polarization can produce its worst consequences in societies once held together by common values. Eckstein defines internal war as a kind of social force, 'exercised in the process of political competition', but *departing from previously shared social norms* (1964: 2). For example, much has been written about the religious violence of the Spanish civil war. Supporters of the Republic killed as many as 7,000 religious personnel, and carried out acts, such as the disinterring of their bodies, which were clearly sacrilegious. Such acts were political and beyond politics at the same time. By desecrating churches, the Republicans were attacking the authority structures within which priests and monks (like landlords) were embedded. What was beyond politics was that the Republicans were themselves also performing a religious rite, and revealing a religious sensibility of their own which allowed for no rapprochement (Graham 2005: 27).

The 'closeness' of much of the violence in internal wars can also be traumatic. The dominant understanding of polarization in social science suggests that the intensity of conflict is a reflection of the importance the actors attach to the issues dividing them, or of the extent to which the claims of groups are incompatible with each other (Kalyvas 2006: 64–6). Ideological conflicts such as the Spanish civil war conform to that model. A Catholic cross could be for a conservative the symbol of Spanish national identity; for a socialist the cross could be the symbol of a hated social order. Yet there is no necessary connection between the brutality of civil war and the ideological distance between the combatants. In his study of the Greek civil war, Kalyvas (2006) compares two villages in the plain of Argos: Manesi and Gerbesi (now Midea), which were of the same size, of a similar social outlook, and shared a common descent and social structure. Egregious episodes of violence (including the killing of children and the elderly) took place in only one village, Gerbesi, in August 1944. In Manesi, the villagers acted to prevent the wider left–right conflict resulting in violence within their village. The difference in this case cannot be explained by ideological divisions between leftists and rightists. Perhaps local animosities or local solidarities were at work.

Another negative aspect of internal war is that a threat that comes from up close is worse than that which comes from afar. The Finnish sociologist Risto Alapuro notes that generally it is insulting in society to come too close. He shows that in Finland in 1918, the White rebels in the southern part of the country under Red rule usually came from the same locality as those who were governing them. Because of the rise of the Social Democrat movement, the local rulers or administrators were farm workers and other lower-class people, who had been personally known to landowners and local notables, who now had to tolerate inspections and confiscations made by them. Not only were these people turning the societal order upside down, the insulting challenge came from common people close to those whose position was now threatened (Alapuro: 2010).

Of the three conceptions of war (civil, internal, and new) discussed in this chapter, only that of internal war is really neutral. The Cold War provided the crucial backdrop, since after 1945 all wars were transformed into civil wars (Koselleck 2005: 56). Yet systematic study of internal war, between 1945 and 1990, was stunted by the tendency to relate everything to the East–West rivalry. Another problem was that many 'internal wars' during the Cold War were actually proxy wars, fanned by external powers. Indeed, a sharp dichotomy between internal and external conflicts is hard to sustain. In September 2013, as more calls were made for intervention in the Syrian conflict, a retired Lebanese army brigadier general, Amin Hoteit, said that once Obama fired the first missile he would lose control of the situation. With 400,000 people in the regular army, 150,000 in the people's army, and 100,000 in the armed popular militias, the infusion of a huge number of ground troops would be necessary to change the course of the Syrian conflict. Yet the fire this would ignite would not stop at Syria's borders, and could even reach Qatar, Kuwait, and Saudi Arabia (*Irish Times* 7 September 2013). The truth is that there has been external involvement in the Syrian conflict almost from the beginning.

If the Syrian state is destroyed, its fate will not have been sealed primarily by internal divisions. Such conflicts are not internal wars.

The difficulty of separating what is internal from what is external suggests that no adjective can really do justice to the complex reality of civil war. When a state in crisis moves to defend itself, it must take steps against part of its own community, and often defines this section as being 'outside the nation'. The internal enemy is externalized, and the distinction reaches the point where it becomes the sole difference in society (Schmitt 1996: 28–32). Finland, with its long border with the Soviet Union, has always possessed an exceptional sensitivity in cultural terms to what was internal and external. What proved especially polarizing about the civil war of 1918, which followed the Bolshevik revolution, was that the Russian factor entered into the definition of what was Finnish (Alapuro 2002: 171). The political question, of who would inherit the tsar's powers (left or right), became the much more insidious question of who was inside the nation or not. The victors defined the losers as 'those with no Fatherland', for they had allegedly been contaminated by Russian Bolshevism (ibid.: 172).

Many astute theorists of modern war were German, writing at a time before World War I when the connection between imperial rivalry and domestic politics was clear (Mališević 2010: 28–45). For Weber himself, the national state was the arena where the drama is played out, but the international system writes the plot. When the state loses out in international conflict, and begins to crack (as before the Russian Revolution), organized groups begin to challenge state power, with civil war the result. Making a distinction between internal and external conflicts is thus like drawing a line on water. Literature is a good source of insights. Liam O'Flaherty was an Irish short-story writer who fought for the Republican side in the Irish civil war in 1922–23. This conflict brought to an end the Irish independence struggle against the British government, which had begun with the 1916 Easter Rising. O'Flaherty experienced the disillusionment that happens when violence directed against a 'foreign' government turns inwards. In his 'The Sniper', two snipers in uniform, night after night, exchange fire across the rooftops in the centre of Dublin, as they would have in a conventional inter-state war (Kelly 2000). Clothed more or less the same, of similar age, and apparently of similar social background, one eventually kills the other, and navigates the buildings to establish the identity of his enemy. When he lifts the lifeless body, he sees the cold face of his own brother. Whereas the modern Irish for civil war (*cogadh siabhalta*) is a literal translation, the civil war of 1922–3 was also known as *cogagh na gCaradh* ('War of the Friends').

Civil wars can happen suddenly to a society, coming 'from the outside in', but they leave their mark within in a way that is internal to a society. The parallel is with medical infections which happen to us, regardless of our conscious choices. Indeed, going back to Hobbes's use of 'intestinal discord', the language is often one of infection (which also comes from outside). The Israeli novelist Amos Oz complained of the avoidance by Palestinians of the 'dirty word' Israel, calling the state instead 'the Zionist entity', 'an artificial creature', the 'intrusion' or 'infection' (Oz 2012: 25). One could write a whole book about how inside–outside distinctions are made during wars. For example, tactically, the military strategy of al-Qaeda was shaped by a dialectic between 'the close enemy' (such as Egypt) and 'the distant enemy', the West. One strategy was to provoke the latter to intervene in the workings of the close enemy, in order to establish its apostasy. Ultimately, al-Qaeda had to recognize that acts of liberation against the distant enemy impressed potential recruits more than a revolutionary agenda against the Middle Eastern states (Filiu 2011: 110). One also can take from these examples fresh evidence of an older theme: the way boundaries (here between what is inside and outside) become blurred during civil wars.

New wars

The two decades after 1989 produced many new conceptions of conflict: 'post-modern wars', 'new wars', 'wars of the third kind', 'complex emergencies', 'resource wars', 'never-ending wars'. The 'new war' concept emerged in the late 1990s, when many assumed that globalization was transforming the nature of war, and some saw new forms of war emerging. The 'internal war' concept had been very Weberian in seeing the violent struggle for state power as the defining feature of civil war. Yet historically, civil war had been possible in all forms of state: city states, empires, principalities, the composite monarchies of early modern Europe, for example. Increasingly, scholars today are forced to consider the nature of conflicts within 'weak' 'failing', 'frozen', 'shadow', 'post-modern', and 'collapsed' states.

The concept of 'new wars' refers to an allegedly new type of war which developed in Africa and Eastern Europe in the 1980s and 1990s (Kaldor 1999). Its emergence in the 1990s suggests again that conceptions of civil war tend to say something about the dominant regime form in their era. It is no surprise that the Greeks of the fifth and sixth centuries BC would make this connection first, for that was a time when power, and changes in power, were first understood (Debord 1995: 91). Aristotle, for example, thought civil conflict arose from struggles to control a polity or its constitution (Price 2001: 31). Much later Thomas Hobbes remarked that Monarchy cannot disagree with itself, out of envy or interest, 'but an Assembly may, and that to such a height, as may produce Civil War' (Pouncey 1980: 154). He criticized starry-eyed scholars of ancient Greece and Rome, who downplayed 'the frequent seditions and Civil Warres, produced by the imperfection of their Policy' (Hobbes 1985 [1651]: 369). In the early twentieth century, in anticipation of the revolutionary state, Leon Trotsky defined a situation of dual sovereign power—underpinned by irreconcilable class differences—as the essence of a civil war situation (Bolsinger 2001: 73).

For the political scientist Mary Kaldor, the phenomenon of 'new wars' reflects above all 'the erosion of the state's monopoly of violence, from above by the growth of international military forces, and from below, by transnational crime networks, diasporas, and the emergence of paramilitary actors' (Kaldor 1999: 20). The spread of international institutions, multinational corporations, information technology, and the global media have also made transnational actors

48

as important as, or more important than, the state. Hence, since the 1990s globalization has contributed another regime factor, making for wars (according to some scholars) that are transnational in character. Jeffrey Checkel's *Transnational Dynamics of Civil War* (2013) covers conflicts in Afghanistan, Chechnya, Rwanda, Sierra Leone, Sudan, and Turkey—conflicts in which the transnational dimension led to significant changes in the rebel groups' tactics, resources, and political ideas. In Sudan, for example, one consequence of the existence of a Sudanese advocacy group in the diaspora was the demobilization of child soldiers in the South Sudanese MPLA, but also the support of the United States for its independence drive (Hamberg 2013: 149–73).

Indeed Kaldor comes close to suggesting that the concept of civil war lost its relevance with the weakening of the nation state. Her choice of 'new' in place of 'civil' was significant. She argues that 'new wars' 'are part of a process, which is more or less a reversal of the processes through which the modern state evolved' (1999: 5). The modern state had grown through war, and financed its war efforts by mobilizing domestic resources. As war became the province of the state, and competitors to the state were gradually eliminated, the growing destructiveness of the modern state in the international sphere was accompanied by growing security at home: 'hence the way in which the term "civil" came to mean internal' (ibid.). The strength of the modern state had allowed for an internal sphere within which civil wars could occur, but if the distinction has collapsed because of globalization, perhaps civil war has ceased to be a major category of warfare. Indeed Kaldor equates civil not with an autonomous internal sphere, but with values of peace and universality (ibid.: 2).

In stark contrast, Kalyvas (2001) questions what is new about 'new wars', but an important sociological intuition does lie behind the concept. The 'new wars' approach has its intellectual roots in the study of the changing character of warfare, which explores the impact of societal and technological changes on the nature of war. There is a need to think creatively about the connection between changing borders, technological change, and armed conflict. Consider the flood of illegal child migrants now making their way, via Mexico, from the Central American states of El Salvador, Guatemala, and Honduras to the United States. In the nine months before July 2014 US border officials came across about 52,000 unaccompanied minors from Honduras, Guatemala, El Salvador, and Mexico, compared with 19,418 in 2009 (*Guardian Weekly* 18 July 2014). They are fleeing countries where there is no rule of law, where the populations are terrorized on a daily basis by gangs, and where parents have lost hope in their future. The UN High Commission for Refugees has called for these Central American children to be treated as refugees displaced by armed conflict, and given international protection. Categorizing conflicts becomes a serious issue when those involved are made aware of the immense practical consequences of a given definition. On what basis can we say they are not armed conflicts? The annual murder rate in Honduras per 100,000 people is 90, compared with under five for the USA (ibid.). Since the gang phenomenon originated in the United States, and is financed from further south by the narcotics trade, is globalization not a major factor, requiring concerted international action of the kind we have seen in Kosovo or Sierra Leone?

Far more than either the civil or internal wars traditions then, the 'new wars' approach brings insights from economics and sociology to the business of defining conflicts. A theme it shares with the older tradition of studying change in the nature of warfare is the deterioration of war itself. Koselleck's image was of societies 'senselessly circling', and not moving forward of their own volition (2004: 49). The advance of the Islamic State of Syria and the Levant (ISIS), Iraq, and northern Syria is a case in point: it points the finger backwards in that it raises questions about the state system imposed on the Levant by France and Britain during and after World War I. At the same time it is a transnational struggle sustained by financial and technological changes which came about only in recent decades. Thus it also points towards the future too. Indeed ISIS exemplifies something about civil war which can be traced back to ancient Greece: its capacity to undo progress by the very means of that progress (Price 2011: 93).

The waves of civil war which can be traced back to the 1940s have shown no sign of abating since the 1990s, when globalization became the concept for the future. Indeed most of the new concepts for understanding conflict which have emerged since the 1990s share a general sensitivity to their longer duration. When the state is defined in terms of its legitimate control of the means of violence, civil war is, by definition, a break-down, a state of exception, something that follows when politics has got out of hand. Yet in some countries conflict was not exceptional; rather, states have become spheres of perpetual war. Wars in places as far removed as Angola, Burma/ Myanmar, Cambodia, Colombia, Mozambique, Pakistan, and Sudan have lasted more than two decades. Indeed, while the 'internal wars' approach had been rather neutral in its attitude to conflict, the older catastrophic connotations of civil war have returned. The 'new wars' literature emerged in a decade where states and nations were seen to be struggling, failing, or collapsing, just as the ancient Greek fear of the consequences of factions reflected an acute sensitivity to the fragility of states (de Romilly 1991). Hence it is appropriate that Yugoslavia and its violent collapse was chosen as the paradigmatic example of a new war.

The 1990s, in particular, was a decade when many states that had been propped up financially from outside during the Cold War were forced to fend for themselves. Civil wars in places like Chad, Turkey, Peru, and Yugoslavia seemed to pit one broad category of people against another, rather than targeting politically active opponents of the status quo (Ferguson 2003: 18–22). Since their nations often turned out to be what the anti-colonial writer Frantz Fanon called 'empty shells' (2001: 19), many concluded that there was a need for new concepts for a range of conflicts that were not civil or internal in any meaningful sense. Consider *Another Day of Life*, the account of Angola in the summer of 1975 written by the Polish war correspondent Ryzard Kapuściński (2001). This book gives a dramatic account of

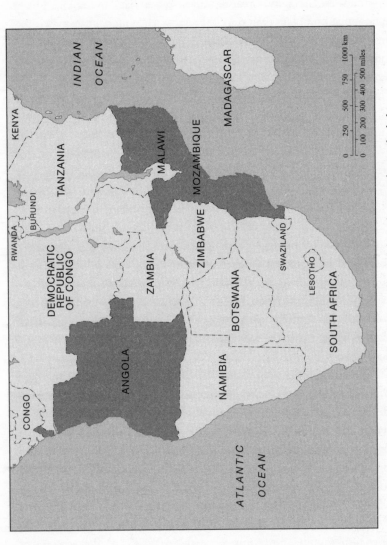

Map 2 Southern African states with Angola and Mozambique shaded in

the early stages of the series of civil wars which took place in a country that was 14 times larger in territory than Portugal, and larger than France, West Germany, Great Britain, and Italy combined. Yet in 1970 its population of less than 6 million was divided into more than one hundred tribes. Kapuściński quotes an Angolan officer recalling his time in eastern Angola during the independence struggle against the Portuguese:

> We had to learn the language of the local tribes and act in accordance with their customs. This was a condition of survival—otherwise, they would have treated us as foreigners trespassing on their land. And yet, we were all Angolans. But they did not know that this country was called Angola. For them, the land ends at the last village where people speak a language they understand. That's the border of their world. But, we asked, what's beyond the border? Beyond that border lies another planet inhabited by the Nganguela, which means non-humans. [Kapuściński 2001: 34]

For such local tribes, state and nation were new and alien concepts, and the borders of their linguistic world more real than those lines on the map separating the new Angolan state from Botswana, the Congo, Namibia, Zaire, or Zambia. If so, how can such a war be thought of as a war between citizens of the same state?

How then to define such wars? When Yugoslavia collapsed, it seemed to many that the different sides were motivated by a nostalgia for a lost sense of community in a world of progressive globalization. When history seems in reverse in this way, 'new wars' had to be defined as an antithesis (of civility, of politics, of state-building, of war). Indeed one common way of defining contemporary wars is by means of contrast with more conventional forms of war. After decolonization, Holsti argued that rather than highly organized armed forces, wars have tended to be fought by 'loosely knit groups of regulars, irregulars, cells, and not infrequently by locally based warlords under little or no central authority' (Holsti 1996: 20). He uses the term 'Wars of the Third Kind' for wars that are as lethal as inter-state wars, but fought over the definition of the political community (ibid.: 19–41). Kaldor suggests that 'Old Wars' fought between states were wars fought 'for a definable political end' (1999: 13–31). In contrast, the newness of 'new wars' consists in them blurring the boundaries between war, organized crime, and large-scale human rights violations (ibid.: 2). Both approaches are especially relevant to inter-ethnic wars which are fought between citizens of the same state—ostensibly over identity issues—but often take the form of inter-state wars across borders, with regular armies, battles, soldiers in uniforms, and unofficial border controls. Bosnia-Herzegovina is a paradigmatic case for being formed out of an 'asset strip' of a failing state (Yugoslavia) by a range of transnational political and criminal networks which remain powerful in the domestic politics of the Federation two decades after the Dayton Agreement brought the Yugoslav wars to an end (Kostovicova and Bojicic-Dzelilovic 2015).

The 'new wars' approach is neutral in the sense that it explains the emergence of 'new wars' sociologically, as a consequence of globalization. Yet it is not neutral in its attitude to contemporary conflict, which it tends to criminalize. Note that it was also true of the nineteenth century that the universal approbation of war was nowhere extended to civil war. What these nineteenth-century views have in common with the 'new wars' literature is the assumption that it is only the state that encapsulates the 'political' in conflict. This assumption is present in the political theorist John Keane's 'uncivil wars' and Kaldor's contrast between 'old' and 'new' wars. Note too that the question 'why do men rebel?' is asked only of internal wars, on the assumption that the nature of a civil conflict needs to be established through the motivations (ideological, economic, or criminal) of the individual combatants. Such a question is never asked for inter-state war, because we assume that if the state is involved, the conflict *must* be political. This assumption, and the contrasts made with classic wars between states, feeds into the images of societies senselessly circling upon themselves, when at war with themselves, and is linked to the view that these are humanitarian crises rather than basically political conflicts.

Indeed the recent appearance of new concepts for conflicts is clearly connected to the recent spread of a humanitarian and interventionist agenda since the 1990s. During the Cold War we could usually count no more than five UN peacekeeping operations in any one year. Since 1990 the annual figure has usually been more than 15 (*The Economist* 9–15 November 2013). The 'new wars' approach is also firmly within the Western historical tradition of seeing the collapse of boundaries, and the overturning of hierarchies, as the worst aspect of domestic conflict. Not everyone accepts the novelty of these wars. Identity conflicts, human rights abuses, and cross-border paramilitary formations were no less a reality in eastern Croatia in 1941 than they were 50 years later. Slavko Goldstein's reconstruction of the earlier conflict between Croatian Nationalists and their opponents, *1941: The Year that Keeps Returning* (2013), covers a decade in which more people were killed in Yugoslavia than in the Spanish Inquisition. Perhaps what really *is* new is the easy availability of external finance, which means that the 'start-up' costs for irregular armies are lower. In less than four years, ISIS went from being a jihadist terrorist group in northern Syria to, potentially, a new state in northern Iraq. External funding from wealthy patrons in Kuwait, Qatar, and Saudi Arabia was one source of income at the start: now a combination of extortion, taxation, kidnapping, and oil revenues have raised its estimated income to more than 1 million dollars a day. If this resource base grows, the region could soon be home to a fundamentalist Islamic state with control over a territory larger than the size of the United Kingdom.

Should we abandon the concept of civil war?

If the analysis hitherto has told us anything, it is that the blurring of boundaries, between what is inside and outside, between different social strata, between the public and the private, has long been recognized as one of the worst aspects of civil war. Consider Goya's 'Los Disastres de la Guerra', which was also named (in its English translation) 'Fatal Consequences of the Bloody War with Bonaparte, and Other Emphatic Caprices'. This series of 82 sketches is divided into three sections; those on the actual Peninsular War between the

Spanish and Napoleon's forces (1808–14), those on a famine which occurred in Madrid during that war, and a set of political and cultural allegories about the aftermath. Goya does not depict the war as being heroic: we see no human dignity in these diabolical images of cruelty, hallucination, madness, and mutilation. Rejecting the use of colour in place of shadow and shade, the backdrop is usually death. Witches are present in about one-quarter of the satirical *Caprichos* (caprices) which were intended to be a commentary on the peace established after 1814. Many sketches are set in the cemetery, the madhouse, and the prison.

Art critics have asked what these prints tell us about our own condition. The world of war is depicted by Goya as an inverted one; no distinction is made between soldiers and citizens: all seem stripped of human dignity. Good and evil appear on neither side of the war. Witches often appear. At times the boundaries between the bestial and the human are blurred in the depiction of mangled and often tortured bodies. Yet the theme of blurred boundaries, and the idea that the commonplace becomes inverted during such wars, go back to the third century BC. Yet it is precisely this blurring of boundaries that makes civil war, as a distinct form of conflict, hard to define. The social science concern with classifying, defining, and measuring civil wars is at odds with the fact that nowhere in the world of politics are boundaries so elusive (Cramer 2006: 84). This problem of definition is compounded by the fact that scholarly interest in civil war has always taken second place to that in other forms of war, notably wars between states and revolutions. The final question for this chapter is whether the very concept of civil war has become obsolete? If not, how can it be rescued?

More than anyone else John Keane has dwelt on the paradox that the popularity of the term 'civil society' has coincided with a growing number of 'uncivil wars' (2004: 109–27). He finds 'a troubling contradiction' in the fact that violence is the antithesis of civil society, but every known form of civil society tends to produce some violent antithesis. Once violence and the civil are opposed in this way, Keane comes to the conclusion that there are actually no civil wars left. As in Hobbes, such wars constitute a form of conflict outside the framework of civil society. According to Keane, civil wars were traditionally contests between groups concerned with the acquisition of state power: violent forms of 'horizontal conflict with vertical aims', in other words. In contrast, the drug wars in Mexico, *la violencia* in Colombia, and the post-communist collapses are 'uncivil wars'. The Latin term *violenta* ('exercise of force') captures the self-perpetuating nature of these wars better than civil war (Keane 2004: 109–27).

Clearly, the concept of civil war *is* paradoxical; these conflicts are experienced as decidedly *un*civil wars. Going back to Thucydides, one could study them, not in terms of their initial causes or the development of social relationships, but as something implied by *violenta*: a progressive deterioration in those morals and social relations that made conventional politics possible (ibid., 113). Yet instead of this progressive deterioration, a tunnel analogy is perhaps more appropriate. Appian's *Roman History* (Appian 1996)—which covered the turbulent years between 133 and 35 BC—saw Rome's civil wars in this way: as a testing-ground of martial valour and political prowess. Conflicts may have stemmed from the unbridled pursuit of power, but the ultimate question was: what qualities—civic or otherwise—allowed the Romans to emerge from this tunnel, and to establish the Empire?

It was once said that the religious and philosophical approaches within the Western tradition to the reality of human evil were either to accept that it was a problem and solve the problem, or to deny it existed altogether (Kolakowski 2012: 161). The 'new wars' literature wants it both ways: it accepts that the world is not becoming less violent, and calls for interventionist solutions, but denies the adjective 'civil' to contemporary violent conflicts. Clearly, the Roman tradition of defining a conflict in terms of the enemy being fought has its limits, not least because not all states are strong enough to make citizenship a meaningful category. Yet applying the adjective civil only to those whose values are 'progressive' and 'universal' (for which read liberal), empties domestic politics of much of its meaning. Indeed the Arab Spring has brought back new content to old concepts of citizenship, and a range of conflicts that *are*, precisely, horizontal conflicts (between citizens) with vertical aims (state power). Different visions of the future have emerged because of social change, and those aspiring to change have the aim of capturing state power in order to realize it. Where revolts first succeeded (Egypt, Libya, Tunisia), the changes were marked with the adoption of new constitutions.

The 'new wars' approach also 'jumps the gun' in thinking that states and state power have ceased to matter in civil conflicts. We have seen a revolutionary state removed by a violent uprising in Libya, a corrupt presidential regime removed by a combination of military coup d'état and popular protest in Egypt, and a state dominated by a religious minority producing a bloody civil war in Syria. These conflicts are not the antithesis of politics, but rather the outcomes of competitions between rival interests, the articulation of historical grievances with the state, and political instability: the very stuff of politics. We do not deny their political character because the Arab states are not so far removed geographically, and their conflicts over religion, democracy, and secularism—i.e. over the nature of the state—make sense to us. We accept their definition of the political, because they are located within our horizon of experience.

There have been many valid criticisms of the use of the term 'state' in comparative politics. Yet some aspects of the state have not diminished in importance (see Ferguson 2003: 9–10). The first is their territorially bounded nature: civil war violence remains within these states for the most part. Secondly, what remains very real is the myth of the state's independent existence (Abrams 1988: 58): civil wars polarize ideas in general and the idea of the state (as friend or foe) can get quickly internalized when these wars begin. Finally, even in societies dependent on natural resources, control of the state is the best means to access them: the state remains the main agent for their exploitation and redistribution. For all the talk of weak states and globalized war economies, the state—'as the pinnacle of the structural landscape' or as a 'magnetized node of wealth and power'—remains important in the post-colonial and post-communist states (Ferguson

2003: 9–10). These states have a weaker resource base but stronger expectations placed on them when it comes to lifting their population out of poverty (ibid.).

If the simple question is whether or not it matters who speaks with the authority of the state during civil wars, the answer in the Middle East and North Africa is definitely yes. The Egyptian, Libyan, and Syrian conflicts are obviously cases which involve rival claims to legitimacy. Since the particular character and manner of expression of claims to legitimacy vary according to the nature of each regime, we should be more alive to the variety of political regimes in this world, and the way they shape local versions of the political, before we deny their conflicts the adjective 'civil'. Both the vertical aspect to an internal war (the claim to a legitimate form of rule) and the horizontal dimension (the claim to represent a community) have always been related during civil wars. They were present in the English civil war which polarized different communities over a vertical issue, kingship, in the 1640s, with such religious implications that the conflict resulted in the establishment of different horizontal bases to the Crown's rule: England and Wales, Scotland, and Ireland. The way this legitimacy crisis was resolved between 1649 and the Glorious Revolution of 1688, has left legacies in Scotland and Northern Ireland that remain important in British politics today.

Kalyvas sees two traditional ways of thinking about the meaning of the civil in civil war (2006: 18). The first, rooted in Thucydides, focuses on the split nature of the polity, and reflects different groups controlling different territories, or rival claims to sovereign authority by different factions. The second, which emerged in larger entities such as empires, uses concepts of sedition and rebellion to characterize civil war. Hence the importance of the legal claims of the actors. In England, before the seventeenth century, a distinction emerged between rebellion, which was an action against an established authority without legal justification, and revolution, which meant the restoration or renovation of an earlier lawful authority. Paradoxically to modern thinking, Cromwell's actions were first seen as the Great Rebellion, while the events of 1688 were termed the Glorious Revolution. These ideas can still be used creatively. In Costa Rica, the idea of civil war as a means of restoring a constitutional *status quo ante* had a powerful influence during their civil war in 1948. The result was the only stable democracy in Central America. In Rwanda, the split nature of the populace was far more important than any constitutional framework. Yet the American civil war emerged in a split polity in terms of north and south, but under a constitutional framework invoked by both sides as a source of legitimacy. It was split in both senses.

The idea of the split polity has received its most sophisticated theoretical expression in the work of the Russian revolutionary Leon Trotsky, who argued that in a class society any genuine transfer of state power from one class to another must pass through a stage of 'dual power' that would end only when one side monopolized all the instruments of rule: the army, propaganda, intelligence, and ultimately economic resources (Bolsinger 2001: 73). The question is how his idea of a split polity can be applied to societies where the social structures and the importance of state power vary. States as conceived of in the 'internal wars' literature, 'internally peaceful, territorially enclosed, and impenetrable to aliens' (Schmitt 1996: 47), *are* fictional in some parts of the world, so we need to know much more about the specific nature of the political communities in which conflicts take place before we decide what is civil, internal, or new about their wars. For instance, Angola—vast in size, small in its population, and rich in natural resources—would seem to cry out for a new concept of civil war. Kapuściński spent some time patrolling with an MPLA unit of 120 men, the only unit on the southern front between the city of Lubango and the border (450 kilometres) and between the Atlantic and Zambia (1,200 kilometres) (2001: 66–74). Yet his depiction of a civil war in a vast country dominated by sparse bushland stands out not for its novelty, but for its consistency with older conceptions:

> In Europe, he (Comandante Farrusco) said, they taught me that a front is trenches and barbed wire, which form a distinct and visble line. A front on a river, along a road, or from village to village. You can trace it on a map with a pencil or point to it on the terrain. But here the front is

CIVIL WAR IN HISTORY

everywhere and nowhere. There is too much land and too few people for a front line to exist. This is a wild, unorganized world and it's hard to come to terms with it. There is no water, because there is a lot of desert here. You can't hold out for long where there are no springs, and it's a long way between springs. Here where we're standing there is water, but the next water is a hundred kilometres away. Every unit holds on to its water, because otherwise it dies. If there are a hundred kilometres between water, that space is nobody's and there's nobody there. So the front doesn't consist of a line here, but of points, and moving points at that. There are hundreds of fronts because there are hundreds of units. Every unit is a front, a potential front. If our unit runs into an enemy unit, those two potential fronts turn into a real front. A battle occurs. We are a three-man potential front now, travelling northwards. If we are ambushed, we become a real front. This is a war of ambushes. On any road, at any place, there can be a front. You can travel the whole country and come back alive, and you can die a metre from where you're standing. There are no principles, no methods. [Kapuściński 2001: 76]

The MPLA Comandante tries to define the essence of this civil war by means of comparison with more conventional forms of war, a tradition exemplified by Hugo Grotius in the seventeenth century. Yet his description of the arbitrariness, brutality, and lethality of the violence is not different from that given by Hobbes in the same century, who suggested that in a civil war one does not fear any particular thing, or any particular moment, but fears for one's entire being due to the absolute closeness of death (Koselleck 1988: 31). In 1940 Ernest Hemingway, the American novelist, published *For Whom the Bell Tolls* about the experiences of a young (fictional) American who was part of an international brigade during the Spanish civil war. The novel had as its theme the brutality of war, but took its title from a meditation by the English metaphysical poet John Donne in the seventeenth century on the themes of health, sickness, and death. Donne's lines were 'Ask not for whom the bell tolls, it tolls for thee.' In the context of Spain this could mean that when someone dies during a civil war part of humanity dies with him. Alternatively if Hobbes was right to stress the absolute closeness of death during civil war, the quote could also be read as a warning: when the bell tolls, do not ask for whom it tolls, it is tolling for you!

For Kalyvas the 'civil' in civil war refers primarily to a divided polity (2006: 17–18), but the people must also be members of a common community at the outset. When one assumes a coherent political unit within which civil wars take place, the link between the vertical and horizontal aspects of politics becomes fundamental: as Trotsky put it, 'civil war gives to this double sovereignty its most visible, because territorial, expression' (Bolsinger 2001: 73). Both state power and the control of territory do matter in most societies, but the idea of a split polity need not in any case assume too much about the strength of social orders. It can be applied to strong as well as weak states. In ancient Greece, the objective definition of the situation (stasis), was linked to the experience (fragmentation) it brings, and the link was especially meaningful in the city states, which lacked centralized structures of coercion. Thucydides thought the laws and institutions of the Greek *polis* could quickly count for nothing once stasis set in (Price 2001: 34). Indeed the ancient Greek world was conceived of as a moral community whose boundaries transcended the different areas of political sovereignty: in contrast to Greek culture, the polity was a subjective and unstable thing (ibid.).

The fear that stasis gave rise to is no different to the way many people think about state collapse and social disintegration today. In Thucydides' account the 30-year Peloponnesian War began as a war between nations, and then became one between individuals. In this downward spiral, each individual's pursuit of survival and self-interest only fragmented the polity further (Pouncy 1980: 145). This is clearly a story of what today we call 'state collapse', even if the Greeks had no conceptions of 'the state'. The Peloponnesian wars may have begun with a declaration of hostilities from one state to another, but the most destructive consequence was fragmentation, another process which connects past and present civil wars, Syria being the latest example. Grotius put it this way: splits become 'insupportable' when the people become so divided into two nearly equal parts that it is doubtful which of the two retains sovereignty (Kalyvas 2006: 18). The difference between Syria today and Russia in 1917 is that in the latter one side eventually re-established and exercised sovereign power.

Since all societies are concerned with self-protection and self-reproduction, civil war divisions almost always evoke a sense of the fragility of these political communities. Such apprehensions often further the polarization we see in civil wars. The epilogue to this book will consider how the theme of fragmentation can be built into a definition of civil war that applies beyond the cases discussed here. The worst consequence of fragmenation, in addition to a split polity, may be a divided self, which makes it very difficult for unity to be restored afterwards. In *The Divided Self*, the psychiatrist R. D. Laing (1960) showed how the loss of selfhood in psychological terms also occurred through fragmentation. Since, as with some forms of mental disintegration, civil war collapses precisely those boundaries which hold a society together, the fear of fragmentation during civil war transcends any era and any specific form of polity. That this negative association of civil war has endured, after the passing of three millennia, presents us with a clear case for retaining, rather than replacing the adjective 'civil' in the term 'civil war'.

Conclusion

When it comes to definitions, was Ezra Pound right that only the emotion endures? The Romans thought war between citizens the worst type of war. After the French Revolution ideological struggle gave such wars their ferocity. For our contemporaries the absence of boundaries between war, politics, and crime make new wars especially destructive. This is clearly an old and enduring theme. The contrast between civil wars and inter-state wars is another. This contrast suggests that the struggle for state power is an enduring characteristic of civil war, regardless of whether soldiers, civilians or criminals are involved. It has taken the Arab Spring to return us to this essential point. And the state remains important because the main danger the state is designed to prevent, the fragmentation of both state and society we have seen in Syria, makes for conflicts of very high stakes. Thus more than the emotion has endured.

On the centrality of the state to the study of civil war, this chapter has shown the tendency for differing conceptions of civil war to reflect the regime trends of their era, including the rise (and weakening) of the modern state. One can think of each conception as a window on the unique worlds they sprang from, but also as a part of a general and ongoing intellectual tradition, which began with the Greeks. Although the word 'state' did not exist in ancient Greek, the Greeks relied on an essentially political conception of what these conflicts meant. Stasis became one of the biggest themes of political thinking in the later part of the fifth century BC, and was conflated with 'political standing', 'faction', and 'civil war'. Stasis was condemned, but also seen as inevitable. The irony was that the Greeks are also credited with having invented democratic politics (Berent 1998: 331). One explanation for this irony is that theirs was 'a stateless community' which promoted political competition and participation, but did not possess a central-ized structure of coercion. The fear of stasis was thus directly related to the absence of a public organ which could check seditious factions (Berent 1998: 333, Cartledge 2009). The analogy in our day is the fears that arise when democratization takes place in weak states, as with the Arab Spring, or when economic crises lead to polarization. Thus, over a very long span of time, another theme has endured: civil war as a product, not of barbarism or poverty, but of politics.

What do these three concepts (civil, internal, and new war) tell us about the sources of human divisiveness? Writing during a military campaign, the emperor and stoic philosopher Marcus Aurelius reflected on the need

> [t]o bear in mind constantly that all of this has happened before. And will happen again—the same plot from beginning and end, the identical staging. Producing them in your mind, as you know them from experi-ence or from history: the court of Hadrian, of Antonius. The courts of Philip, Alexander, Croesus. All just the same. Only the people different. [Aurelius, 2003: 139]

This suggests, again, that political conflict will have a recurrent char-acter, regardless of levels of social development and regime forms. Yet few civil conflicts have occurred in the developed countries of the West since 1950 (González Calleja 2013: 25). In the countries of the European Union and North America, and states like New Zealand, the sources of conflict do seem far away. Perhaps economic and political development reduces the risk of civil war over time. One important study which refines this view (Hegre et al. 2001), suggests that pure democracies or pure autocracies, once stabilized, are equally less prone to large-scale violence. Civil wars are more likely to happen when regimes enter into uncertain transitions, or when they are 'institutionally inconsistent'. In other words, the evidence suggests that, regardless of economic development, only some regimes are really vulnerable to civil war. It may be cold comfort for those in the Arab world to be told that while transitions are risky, one long-term benefit of a consistent democracy is peace. Aurelius (in the quote above) emphasized the permanent nature of all human conflicts, regardless of how power is exercised. At this stage, it suffices to say that this is not the last time the reader of this book will encounter the difference between an approach which sees the divisiveness of civil war as the natural expression of human nature, and one which provides a contextual explanation for such conflicts.

3

PATTERNS OF CIVIL WAR
SINCE 1945

The poet Seamus Heaney once remarked that after the US-led invasion of Iraq in 2003 the whole world had become 'a big Ulster' (*Irish Times* September 7 2013). This was not the first time that a form of conflict has stood as a metaphor for the violence of an era. Exaggeration has always played a major role in the study of conflict. It has produced book titles like *The European Civil War* (Nolte 1987), *Age of Extremes* (Hobsbawm 1995), *Cataclysms* (Diner 2008), and phrases like 'Global Civil War' (Hardt and Negri 2004) for the history of our era. No doubt the twentieth century was very violent and civil wars have, increasingly, played a large role in that violence, happening in every region of the world at some point, and seemingly growing in destructiveness. Yet if one promise of the systematic approach to the study of conflict is its capacity to identify specific patterns, what follows will reveal whether civil war should stand as a faithful metaphor for the history of the past century.

The idea of the whole world becoming a big Ulster also raises the question of whether there is a global pattern, in the sense of the European experience up to 1945 being the forerunner of what comes later in other parts of the world. The recent literature on civil war has shifted the attention of scholars of conflict away from the three conflicts which defined Europe's twentieth century: the two World Wars and the Cold War. Yet did these conflicts not extend European patterns of conflict and violence to the rest of the world after 1945, making this not a European, but a global cycle of conflict? These wars had first made Europe 'a dark continent' (Mazower 1998), forcing countless millions to live as if stuck in a dark tunnel in which the boundaries between war and peace were blurred for much of their lives. Landmark books such as Elie Kedourie's *Nationalism* (1960), Michael Mann's *The Dark Side of Democracy* (2005), and Andreas Wimmer's *Waves of War: Nationalism, State Formation and Ethnic Exclusion in the Modern World* (2013) suggest that those who would enter this tunnel after 1945 were not only Europeans.

On the other hand, there may be no patterns. When we hear news of violence from Iraq—an improvised device exploding at a roadside in one part of Baghdad, the detonation of a car-bomb in another—our impression is of chaotic, unpredictable, and indiscriminate violence. Moreover, patterns look different depending on the perspective of the observer. The former US Secretary of State, Robert MacNamara, once said of Vietnam that to us it was part of the Cold War, but to them down below it was a civil war (Morris 2003). The view from below requires us to study patterns, not from above, but region by region, and then within regions. When we do, the shift of perspective will qualify the view that the world has become 'a big Ulster'. Some regions, such as South America, have actually become more peaceful. In contrast, the Middle East retains the potential to cause major inter-state conflict. Variation within regions is also pronounced. Burma was one of the wealthiest countries in South-East Asia before 1960. Largely because of economic mismanagement by the military regime, it is now 'a crisis state'. Ultimately, the patterns of civil war show a great deal of variation within an admittedly very violent experience of modernity.

Violent modernity

The twentieth century was dominated by the experience of war, by images of war, and by talk of war. At its heart are the two World Wars, which resulted in more loss of life than any previous conflicts in world history, perhaps comparable in their impact to the bubonic plague in the Middle Ages, or to some natural disasters in Antiquity. They took place at the heart of Europe—were 'German wars' in some sense—but ideological principles important to non-Europeans were also at stake. The ideas of empire, national self-determination, revolution, equality, and democracy would continue to unsettle the world after 1945. While Europe itself found peace in the shadow of the Iron Curtain after 1945, the lives of people in sub-Saharan Africa, Central America, the Indian subcontinent, and South-East Asia, became plagued by civil war. We can see two spikes in the incidence of civil war as part of this cycle of conflict: one immediately after 1945, and then a second peak after the collapse of communism in 1989. As the Cold War ended, the West took on the mantle of global policeman, committed to intervening (in the Balkans, Africa, Central America, and the Middle East) where it thought necessary, but also, in the war on terror, creating wars which were neither inter-state wars nor civil wars.

Before considering the place of civil war within this cycle of conflict, note the paradox: we live in a world dominated by talk of democracy, human rights, progress, and internationalism, but the past century has been unprecedented in the scope and intensity of its violence (Mališević 2010). One historian has concluded that while at the beginning of the Middle Ages the death toll of all previous wars in history amounted to a mere 60,000, the twentieth century alone resulted in more than 110 million deaths caused directly by warfare in general (Eckhardt 1992: 272). The total number killed in all wars (187 million according to Eric Hobsbawm) was more than 10 per cent of the world population as it was in 1913 (Hobsbawm 2007: 15). Other facts are not reassuring. The share of civilian casualties in war rose from less than 5 per cent in World War I, to 66 per cent in World War II, to more than 80 per cent today (ibid.:18).

In addition, there has been a general tendency for large numbers of people to be killed by their own governments, typically when authoritarian states become involved in war. Data collected by an American political scientist, Rudolph Rummel (1994), suggests that after 1914 deaths suffered at the hands of one's own government have been comparable to casualties in wars between states. Rummel showed that the states that killed their citizens tended to be autocratic, and revolutionary states were the most homicidal, especially when involved in major wars. The worst offenders were China (Communist 1959, 1967, and Nationalist 1928–49), Nazi Germany (1933–45), and the Soviet Union (1917–87). Together with Cambodia, Yugoslavia, and Vietnam, between 1900 and 1987 these three states accounted for a total of 128 million killings, or 84 per cent of the total (Rummel 1995: Table 1, 3). 'Death by Government' has thus formed a major part of this violent modernity.

Nor was there a pause. Eric Hobsbawm cites Hobbes' definition of war: 'consisting not only in battle or the act of fighting, but in a tract of time wherein the will to contend by battle is sufficiently known' (2007: 16). This definition allows him to characterize the whole period since 1914 as one of constant war: 'the German War 1914–1945, the Cold War 1945–1989, and now the War on Terror' (ibid.). The Bolshevik revolution was the pivotal event, kick-starting a whole series of revolutionary wars around the globe. Entire family histories become dominated by this cycle of conflict. *Requiem for the East* (2002) is a novel by the émigré Russian writer Andreï Makine. The book begins with the grandfather who deserts from the Red Army during the Russian civil war, and ends with the grandson, the book's narrator, working as a medic and then an intelligence gatherer during Cold War conflicts in Africa and the Middle East. Being first a biography of a Russian family, the book also works as a biography of the Soviet revolution, the story beginning in its initial stages, and ending with the Cold War that saw the defeat of the Soviet system. The father, Pavel, fought in and survived World War II. Just as the revolution provides the link between the different wars that Russia experienced, Pavel is the link between the generations in this story.

So continuous was the experience of conflict after 1900 that a tunnel analogy could be applied to the international history of the twentieth century: with World War I laying the seeds of World War II, which then culminated in the Cold War. One theme in Thucydides is the way language changes as a consequence of war. An example is the everyday use of the term 'war' for non-military issues: the war on drugs, the war on poverty, the war on crime and so on (Hobsbawm 2007: 21). The current 'war on terror' has also mobilized countless governments in a war that had a clear beginning in the events of 9/11, but which also feels like a war without end. The philosopher Hegel posed the question of whether the wounds of history could heal without leaving scars. The Western order which emerged victorious in 1989 still carries at least linguistic scars from its violent past.

The violence within this tunnel was not a throwback to the medieval era. In principle the modern age has little tolerance for the use of violence against fellow human beings: states everywhere are under pressure to conform to universal human rights standards, and events like hangings and floggings are regarded as barbaric (Mališević 2010: 10). Yet the track record of political causes espousing universal ideologies rooted in the European Enlightenment has been no better. The Marxist conception of revolutionary violence was that its use would allow for the elimination of all violence and injustice in the long term (Mališević 2010: 23). Leon Trotsky prophesied that the Russian Revolution would produce the last civil war. As revolution spread itself outward from its new epicentre in Russia—bringing to an end the oppression of the working class—the defeat of capitalism would eventually make future civil wars unnecessary. Yet Trotsky was wrong: there has been no end to domestic conflict and the Marxist regimes in China and the Soviet Union were far more violent than those they replaced. They shared with Nazism the tendency towards state worship, and a willingness to justify mass murder in the name of ideas. For Trotsky a revolutionary transfer of power—from one class to another—required as a precondition 'a real contradictory situation', most of all in the form of dual power (Bolsinger 2001: 73). Yet in Russia neither the ending of the dual-power situation—through the victory of the Bolsheviks in the civil war—nor the abolition of private property led to the 'withering away' of the state. Rather these revolutionary regimes exercised state power like no other.

According to the Polish moral philosopher Leszek Kolakowski the twentieth century was not unique in seeing millions of people murdered in the name of political goals (2012: 74–91). Where it stood out was in the elaboration of sophisticated ideologies to justify such measures, and their consistent appeal to political elites of every disposition. Sinişa Mališević, a sociologist, adds that lethal violence on such a scale requires social organization. Prior to the modern age human beings were rather 'bad at violence', however much they glorified it. Lethal violence on a mass scale requires social organization, which modern conditions have given rise to in two important ways: (1) the application of bureaucratic principles of organization to militaries, which made them 'able to act swiftly and murder millions in a matter of months if not days', and (2) the ability of states and other organizations to ideologically penetrate the minds of large numbers of people in an era of mass culture (Mališević 2010: 118–46).

There has nonetheless been a dramatic decline in major international conflict since 1945. In *The State, War, and the State of War* the International Relations scholar Kalevi Holsti shows that since 1717 there has been a steady rise in the number of states, but not in the number of inter-state wars (1996: 24). Moreover, the number of states did rise sharply between 1945 and 1995—from 30 to 140—but the same period only saw a rise from 25 to 38 inter-state wars. The problem is that there has been no reduction in the amount of civil war. The sociologist Anne Hironaka showed that while from 1816 up to about 1940 the number of inter-state wars, and the number of civil wars, roughly corresponded, after 1940 only the civil war figures shot up (2008: 6). Most significantly, after 1940 both the number of civil wars, and the number of former colonies which became independent, took off in the same direction. Some useful statistics were presented in a short article by Charles Tilly, first published in 2002. His findings are summarized in the box below. The most intriguing pattern is that the dramatic decline in conventional inter-state war has been accompanied by a cumulative growth in the number of intra-state or civil wars. Africa exemplifies the pattern best; civil wars have become very common since 1945 in a continent which has only produced a handful of wars between states.

What explains the pattern of more civil war, but less inter-state war? First, the nuclear stand-off between the United States and the Soviet Union meant that proxy wars became a less costly method of waging war after 1945. Hence a 'displacement effect' of the Cold War was countless civil wars, ranging from Central America, to South Asia, to Southern Africa. The worst of these, Angola, China, Cambodia, Greece, Korea and Vietnam, were decisive events in the evolution of the Cold War.

'Violence, Terror and Politics as Usual'

Research question: What explains the most striking trends in collective violence, the decline in inter-state war, and the prevalence of intrastate violence with an increasing involvement of irregular forces (mercenaries, militias, and paramilitaries)?

Facts: Between 1900 and 1999 there were about 250 new wars (international or civil).That means that there were two or three big new wars every year. These wars resulted in about a million deaths per year. Additionally, the number of independent states also arose from about 100 in 1960, to 161 in 1999.

Approach: The article explains patterns of civil war in terms of respective strengths of state and society. It also shows the growing effectiveness of bottom-up violence, which is seen as another form of collective action.

Argument: The main factor influencing the current trends in collective violence is the large number of weak states, and the fact that weak governments in those states have to face increasingly better-financed and better-armed opponents.

(Charles Tilly 2002)

Second, the Cold War destabilized large parts of the world. Its early stages produced the highest global casualties resulting from civil war since the Russian Revolution: total deaths per annum rose to around 200,000 persons per year between 1945 and 1949. After 1950 this figure declined dramatically (*The Economist* 9–15 November 2013). The 'new wars' literature suggests that the end of the Cold War created a wave of new wars, which peaked in number between 1990 and 1993, and were novel in their destructiveness. However, a statistical comparison of the two periods (1946–89 versus 1990–2002) showed that the Cold War led to far more destruction and violence in terms of battle deaths and violence against civilians (Melander, Öberg, and Hall 2009). Hence, contrary to popular belief, the Cold War was more destructive than globalization. Many affected countries are yet to recover.

Thirdly, the impact of this violence was greatest in poorer and new states that did not have the strength to project their power externally. Their violence would remain directed inwards. Holsti sees the post-1945 context as one that generally favoured micro-nationalisms, insurgencies, and warlords in their struggles against the state (1996: 41–61). His figures show that between 1945 and 1995 there were an average of 0.85 internal wars per state, and the states affected were mainly post-colonial (ibid.: 24). Regions are of course distinct: North America is also post-colonial, but has seen no major civil war or inter-state war in this period. Nonetheless the link between decolonization and civil war has been important in most regions of the world. It has been estimated that 77 per cent of the civil wars which occurred after 1945 have taken place in new states (Newman 2014: 184).

To return to the initial question: were the conflicts in the new states the product of Europe's experience of modernity and violence being externalized, and its methods and ideologies of mass violence extending (south and east) after 1945? At first glance the answer is yes. Stanley Payne's *Civil War in Europe 1905–1949* (2011) is a study of revolutionary civil wars in Europe, from that of Finland in 1918 to Greece between 1946 and 1949. Revolutionary (and counter-revolutionary) violence over the issue of communism provides the link between the cases he covers. These wars emerged in three contexts: peripheral countries struggling to modernize, newly created states, and those traumatized by outside conquest or defeat in war. The same contexts would produce more revolutionary violence further afield after 1945 (Payne 2011: 226).

On the other hand, conflict histories have clearly diverged since 1945: Europe generally stabilized after the Greek civil war which ended in 1949. No major civil war would occur on either side of the Iron Curtain between then and the collapse of communism in 1989. Compare Europe's experience since 1945 with that of sub-Saharan Africa. Between 1914 and 1945 this part of Africa was largely unaffected by Europe's conflicts, between 1945 and 1989 violence made its entry, and after 1989 we see a host of conflicts at a time when Europe became reunited. Since 1989 almost half of all battle deaths involving states in the world have been the result of conflict in sub-Saharan Africa (Uppsala Conflict Data Programme (UCDP) Conflict Encyclopedia). All but three states in this region have experienced some form of violent conflict since the inception of the Uppsala Conflict Data programme in the 1970s. Hence, as the European continent became pacified, the divergence between different parts of the world actually became more pronounced. The 75 years between 1914 and 1989 have been called 'the historical twentieth century' by the Hungarian historian John Lukacs (2012: 42). Its landscape was dominated 'by two enormous mountain ranges; the First World War, that led to the Second World War, that led to cold war, ending in 1989'. Sub-Saharan Africa may have shared the same chronological time as Europe, but was not part of this 'historical century'. Its experience was dominated by mountain ranges of a different kind.

The key difference is that while violence in Europe in the past two centuries was very much the work of its larger long-established states, and reached its excesses during major international conflict, outside Europe violence found its worst expression in domestic conflict. For Tilly (1995), in the more successful European states the pattern had been for the state to pacify its population over time, to the extent that traditions of protest and mobilization became more peaceful. Indeed, states such as France were able to prevent, eliminate, or neutralize civil war, falling prey to 'state weakness' only in trivial ways. One consequence was that deaths occurred largely in international and colonial rather than civil wars. Yet almost exactly the opposite processes have been happening in many parts of the developing world (Tilly 1995: 185–6).

One indicator of this difference is the longer duration of contemporary civil wars. In *Neverending Wars* Hironaka argues that the average duration of civil wars has tripled since 1945 (2008: 33–73). Table 3.1 shows the extent to which some conflicts became self-perpetuating in

Table 3.1: The duration of civil wars 1945–2013*

More than a decade	More than two decades	More than three decades
Burundi	Angola	Afghanistan
The Congo	El Salvador	Chad
Indonesia (West Papua)	Guatemala	Cambodia
Lebanon	India (Kashmir)	Colombia
Mozambique	Indonesia (Timor Leste and Aceh)	Ethiopia
Rwanda	Iran (Kurds)	Israel/Palestine
	Iraq	Myanmar
	Northern Ireland	Philippines
	Peru	Somalia
	South Africa (Namibia)	Uganda
	Sri Lanka	
	Turkey	
	Vietnam	

* Sudan could have been included, but was omitted from this group presumably because those conflicts which took place between 1963–72, 1983–91, and 2003–6 were not considered one conflict.
Source: 'Daily Chart: Inner Turmoil', *The Economist*, 13 November 2013.

this period. Twenty-nine civil wars lasting more than a decade are included. Twenty-three lasted for more than two decades. Twenty-two took place in independent states that were formed in the twentieth century. Notably, Northern Ireland is the only European case included, but the only European parallels for the massive humanitarian disasters experienced in a case like Sudan since independence, are probably those conflicts fought in Russia and Ukraine after the Bolshevik revolution.

The transition to the nation-state model and the ideological heat of the Cold War are two facets of Western history which combined to produce an explosion of civil war elsewhere in the 1940s and 1950s. The spikes and troughs in the incidence of all wars over the past two centuries reflect historical turning-points in the transition to the nation-state model, as with 1918, 1945, or 1989 (Wimmer 2013: 25). It is also true that the factors which had polarized Europe—radical ideologies, social conflict, foreign manipulation, and ethnic conflict— were more prevalent in other parts of the world after 1945 (Payne 2011: 230). Nonetheless, it is not sufficient to invoke European precedents for what happened in the other regions of the world since 1945: we have to identify causes unique to this period, or a factor which has gained significance since then. Indeed there is general agreement on the emergence, since 1945, of a new domestic and international environment in which the balance between state and society became tilted against the state. The pattern has led people to speak of a conflict cycle, in which factors such as opportunity, grievance, and inequality have made post-colonial statehood a debilitating experience, extending far beyond the life experiences of those who gained independence initially.

Patterns of internal war in the new states

The significance of decolonization can be grasped by considering the rate at which new states became formed. Between 1870 and 1914 there were around 50 sovereign states in existence. Things changed greatly between the two World Wars. While the League of Nations had 42 member states when it was set up in 1920; its successor, the United Nations began with 51 member states in 1945, but membership increased to 82 by 1960, 135 by 1973, and 184 by early 1994 (Alter 1994: 70). Arguably, the dramatic expansion in the number of states has created an unprecedentedly new context in which violent conflicts could proliferate.

Since 1945 we have seen multiple struggles for state power: made worse by the fact that the new states were generally new and insecure vis-à-vis the populations they govern. A three-step sequence could be observed: over a hundred new states were formed out of the collapse of the European empires; they often had to exercise force to establish or expand their authority; and in some states later ethnic/secessionist challenges perpetuated the conflict cycle. In a minority of cases secession constituted a fourth step. This sequence implies the existence of an endless struggle to establish viable states and nations in the wake of Empire. Just as none of the multinational empires which were in existence in 1900 have survived, it has been no easy task to find a formula for legitimacy for many new states.

There are different philosophical perspectives on why civil war would follow the creation of so many new states. For the French philosopher, Jean Jacques Rousseau, human beings were naturally pacific, but the state, unlike human beings, possessed no limits to its ambitions. More states would simply mean more war. This has indeed been the case since 1945—but only in the form of more civil war. The difference returns us to Hobbes, for whom civil war was the natural activity of humankind, absent external restrictions. Hobbes' perspective suggests that the occurrence of civil wars should be explained in terms of the strength or weakness of the state. Yet when a new state is formed civil war could also be motivated by desire, rather than fear. For the literary scholar René Girard (1995), desire is imitative, oriented to objects that others desire. This desire can lead to rivalry about women, land, or states; it often escalates to the point that it comes to dominate the relationship of the rivals, even to the extent that the

77

original object loses its importance. A new state is a new object for people to desire.

In terms of the empirical patterns, what types of conflict have the new states experienced? Historically, civil wars primarily took three major forms: succession conflicts, revolutionary wars, and secessionist struggles (Payne 2011: 1–12). If René Girard was right, one would expect the oldest form, succession conflicts, to produce civil wars relatively soon after independence. Table 3.2 contains data on the 31 decolonized states (out of a total of 133) in which civil war took place soon after independence. The table includes both the first instance of civil war after independence, as well as conflicts which emerged during the independence struggle. The states in the left-hand column are grouped from top to bottom, according to how close the first instance of civil war was to the gaining of independence. Table 3.2 also gives the dates for the outbreak of these civil wars, the years these states became independent, and the months between independence and the outbreak of civil war.

The main source is the Correlates of War database on intra-state war for the period 1816–1997. This database is one of several constructed at the University of Michigan since 1963 which try to systematically trace the reasons for the outbreak of all wars since 1816. The database also contains data on the number of independent states that emerged since 1816. Table 3.2 covers only new states that became independent since 1930. Yet since different datasets define civil war differently, in order not to miss out on significant conflicts, information from the Uppsala Conflict Data Programme and the online UCDP Conflict Encyclopedia is also included. The figures are not generally agreed, but the table does show how quickly civil wars can develop in new states: two-thirds of these states (20 out of 31) experienced civil war within ten years of independence; 18 out of 31 started within ten years; 11 out of 31 started within five years; and 9 out of 31 started within one year of or in the same year as independence. For only 5 out of these 31 conflicts could it be said that they were not succession conflicts of some kind. Yemen stands out in experiencing civil war 76 years after independence.

Table 3.2: Decolonization, succession crises, and the timing of civil war*

State Name	YrIndep	YrBeg	MonBeg	BrkOutPrd	YrEnd	MonEnd	Subsequent Civil Wars?
Zimbabwe	1980	1972	12	−8	1979	12	1983–7
Saudi Arabia	1932	1929	3	−3	1930	1	No
Algeria	1962	1962	7	0	1963	1	1992–9
Congo Democratic Republic	1960	1960	7	0	1965	9	1997, 1998–2002
Angola	1975	1975	11	0	1991	5	1992–4, 1998–2002
Georgia	1991	1991	12	0	1994	5	2004, 2008
Bosnia-Herzegovina	1992	1992	3	0	1995	11	No
Rwanda	1962	1963	11	1	1964	2	1994, 1997–8, 2001
Indonesia	1949	1950	5	1	1950	11	Multiple**
Tajikistan	1991	1992	5	1	1997	6	No
Azerbaijan	1990	1991	12	1	1994	7	No
Mozambique	1975	1976	6	2	1992	10	No

(continued)

Table 3.2: Continued

State Name	YrIndep	YrBeg	MonBeg	BrkOutPrd	YrEnd	MonEnd	Subsequent Civil Wars?
Uganda	1962	1966	5	4	1966	6	No
Chad	1960	1966	11	6	1971	6	Multiple**
Philippines	1946	1950	9	6	1952	7	No
Laos	1954	1960	10	6	1962	7	1963–8, 1976–9, 1989–90
Sudan	1956	1963	10	7	1972	2	1983–91, 2003–6
Nigeria	1960	1967	7	7	1970	1	1980–1, 1999–2000, 2004
Liberia	1980	1989	12	9	1990	11	1992–5, 1996, 2002–3
Burundi	1962	1972	4	10	1972	5	1993–8, 2001–3
Lebanon	1943	1958	5	15	1958	9	Multiple**
Cambodia	1953	1970	3	17	1975	3	1989–91, 1993–7
Yemen People's Republic	1967	1986	1	19	1986	1	No
Somalia	1960	1982	4	22	1997	12	2006–8
Jordan	1946	1970	9	24	1970	9	No

Iraq	1932	1959	3	27	3	1959	Multiple**
Sierra Leone	1961	1991	3	30	4	1996	1998–9 (2000)
Ethiopia	1941	1974	1	33	5	1991	1999, 2002–3
Congo	1960	1997	6	37	10	1997	1997, 1997–8
India	1947	1985		38		1997	Various territorial conflicts
Yemen	1918	1994	2	76	7	1994	2004–5

* (a) This table includes only larger conflicts. In some countries for which this table states no subsequent civil war took place, there were territorial conflicts of smaller extent which took place well after independence. This is the case in the Philippines, India, and Yemen. However, for the purposes of classification those conflicts have not been considered civil wars. Smaller episodes of conflict—a two-week conflict in Saudi Arabia in 1979, violence against civilians in Laos between 1989 and 1990, and the violence between the Movement for Peace and government forces in 1998 in Tajikistan—are not included. (b) The table is mainly based on the Correlates of War dataset (COW). The timing of particular conflicts in the second most influential dataset, the UCDP Conflict Encyclopedia, is sometimes different. Hence, not all the dates and periods above are uncontested. The reason is that the COW and UCDP datasets use different methods of defining war. COW defines a war as a sustained combat, which involves organized armed forces and results in a minimum of 1,000 battle-related fatalities within a 12-month period (COW Codebook, by Meredith Reid Sarkees). The UCDP in contrast requires a minimum of 25 battle-related deaths per calendar year in order to include it in a dataset. Among the problematic cases are the Abkhazia conflict in Georgia, Rwanda, and the wars in Chad, Somalia, and the Philippines. There are also differences in the timing of the second Sudan conflict, as the COW places it between 1983 and 1991, whereas the UCDP writes about it continuing, on and off, until 2004. The UCDP also considers the first episode of intra-state conflict in Liberia as one which occurred between 1989 and 1996. The year in which the first war in the Democratic Republic of Congo ended is also contested. Finally, the UCDP describes the Lebanese civil war as an on-and-off conflict between 1975 and 1990.

** The dates for the multiple subsequent civil wars are: Indonesia (1953, 1956–62, 1965–9, 1976–8, 1976–9, 1989–91, 1999–2002, 2003); Chad (1980–4, 1989–90, 1998–2000, 2005–6); Lebanon (1975–6, 1978, 1983–4, 1989–90); Iraq (1961–3, 1965–6, 1969–70, 1974–5, 1985–8, 1991, 1994–5, 1996).

Sources: Correlates of War, 2010; COW Intra-State War Data, 1816–1997 (v 4.1); UCDP Conflict Encyclopedia: http://www.ucdp.uu.se/gpdatabase/search.php.

Yet the majority of the decolonized territories did not experience wars of succession. Many of their future conflicts reflect rather frustration over time with the actual experience of self-rule. Even their succession problems could be viewed as being part of a longer cycle of conflict. To underscore this point, the extreme right-hand column of Table 3.2 gives information on whether these conflicts have reoccured, or returned in new forms later on (as in Algeria, Burundi, Chad, Congo, Iraq, Lebanon, Nigeria, the Philippines, Rwanda, Sudan, and Uganda). This column shows that in a large majority of cases conflict reocccurs.

True, decolonization had created a perfect storm that non-state actors could take advantage of at the moment of state formation. But this does not explain why their challenges were effective and sustainable over a long time: the real question is why has civil conflict been endemic in some states and regions? For example, Nigeria was once a model for how a state could overcome its violent birth pangs. It overcame the secessionist challenge of Biafra during a bloody civil war between 1967 and 1970. Yet half a century later, it has lost the monopoly on the use of force over its territory, and is ranked by international agencies as a crisis state continuously at the mercy of religious violence in some northern provinces. Problems of succession do not explain such cycles of conflict.

Intractable conflict is not new. René Girard's point was that conflicts which begin with desire can sustain themselves long after the original bone of contention has lost its importance. As each side becomes fascinated with each other and winning becomes a question of pride, the issues cease to be negotiable (Kalyvas 2006: 64–6). Madrid's Museo del Prado holds a painting by Goya, of two men fighting, called 'Riña a garrotazos' (brawl with clubs or cludgeons). The painting was painted onto the wall of Goya's house, sometime between 1819 and 1823, as part of a series of 14 paintings. Some call it 'Duelo a garrotazos' but while a duel is usually fought according to rules—with the expectation that it will be brief and conclusive—Goya's intention was to stress how totally obsessed the two men had become with each other. The brawl could have begun as a dispute over land—many are—but this fight will not end in compromise; the two men have been consumed by their enmity to the exclusion of all else. To suggest this, both men were later painted as being knee deep in marshy ground and as totally indifferent to the surrounding countryside. Indeed the field, the surrounding hills, and the sky were painted in generally bright colours. The darkness of the painting lies in the subject matter, not in the colours themselves.

Unlike succession crises, events one can regard as being of an exceptional nature, the suggestion in much of the recent literature is that civil war can become a way of life, encouraged by a situation of state weakness, a relatively permanent but novel condition strongly associated with vulnerability to ethnic and irredentist wars. Indeed another pattern is the increasing prevalence of such conflicts, which commonly take the form of insurgencies with a support base in the rural population. Revolutionary civil wars, which sought to radically alter systems of government, or to introduce new ideas into politics, had been rare or non-existent historically. They then emerged in most parts of the modern world after 1900. The major civil wars of the Cold War period (Angola, Cambodia, China, Cuba, Colombia, El Salvador, Ethiopia, Guatemala, Korea, Mozambique, Nicaragua, and Vietnam) were also wars of this kind. Nonetheless, the end of the Cold War marked a turning-point: wars of secession have largely replaced revolutionary wars in most of Asia and Africa. Africa has seen major ethnic conflicts in Angola, the Congo, Sudan, Ethiopia, Nigeria-Biafra, Rwanda, and Burundi. In Asia violent conflicts in Burma, India, Pakistan-Bangladesh, Sri Lanka, and Indonesia also have had a strong ethnic component.

State weakness may be an inherited condition. Holsti argues that when nationalism strengthened the state and unified populations, it did so organically, when it had time and space in which to grow (1996: 41–61). In contrast, the European colonial empires had had no interest in state-building, they did not prepare the colonies for independence, and the new states did not correspond to older cultural borders. Here an aspect of their weakness was their artificiality, which made them especially vulnerable to secessionist and irredentist conflicts. Hironaka also sees the tolerance of the current international system for weak and failing states as a crucial factor (2008: 2). By committing states to mutual recognition and the peaceful mediation of disputes, the UN system has regulated and prevented wars between states. Yet it has also given weak states a status shared by all states and thus protected them, even when they are not supported by their populations. Her book's subtitle is *The International Community, Weak States, and the Perpetuation of Civil War*.

Alternatively, if we need to explain why a country in conflict in 1965, such as the Sudan, remained so four decades later, some try to identify the relatively permanent conditions under which insurgencies sustain themselves, and especially the role of material resources in their perpetuation. Of the sources of funding insurgent groups could take advantage of, Tilly (2002) lists: cocaine, heroin, sexual services, illegal migrants, dirty money, rubber, oil, diamonds, and other minerals. The low level of democracy has also mattered. Upon independence, the rulers of the new states did not possess much repressive capacity to begin with, so grievances were more easily expressed than under colonial rule. At the same time, demands were rarely met through open institutional channels. Their poor economic performance subsequently meant that structural factors, such as inequality, were not easily overcome, and the conflicts could not easily be resolved by political concessions.

No one observing the rapid collapse of a state like the Central African Republic today, and the way anarchy and civil war almost become equivalent experiences, can dismiss the state weakness perspective on the new state's lasting vulnerability to violent changes. As newly independent states like South Sudan seem to inherit this condition of artificiality (in this case, from the earlier Sudanese state), the prospect that more states will simply mean more war has not diminished at all in some parts of the world since 1950. Yet state weakness should not be allowed to stand as a metaphor for the experience of the whole of the post-colonial world. The image of a weak state is that of a state floundering in troubled seas, but the patterns remain varied across and within regions. The empirical question cannot be why more than 130 new states are generally 'vulnerable' to conflict, but the more precise one of why decolonization resulted in civil war in one state and not another: in Algeria but not in neighbouring Tunisia for instance? Many countries that were in trouble in 1945 remain so today. In South Korea, Taiwan, and Vietnam however, state identity is strong, despite their early experience of conflict. The next section shifts perspective to the regional level in order to trace these patterns more closely.

Patterns across geographical regions

The mass media has certainly raised awareness of a multiplicity of conflicts taking place concurrently in many parts of the world. In the last week of September 2013, it broadcast shocking images of religious massacres in three different countries: Kenya, Iraq, and Pakistan, over one weekend. The impression was that of a global trend in the use of terror against civilians. Every incident was new and shocking, but still related to a general trend of unstoppable momentum. It is as if the whole world had become like a huge and complex city such as that evoked in Peter Ackroyd's novel *Three Brothers* (2013), which projected an image of London as a web so taut and tightly drawn that the slightest movement of any part would send reverberations throughout the whole city (*The Times* 5 October 2013).

The question posed in this section is whether patterns of conflict are sufficiently regular across regions to justify this image of a global or 'web-like' pattern of conflict. Are these regions experiencing similar types and patterns of war? Is there really a global trend, constant across regions, towards more internal and less inter-state war? Arguably, no such trends exist. Indeed Holsti shows that whole regions, but not others, can go from being zones of war to zones of peace. Moreover, patterns within geographical regions show variation, both in terms of the forms of war they experience and in terms of rates of violence. The differences within regions pose the question of whether patterns can be better explained by paying attention to more local sources of conflict.

We have already seen that between 1914 and 1945, Europe saw two World Wars, the Russian Revolution, the collapse of three traditional empires, and Hitler's genocide against the Jews. Yet the Iron Curtain largely stabilized things, despite the large number of states on either side of this division. Alongside the existence of a security system backed up by the Soviet Union and the United States, prosperity became a major source of stability. Indeed the 48 richest states in the world experienced only two wars amongst them since 1949 (the Soviet invasion of Hungary in 1956), with the short conflict between the United Kingdom and Argentina over the Falkland islands, in 1982, being another (González Calleja 2013: 25). The ethnic conflicts—in the Basque region, Cyprus, and Northern Ireland—did not impact on mainstream society as before 1950. Unlike the earlier civil wars in Finland, Greece, Hungary, Ireland, and Spain, control of the capital city was never at issue. What the periphery has been unable to do is to bring violence back to the core, as happened when Gavrilo Princip assassinated Archduke Franz Ferdinand in Sarajevo in 1914. Now it is only through the collapse of financial markets that the periphery can destabilize the core.

Latin America has also had an exceptional experience of conflict transformation, with no wars of secession, and only one major international war since 1941 (Holsti 1996: 150). This contrasts with the violent early record of colonialism up to 1900, when disputes between the new Latin American states over borders were a common source of contention. Remarkably, between 1816 and 1900 the region produced no less than 42 military disputes (Holsti 1996: 151). Considering that there are 12 large states in South America, the pattern is striking. Some credit strong militaries, others the inclusive nature of immigrant cultures, and some scholars stress the existence of legal traditions of dispute resolution between states. Yet the South American trend now is both towards less war and less civil war. The most intractable conflicts were in Central America and also in Colombia, where levels of violence have remained high despite peace being agreed in the early 1990s in El Salvador, Guatemala, and Nicaragua.

In stark contrast, there is no trend towards less war of any kind in the Middle East. Holsti counts the number of wars (of all kinds) in this region between 1945 and 1995 at 33 (1996: 22). Others would put the figure closer to 50. Due to the Israel–Palestine conflict, the local axes of conflict are linked to the international rivalries, giving rise to a series of interconnected conflicts. Indeed hybrid forms of war have flourished in the region (the Arab–Israeli wars in 1948, 1967, and 1973; both Gulf Wars of 1990–91 and 2003 to the present; the Israel–Lebanon war in 2006; and the recurrent Israel–Gaza conflicts, 2004, 2006, 2007, 2008–9, 2012, 2014). The whole future of the inter-state system in the Levant has now been placed under a question mark because of the challenge of ISIS. The Ottoman Empire was replaced by a cluster of fragmented and weak states with contested borders, hostile neigh-bours, and minimal popular support. The partition of Palestine is one obvious source of conflict, but Syria has never given up its claim to Lebanon, Saddam Hussein claimed a historic right to reclaim Kuwait (and its oil) for Iraq, and the replacement of British with Greek authority over Cyprus was always unpopular with Turkish Cypriots. In terms of classic civil wars, Algeria, Lebanon (1958 and 1975–90), Yemen, and Syria have experienced them. Libya can now be added to this list.

Africa stands out for its combination of many internal, but few major international wars. For the period between 1945 and 1995 Holsti gives a figure of 44 wars, seven of which were inter-state wars (1996: 22). Of the 37 internal wars more than half (21) involved an attempt at secession. The numbers of wars per state (44 to 43) makes Africa one of only two regions in the world where the number of wars was greater than the number of states. A comparison could be made with Central America, where the number of conflicts over the past century was also greater than the number of states there. Many so-called civil wars have had important cross-border dimensions, such as those in the Congo, the Central African Republic, Mozambique, Rwanda, Sudan, and Uganda. This means there is no evidence of a secular decline in any form of conflict in Africa. The complex conflict now unfolding in the Democratic Republic of Congo, with seven states involved, is comparable to the Palestine–Israel conflict in its potential to create a regional war between states.

Holsti divides Asia into South, South-East, and East Asia. Together these produced 49 conflicts, only 12 of which were inter-state wars, or wars with external intervention. The number of internal wars (37) is also much greater than the number of states in these subregions (Holsti 1996: 24). It was in East Asia that domestic divisions had the greatest international ramifications during the Cold War: peasant revolutions led to the creation of communist regimes in China, Vietnam, and North Korea, all of which have shown staying power. South Asia has the largest number of conflicts of any world region in Holsti's study. Secession was an issue in 10 of its 14 internal conflicts: those in Afghanistan, India, Pakistan, and Sri Lanka have lasted decades. Another study of the period between 1960 and 1999 judged Asia as a whole to be more peaceful than Africa, and increasingly so, but found that civil war could be more prevalent in East and South Asia than in Africa (Elbadawi and Sambanis 2000: 251–5). It concludes that the East and South Asian experience reflects high levels of ethnic polarization (ibid.: 254).

In fractal geometry the principle of 'self-similarity' means that when we consider an object, the degree of complexity or simplicity, or roughness or smoothness, is similar regardless of whether you observe it from a microscopic or macroscopic perspective. The international historian John Lewis Gaddis gives the example of a cauliflower: when you pull it apart into smaller and smaller pieces, the patterns remain the same (2002: 82). We cannot say this of civil war: when patterns of conflict are viewed at the regional, the national, and the local levels, they do not conform to one global pattern. Inter-state war has become less common in most parts of the world, and in three

88

regions (the Americas, Europe, and South America) all forms of war have become less frequent. In these regions the patterns *are* the same regardless of the scale of politics we are looking at. Elsewhere, the Middle East has experienced many armed conflicts since 1945, but its conflict dynamics are hugely shaped by international rivalry. In Africa and East Asia, persistent civil war seems disarticulated from international war. In short, only some regions of the world show similarity between patterns of conflict at different levels of world politics.

When you consider patterns of conflict region by region, variation also remains very pronounced. Some areas are very violent (Africa, parts of Asia, and the Middle East), while others (Europe and South America) exhibit a pacific trend. Within regions, too, there is variation: Central America is more violent than South America, and South Asia more at risk of civil war than East and South-East Asia. Yet the mere existence of ethnic or regional conflicts in new states should not blind one to the presence in every region of comparatively successful state-building projects. In South-East Asia 'improbable' new states such as Malaysia have survived, and Timor Leste's independence from Indonesia is the sole example of actual secession (Sidel 2012: 143). The collapse of communism created a number of conflicts in Central Asia and Eurasia—such as that between Armenia and Azerbaijan—but a combination of geopolitics and international intervention made for relative peace after the initial wars in the 1990s.

One explanation for the absence of self-similarity is obviously the emergence of regional security systems, which operate at the interstices between international and domestic conflict. In discussing why South America became a zone of peace over the twentieth century, Holsti refers to concepts like 'a distinct international system', 'international political sub-system', and 'regional security complex' (1996: 151). In Table 3.1 the African cases (the Democratic Republic of Congo, Algeria, Sudan, Rwanda, Chad, Uganda, and Nigeria) all experienced civil war within seven years of independence, and most are still in turmoil. In contrast, 3 from 15 former Soviet Republics (Azerbaijan, Georgia, and Tajikistan) suffered from civil war within ten years of the collapse of the Soviet system. The political scientist Charles King also considered the wars in the former Yugoslavia in the 1990s to be successionist wars (2001: 166). They needed little time to develop: indeed the other post-communist conflicts began within two years of independence. Nonetheless a combination of cooperation with the EU and NATO military forces has largely been sufficient to limit the effects of the post-communist conflicts which took place towards Europe's south and east. The current crisis in the Ukraine raises questions about how durable this peace will prove, but the transition from Soviet rule was generally better managed than that from colonial rule.

Another reason for the lack of a clear pattern across regions is that even if there were regularities in the causes of civil war, their actual occurrence will inevitably be unpredictable. Most conflicts since 1945 have been shaped by structural changes, the spread of capitalist markets and the nation state to the Third World being examples. Yet a basic insight of complexity theory in physics is that while big structures unsettle established patterns wherever they move, they still collide and explode in unpredictable ways, and at different levels of the atmosphere. Actual conflict emerges only when dynamic factors (such as human agency, organizational traditions, and ideology) interact with these static environmental factors (such as physical attributes, economic conditions, or social structures). Self-similarity would exist under the demanding condition that both the objective context and the local understanding of that context were similar across states, which is very unlikely to happen.

Patterns only refer to conflicts which occur with sufficient regularity to make themselves apparent to us (Gaddis 2002: 30). They cannot be the basis of theories of why civil wars occur in the same way as, for instance, the theory of relativity in physics or the theory of natural selection in biology. Even regions themselves—while valid geographical concepts—do not, politically, mean as much as their colloquial use implies. Political scientist John Sidel's survey of South-East Asia identifies contrasting patterns of nationhood between peninsular

(Indonesia, Malaysia, the Philippines, and Singapore) and mainland (Burma, Cambodia, Laos, Thailand, and Vietnam) areas of the region (2012: 116–17). Were these patterns the product of a specifically South-East Asian experience? The factors that explain the differences (legacies of colonial rule, incorporation into the world capitalist economy, and the international politics of the Cold War) are hardly unique to the region, even if differences established during an earlier period of South-East Asian history have been important (ibid.: 143–4). Nonetheless, a region-to-region comparison is useful to the extent that it holds up the mirror of experience to some of the hyperbole that flourishes in this field. The world has not become 'a big Ulster' and hopefully never will. Concepts like that of 'a global civil war'—argued for in a 2004 book by Michael Hardt and Antonio Negri—have a metaphorical rather than analytical value. They are valid only in Hobbes' sense of the modern era being a tract of time, where civil war was a possibility all the time, and actually present somewhere, some of the time.

Patterns within conflict zones

The final step is to consider patterns within conflict zones. If patterns are not the product of general factors, or of 'higher levels' of politics, they are more likely to be influenced by past conflicts, or of something specific to the local environment. The concept of a conflict zone is a more local way of explaining recurrent conflict. It directs our attention to those demographic, geographical, cultural, and historical factors which give any local area its special character. In his history of the Mediterranean, the French historian Braudel argued that environmental factors led to historical trends, political events, and wars, not the other way round (2002: Introduction). 'Environmental' is used here because many dimensions of social life, not just the state, matter in reproducing patterns of conflict. This approach is appealing because since 1945 in many countries civil or internal wars have shown a capacity to persist despite the changes in the international system occasioned by the emergence and conclusion of the Cold War.

The concept of a conflict zone suggests that some places (and their populations) are receptive to sources of conflict, whether or not they originate from outside that zone, over more than one generation. Fractal geometry has shown that patterns in physics need not originate high up the scale: they can emerge and sustain themselves at lower levels. For an area to be a conflict zone, the patterns of conflict must be self-sustaining because of factors operating at the lower level of analysis. Moreover, this lower level must explain the tendency for some conflicts to become endemic. Consider the opposition to the US-backed administration in Afghanistan. This resistance could be explained in terms of the failure of specific Western policies, or as a consequence of transnational Islam. Yet since earlier external state-building efforts (by the British and the Russians) also faced such opposition, the patterns of conflict extend, not just across borders, but across time.

Human geography is a perennial factor, which remains relevant to a world where scarcity of oil and water, global warming, climate change, and the demographic explosion are producing resource wars of many kinds. Think of the current civil war in Syria. Turkey's potential control of the water supplied by the Euphrates and the Tigris rivers, the location of oil in the Kurdish areas of Iraq and Syria, the vital position of Aleppo (with stronger connections to Mosul, Baghdad, and Anatolia, than to Damascus), and the lack of sealed and natural borders in an Iraq of many communities, are facets of human geography that have made this conflict a truly regional one. So important have these factors been that one can now see the formation, potentially, of an Islamic state cutting across the original border between Iraq and Syria.

A conflict zone—Northern Ireland within the United Kingdom, for example—may stand out in a wider region of peace. Alternatively, a territory may find itself in a larger region with the same characteristics, as with the Bekaa Valley in Lebanon. Eastern Anatolia in Turkey is a conflict zone of the first kind. It consists of the eastern part of the Anatolian land-mass that has been the territorial heartland of the Turkish Republic since 1923. The zone includes south-eastern Turkey,

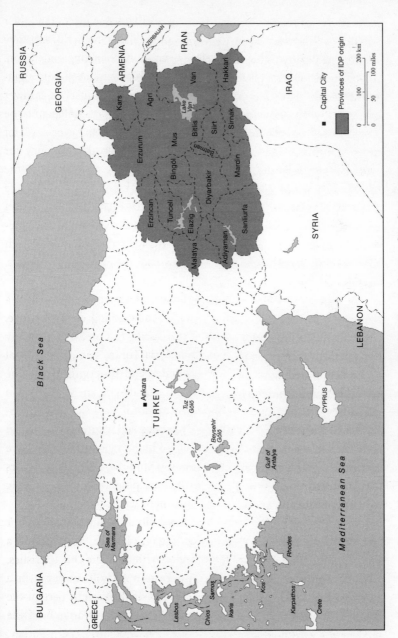

Map 3 Internal displacement (IDPs) in the south-east of Turkey, 1987–2000

in its degree of religiosity very similar to the Middle East, but an area where Kurdish nationalism was sufficiently strong for the dominant Islamist AKP party to lose their electoral majority to the Kurdish BDP (Peace and Democracy Party) in 2011 and see its vote share fall even further to the HDP (People's Democratic Party) in June 2015. With borders now shared with two collapsing states, Iraq and Syria, this area, from Diyarbekir to the Iraqi border (which includes the provinces of Batman, Bitlis, Hakkari, Mardin, Sirnak, Siirt, Tunceli, and Van), has also been the scene of the most persistent fighting between the Kurdish armed group, the PKK, and the Turkish security forces since 1984 (Jongerden 2015: 154). The conflict, which lasted from 1984 to 2013, and has now resumed, was not generally known before the recent battles over the Syrian border town of Kobani. Yet it has spanned four states (including Iran, Iraq, and Syria) and has claimed over 40,000 lives.

One aspect of its human geography is that there is no indigenous majority in an area that has been a crossroad for exchanges between civilizations for thousands of years. During the late Ottoman period, the majority of people in the area stretching north-east from Lake Van to the border with Russia were Armenian. With over 1,600 kilometres between Istanbul and the Iraqi border, much was at stake for the local population, Russia, and the emerging Turkish republic when the Ottoman Empire began to collapse between 1915 and 1923. The historian Mark Levene (1998) argued that the history of eastern Anatolia has been fundamentally marked by competition between the Russian and Ottoman Empires and Iran. In the late nineteenth century this rivalry ignited rival nationalisms among the area's multi-ethnic population. According to him it was this combination of imperial collapse, outside interference, and rival nationalism that led to the genocide of the Armenians in 1915.

The collapse of the Ottoman Empire saw its replacement with several nation states in the region that were committed to imposing national homogeneity on their populations. One can observe the remorseless way in which the nation-state formula becomes diffused downward, from the level of the international system, to that of the nation state, to that of a micro-region, fragmenting political space in the process. Yet if the initial sources of conflict were external, they have been reproduced at the local level since 1923. Over the next century Armenians, Turks, and Kurds, under the banner of self-determination, would all claim ownership of some of this area. Turkish nation-building policies were at their most repressive where, in the east, the elements of human geography posed the greatest barriers to assimilation and the standardization of culture (Üngör 2011). The period between the two World Wars saw two Kurdish revolts in 1925 and 1937, and massacres of Kurds and Alevi Muslims by the Turkish army in Dersim (now Tunceli) in 1937–38.

The pattern of conflict has also been extended over time in the sense that the Kurdish insurgent organization PKK (*Parti Karkerani Kurdistan/* the Kurdish Workers Party) claims continuity with the earlier short-lived Sheik Said (1925) and Dersim revolts (1938). Each revolt occasioned severe state repression, and Kurdish resentment at official policies of linguistic assimilation and martial law (combined with economic grievances) remains strong. Yet an all-out civil war between Kurds and Turks did not materialize in the 1990s; the PKK campaign took the form rather of an insurgency: it involved 'the organised use of subversion and violence to seize, nullify, or challenge political control of a region...through the use of force, propaganda, subversion and political mobilization' (the US Bureau of Political-Military Affairs 2009: 6). Environmental factors, including the mountainous nature of the south-east, the availability of sanctuary across the border (with PKK training camps first in Syria, then in Iraq), the area's status as a conduit for drugs from east to west, and the large refugee and diaspora population in Europe, help explain why this current conflict has gone on so long. The borders with Syria and Iraq are largely fictitious: taken together they extend over 1,500 kilometres. Not only can people cross them freely, but families can straddle them, especially in the Hatay province of Turkey, which was once part of Syria. Many PKK recruits come from northern Syria and the area around the disputed town of

Kobani. In contrast to these relatively permanent features of human geography, the ideological stance of the PKK has shifted from Marxist-Leninism to nationalism (sometimes with religious overtones), to democracy and equal citizenship today.

My stress on human geography should not be taken to mean that because there is a Kurdish-speaking population, or a land which people call 'Kurdistan', such a conflict zone within Turkey *had* to emerge. A useful distinction is made by the historian Pierre Vilar when posing the question of whether his subject is the history of Catalonia or of the Catalan lands (which includes parts of France and Spanish regions like Valencia where Catalan nationalism is weaker) (2012: 34–5). He suggests that the 'hecho Catalan' ('the Catalan fact'), which manifests itself among the geography of European ethnic groups, is of a linguistic and ethnic kind. This fact has impressed itself on the map over a long period of time, and has survived political events which have tended both to unite and separate the various parts of this reality. In contrast, 'el fenómeno catalán' (the Catalan phenomenon), the recent product of the nineteenth and twentieth centuries, can be compared in its combination of political demands and cultural renewal to other European nationalisms. It came to play an important, even fundamental role in Spanish history only in the twentieth century. In the Turkish context we can also ask whether the history of conflict is that of eastern Anatolia of something called Kurdistan. As with the Catalans, there is an enduring Kurdish reality or *hecho* of the ethnic and linguistic kind, but the emergence of Kurdish nationalism as a phenomenon—with the potential to unify and separate Kurds across the different borders—is recent, and can be compared to a variety of ethnic struggles that have emerged in the second half of the twentieth century.

In order to explain its relatively late emergence, one needs to take into account not only the linguistic and cultural realities, but the early history of the Turkish Republic which was founded in 1923 by Mustafa Kemal (Atatürk) in 1923. Committed as it was to the creation of one Turkish nation, the new Turkish Republic refused to accept Kurdish

PATTERNS OF CIVIL WAR SINCE 1945

aspirations and equated citizenship with Turkishness, meaning that minorities had to qualify as Turks before they could enjoy equal citizenship (Barkey and Fuller, 1998: 10). In *Nations as Zones of Conflict*, Hutchinson develops a non-spatial concept of a conflict zone, which he applies to communities in a continuous process of conflict over their foundation myths (2005: 77–115). The worst crises of the post-colonial state occur during the early stages of state-building and their sharpest political conflicts tend to be those fought over the birth pangs of the political community. Consistent with Hutchinson's stress on foundation myths, during the crisis of 'Kemalism' in the 1990s, Kurdish nationalists came to challenge both the official interpretation of the Turkish Republic's founding, and the official language protected by its current (1982) constitution. The fact that the challenge came late does not mean it was not motivated by historic grievances. All their organizations now share a minimum demand for the state to enable the Kurdish language to be revived through public instruction in both private and public schools.

The importance of these founding events brings into the discussion the idea of 'sensitivity to starting conditions' (Gaddis 2002: 64), in which particular actions at the start of a process have larger consequences further down the line. As participants during the war of independence against the Western powers and Greece (1919–23) some Kurds felt betrayed when deprived of special status under the Republic, and resented the subsequent policies of assimilation, centralization, and repression. The early decades of the Republic could also be considered formative in that eastern Anatolia remained a peripheral region economically; the developmental impetus of the new Republic was westward. Ever since 1923 the line stretching from Istanbul in the north-west to Diyarbekir in the south-east, has represented a developmental continuum, with the extremes of both wealth and poverty concentrated at both ends.

Only one part of Turkey can be considered a conflict zone; the patterns of conflict since 1923 reflect the fact that the contradictions of the Republic are felt most acutely in eastern Anatolia (Üngör 2011).

Elsewhere Turkish state- and nation-building have largely been successful. But in eastern Anatolia state-formation and initial repression led to historical grievances among the Kurds, which were renewed in the early 1990s when both the PKK violence and the state's response became very brutal in the south-east. In terms of 'the sensitive dependence on initial conditions', perhaps the emergence of an authoritarian Republic under Atatürk constituted a point at which small shifts at the beginning of the process produced large consequences at the end of it (Gaddis 2002: 120). Had the Republic initially been more accommodating, culturally or politically, perhaps a less polarized form of politics might have developed. With respect to patterns of violence in conflict zones what eastern Anatolia shows is that, even where the original sources of conflict originate outside a state (in imperial rivalry), conflict becomes extended over time because of the facts of human geography and the sensitivity of this pattern to initial starting conditions.

The evidence of patterns of conflict within a specific zone raises issues of definition. What is it that a historian of Kurdish nationalism in Turkey in the 1990s would be observing: an event (called civil war, terrorist campaign, or insurgency) or simply a pattern of conflict extended over time? To assess causes and consequences the social scientist usually defines a conflict with clear beginnings and ends. Yet to study patterns within a conflict zone, the periods of peace between conflicts, and the changes they bring are less significant than those constant factors that give a region its status as a conflict zone. The idea of the 'conflict zone' allows different instances of conflict to be linked, but says little about the politics that produce each specific instance of conflict (in Turkey 1925, 1938, 1984, 2015). This is because any theory which tries to explain a pattern of conflict extended over time, and which stresses relatively permanent factors like geography, ends up defining conflict in more general rather than more specific terms: what matters are not specific conflicts, but a wider process in which the individual instances of conflict have been produced by those over-arching environmental factors.

The reality that this conflict has been extended over long periods of time also raises important questions about how to interpret such a contemporary conflict, historically. If the current Kurdish conflict (1984 to 2012) is the latest in a succession of rebellions going back to 1925, some historical questions follow. Have political and economic changes since then made no difference? Did the current conflict begin in 1984, 1999, or the 1960s (Yeğen 2011: 138–9)? Was the last military coup in 1980 not a watershed? Alternatively, in place of these historical questions, we could also explain these recurrent conflicts sociologically, in terms of some relatively unchanging features of the social and physical environment that characterizes the south-east of Turkey. In Turkey some of these factors have become more important as a consequence of globalization. The possibilities for drug smuggling, the financial support of the Kurdish diaspora, the existence of lengthy borders with failed states (Iraq and Syria), and the availability of sanctuary in the mountains for the Kurdish guerrillas (the PKK), have made this ethnic conflict well-nigh intractable.

Indeed most would accept that environmental factors help explain why a small-scale organization (the PKK), which was listed as a terrorist organization by the EU and the United States, could grow beyond its origins in the divisions of the Turkish left in the late 1970s, and remain undefeated by such a strong state. Yet the idea of a conflict zone should not be used in a reductionist way, implying that environmental or spatial factors simply produce patterns of conflict. Braudel thought that geography could be a marvellous explanatory tool, so long as it is used without determinism (2001: 157). Looking at patterns of conflict geographically can formulate and clarify questions. Since Turkey is a huge country, and since many Kurds live west of Ankara, the question is why conflict has become intractable only in this eastern region. Do its physical characteristics—mountainous terrain and porous borders with Iraq and Syria—provide too good an opportunity for insurgency or too insecure an environment for the state? Although Turkey is a strong state in this region, perhaps the problem is that the long borders with Iran, Iraq, and Syria, (which extend as long as the distance between Istanbul and the most eastern part of Turkey) make it paranoid about its security. Or is relative poverty the reason Kurds vote in large numbers for the BDP (and now the HDP) in the south-east but generally not elsewhere? Braudel stressed that mere geography cannot resolve such issues of interpretation: 'men and their history complicate the picture and confuse the issue' (2001: 157). To what extent has the late emergence of Kurdish nationalism been conditioned by the weakening of the left since the military coup in 1980? Had there been no coups, perhaps a religious party like the AKP would have gained an electoral hegemony in the south-east before now. In contrast, the journalist Nuray Mert (2013) argues that 'the radical line' in Kurdish politics appeals to so many precisely because it involves two revolts: one (that we know of) against statist assimila-tionist projects, and another (within the south-east and its social structures) against the paternalist, patriarchal and elitist/cooptational survival strategies of past Kurdish elites.

Summary

So numerous are the conflicts that patterns of civil war can now be studied statistically. Enquiry into the duration of wars in different periods, the changing level of casualties over time, the likelihood of civil war at any given time in a region, and the role of factors widely associated with civil war—such as poverty—has produced solid find-ings. This chapter has identified some patterns: the decline in inter-state wars, the location of the lion's share of internal conflicts in recently decolonized territories, and the tendency for insurgency to underpin other forms of internal war. Nonetheless, in a spirit of deconstruction, patterns have been examined here in order to hold up the mirror of experience to some of the hyperbole that flourishes in this field. The principle of 'self-similarity' can require that an object is composed of subunits and sub-subunits on multiple levels that (statistically) resemble the structure of the whole object. Yet there is no one conflict history of the world since 1945, and a self-similar pattern in that structural sense does not exist. Indeed it is hard to avoid the conclusion that our assumption that there should be a global pattern is the product of media representation. Although we remain in our armchairs, the spread of social media and of global news coverage encourages us to feel not only that we are everywhere at once, but that we are well-informed about everything.

Human beings are pattern-seeking mammals. Their quest is often for coherence among chaos, and the search for patterns in the universe usually comes down to questions about its ultimate origins. When it comes to patterns of conflict however, the 'big picture' answers that flourish in religion, and some branches of science, will provide only shallow explanations. One reason is that any individual conflict can be recruited into more than one general account of what has made the modern world so violent. Consider the origins of the civil war in Mozambique. The conflict which began in 1976 so soon after independence is usually considered an internal or civil war. Yet it required external intervention to start the Renamo insurgency. Its rapid absorption into the vortex of the Cold War followed, and it was only when outside support began to dry up that a war-weary public got the peace it deserved in 1992. Mozambique *can* be recruited into a general story about the connection between state weakness and civil war, because the border with Rhodesia was porous in 1975–6. This internal wars perspective is Hobbesian in the sense that—absent strong state authority—the sources of conflict were never very far away when independence came. Yet if the sources of conflict were actually other states (which were not far away either), Rousseau (who mistrusted states) is a better guide than Hobbes, and the pattern could also be one of inter-state conflict extending itself into one of the poorest countries of the world.

Another reason why it is hard to see general patterns is simply because conflicts by their nature are not easy to categorize. In geometry, when a fractal object has a fractional dimension, this means that something should look the same from near as from afar. Yet the closer we get to individual conflicts, the less clear the object under view becomes. Andreas Wimmer argues that the replacement of empire with the nation state is correlated with the patterns of all wars, including civil wars (2013: 7). His thesis is a good candidate for a fractal approach, because the nation state became the dominant regime form at the global level; it transformed inter-state relations at the regional level, and the successor nation states then found themselves facing the challenge of micro-nationalisms. In order to trace this process, we use categories like national, ethnic, and secessionist conflict. Yet categorizing conflicts in this way tends to homogenize distinct phenomena. Angola's conflict, for example, could be considered an anti-colonial, an ethnic, or a resource war (Cramer 2006: 11). This conflict also underwent several transformations, including the resumption of hostilities after the rejection of a democratic election in 1994 by the UNITA leader Jonas Savimbi. As Harry Eckstein emphasized, internal wars contain many types of conflict within them, and deciding of which patterns of conflict they are an instance is not easy.

Ultimately, the categorization of conflicts—and hence the tracing of patterns—is prone to what is known in physics as the uncertainty principle; the act of observation alters what is being observed. Ideologies and belief systems are frames through which *both* the participants and the outside scholar studies events. At a certain level of abstraction these frames are similar. Yet they become very blurry the closer one gets to the conflict itself. This makes it very hard for patterns of conflict to meet the test of self-similarity in fractals; ideology and conflict do not look the same close up as from afar. In his history of cataclysms, for example, Dan Diner (2008) suggests that the end of the Cold War rendered the class-based explanations of the past temporary, since in place of the language of class and democracy came a near-universal rhetoric of territory and ethnicity, distinctiveness and memory. Yet this conclusion assumes the validity of the dichotomy between class and nation. The reality is that conflict often occurs when both of the axes reinforce each other. Diner himself suggests that Polish history, for example, presents us with an exceptionally decisive fusion of two axes of interpretation—a fusion of elements of national strife with elements of universal civil war (2008: 8).

What does this literature tell us about the future? People will want an answer to the question of how much civil war the future will bring. Both the rise of the modern state and the integration of different cultural groups into nations have been extraordinarily violent processes. Perhaps there is a link between the sheer amount of violent group conflicts today and the objective requirements of cultural homogenization in an industrializing age (Gellner 1983). The pessimist will note that this process has only just begun in most of Africa, and that such a future awaits the Middle East—a region created by an imperial system, but yet to be economically or politically integrated. Communications, and ties within this region, have yet to reach the level of social density that would allow for civil war, in the sense of a conflict fought primarily among fellow citizens. What if the template for its future is the more commercialized state of Lebanon? The Lebanon was the first Middle Eastern society to descend—after the arrival of Napoleon and in the context of much outside meddling—into a series of insurrections and sectarian conflicts lasting until the 1860s. The country later experienced two civil wars after 1945; a short one, beginning in 1958, and another lasting from 1975 to 1990. This latter conflict is known in Arabic as *Al-Harb al Ahliyyah al Libnàniyyah*/ the Lebanese People's War.

On the other hand, there are grounds for optimism in the fact that what makes a country or region stable is necessarily affected by various factors, such as climate change, human demography, and technological development, that have the power to upset very robust structures in new ways. Indeed the poet T. S. Eliot went further and maintained that knowledge derived from experience had in fact a limited value (1974: 199). For such knowledge imposed a pattern which falsifies experience, and the pattern is in fact new in every moment, with each new experience bringing a shocking evaluation of what has gone before. Before the annexation of Crimea by Russia in March 2014, the assumption was that the Cold War had ended. Three years ago most Egyptians felt they had lived through a democratic revolution: in March 2014 over 500 members of the Muslim Brotherhood were sentenced to death by a state court. Mexico accomplished a democratic transition during the 1990s. Now its decentralized system of government is under the strain of drug violence as lethal as that in Afghanistan. Mexico's twentieth-century solution to instability had been a combination of presidentialism and the bureaucratic domination of one party (Paz 2005: 337). Will democracy prove a better solution, or will the current violence and the prospect of a 'narco-state' necessitate a return to the *caudillos* of the eighteenth and nineteenth centuries, who assumed power as an antidote to instability, only to perpetuate it?

If our expectations are based on experience, as specific regions become more integrated into the world economy, we can expect the number of civil wars to rise. The very concept of civil war is modern in the sense that it assumes some level of social and political integration to begin with. Yet this chapter has argued against the idea that there is one global conflict history, or that the history of the West before 1945 became the future of the rest after that year. The modern experience of civil war can be compared not to one dark tunnel but to many: a set of tunnels not always intersecting. At some point every society will go through the experience, but the point at which they enter these tunnels, and the time they take to find the light, will be varied. Predictions aside, even identifying the point in the past at which a society entered one of these tunnels will be no easy task. Consider the case of Angola. By the time Portuguese rule had collapsed in Angola in late 1974, the territory had already experienced three and a half centuries of colonial exploitation, which began with the Portuguese military conquest in 1573. Apart from the fact that the Empire itself was continually engaged in wars, the slave trade, the occupation of parts of Angola by Germany and South Africa, the deportation of criminals and outcasts from Portugal to Angola, and the coercive use of agricultural labour were all sources of violence that long preceded the transition to independence and must have influenced what happened later (Kapuściński 2001: 134–8). The pattern could be, not simply for decolonization to result in civil war, but for past conflicts to continue in the form of present ones when the opportunity arose.

Conclusion

My aim in this chapter has been to trace the empirical patterns of conflict in a world allegedly at civil war. One could see in the literature on this topic the danger of 'semantic bleaching': the universal and indiscriminate use of the concept (civil war) such that it has become virtually meaningless (Richter 1995: 56). The most striking pattern generally agreed upon is the decline in the number of classic inter-state wars and the huge rise in intra-state wars since 1945. The distinction between 'intra-state war' and 'inter-state war' allows us to see this pattern; indeed it is the organizing principle behind several large datasets. Yet the distinction could misclassify a huge number of conflicts—Mozambique being one—which were both internal and international. Indeed there is another very important (perhaps fundamental) pattern, recorded in the Correlates of War dataset and exemplified by Mozambique: the tendency for anti-colonial wars to produce further conflicts, which are sometimes classified as internal wars, even though their roots lie in systemic relationships within a colonial system. What makes the tunnel analogy appropriate here is the fact that more and more peoples were dragged into the tunnel; as anti-colonial wars were transformed into post-colonial wars during the Cold War, these became resource wars, and so on. Before 1961 Angola had experienced centuries of colonial violence, notably connected with the slave trade. It was then the scene of an anti-colonial war from February 1961 to independence in January 1975, and would experience civil war for most of the subsequent two decades.

With respect to the state, the two most important patterns have been for recent civil wars to occur mainly in the new states, and for civil war to become endemic in some of them. The concept of state weakness provides a link between the experience of colonialism and the occurrence (indeed recurrence) of the civil wars after independence. Yet it matters whether the weakness of the state is temporary or relatively permanent. Conflicts will naturally occur in that short period of time when the coercive power of the empire is withdrawn, but that of its successor has yet to be established. In this interregnum, the use of the authority of the state to resolve the succession crisis is crucial; there is no need to talk about state weakness. These are simply succession conflicts. Alternatively, if the crisis is not resolved, and a mixture of environmental and political factors perpetuate this situation, then state weakness might be a useful concept. The question that follows is how long a state has to have been formed to have reached a point beyond which we can longer call its internal wars succession conflicts? Since a Ukrainian civil war began in 2014, almost a quarter of a century after Ukraine regained independence from the Soviet Union, 30 years seems sufficient for the period between 1989 and now to qualify as an interregnum. Yet this enlarged time span would also make conflicts such as Algeria in 1992 a succession conflict, and make state weakness a less convincing explanation for the patterns we see after decolonization.

With respect to human divisiveness the patterns point to a striking paradox: as the world became increasingly integrated after 1945 the overall number of conflicts steadily increased for more than half a century. In parts of Africa, Asia, and the Middle East the spread of international law, international institutions, and universalist conceptions of human rights—globalization in general—have not reversed this trend. The simplest explanation is historical: decolonization has simply created more units for people to fight over. Yet it is also true that convergence and fragmentation have always stood in a dialectical relationship with each other. Schismatic religions, language movements, and would-be nations stuck in larger states all like to stress their potential contribution to the cultural wealth of humanity. The incidence of ethnic conflict on the outer rim of Europe during European integration is a good example of this dialectical relationship.

Likewise, the way in which the Arab Spring has served to accentuate cultural and religious tensions within specific societies, as part of a regional movement for more universal rights and freedoms, is another. In the long run, more development and more democracy may mean more peace and fraternity, but apart from the fact that this dialectical relationship seems to be part of human evolution, such long-run predictions are still no consolation to those stuck with violent conflict and its consequences right now.

4

CAUSES

Although they are ubiquitous in human history, little of a systematic nature was written about civil wars before the 1990s. There was no unified body of literature on their causes, the assumption being that these were specific to each society. The scholarly work that exists reflects different intellectual traditions in different countries. Thucydides, for example, focused on the psychological consequences of internal strife, believing that constitutional ideals were pretexts for other ambitions. On the English civil wars of the seventeenth century, historians stress constitutional factors as the prism through which the conflicts should be viewed. Some landmark books in this field focus not on causes at all, but on the changing nature of warfare, the variation in violence within conflicts, and whether conflict retards development or not (Cramer 2006, Kalyvas 2006, Holsti 1996).

Structural theories

It is one thing to know the causes of population growth, of rises in inflation, of changes in voting behaviour, but can we also know the causes of civil wars? This section focuses on a literature which assumes that there are general causes that link the many instances of violent conflict that we see on our TV screens. It begins with the assumption that their proliferation since 1945 has been the product of something systematic. Hence it tries to identify causal factors that are general, in the sense that they may apply to more than one case. Structural factors meet this general requirement, since they can be present in more than one case and link different instances of conflict.

Harry Eckstein (1965: 140) distinguished between 'preconditions' and 'precipitants', and argued that the actual causes of internal wars (here the precipitants) may be too numerous to allow for scientific treatment. He used the analogy of a cigarette lighter. It took the physical act of ignition to produce the flame, but this flame could not have been produced without the internal structure of the lighter.

The preference for structural explanations reflects the geographical shift of scholarly focus in Conflict Studies already mentioned in the introduction. Earlier social science research into the question of 'why men rebel' had wanted to show that, even underneath the surface of advanced capitalist societies, there was a mass of seething discontent, reflected in the activities of groups like the Baader-Meinhoff, the Black Panthers, and the Red Brigades. Since 1989, especially due to the interest shown by many economists in African civil wars, the focus has been on mainly poor and formerly colonized territories, mainly in Asia and Africa, where violence was seen as a problem for economic development. Research came to involve an implicit 'compare and contrast' exercise between structural conditions in developed and developing societies. In particular, what are known to social scientists as 'large N' statistical studies (the 'N' refers to the number of cases) in particular try to explain the variation in the incidence of civil war across very different countries, in terms of the objective characteristics of different societies.

This ambition usually means that bad leaders and their ideas are not a central part of the explanation. Violent conflicts can be explained either by the motives of which the quarrelling parties are conscious, or by objective situations and processes. The theories reviewed in the first part of this chapter are of the second structural kind: their focus is on the causes rather than the causers of civil war (Kissane and Sitter 2013: 39–43). A classic example is the theory that the Yugoslav conflicts (1991–5) were the result of a 'security dilemma', in which the primary motivating factor was not ideology or identity, but fear (Posen 1993, Woodward 1999). When Yugoslavia collapsed, the first temptation had been to invoke 'ancient hatreds', seeing its demise as an expression of ethnic identities deeply rooted in history. Yet it took the collapse of a central structure (the state) for these animosities to be expressed. Hence the suggestion that mutual fear, not cultural differences, caused the Bosnian civil war (Woodward 1999).

Because of the territorial and demographic composition of Yugoslavia, the consequence of the state structure collapsing was that the different ethnic groups—excepting the Slovenians—were left in a self-help situation when it came to protection. They had no choice but to provide their security pre-emptively, based on the expectation that others could strike first. This makes for the dilemma. The vulnerability of islands of Serbs in parts of Bosnia-Herzegovina and Croatia also triggered the radicalization of Serbian nationalism as a whole (Van Hook 2013). Under the 'security dilemma' two or more groups come into conflict, not because they actively pursue this course of action, but because the measures they take to protect themselves constitute a threat to the other groups. During a process of state collapse, people will only decide to withdraw their allegiance from the existing state if they know (a) that others will do the same, and (b) that there will be an individual benefit (protection and security) resulting from the formation of a new state (Laitin 2007: 29–61). The security dilemma suggests that very destructive conflicts may be the result of individuals acting rationally under certain circumstances. The paradox is that the outcome may be collectively irrational.

This is a structural theory: had the central state not collapsed the Yugoslav conflict would not have developed in the way it did. The British prime minister at that time, John Major, agreed: the conflict which began in Bosnia in 1992 was 'a product of impersonal and inevitable forces beyond anyone's control' (Mazower 2001: 143). This much is true. Yet because perceptions of threat are key, it is hard to establish the truth of this argument empirically. Moreover, there were a range of motivations at work. Under the 'security dilemma' fear is the dominant emotion, but elites also played on those fears to further their ambitions, and paramilitaries had predatory motives with respect to their neighbours. The massive sexual violence against women was a product of aggression and hatred, not fear. Earlier violence between Croats and Serbs, between 1941 and 1945, had exceeded the total casualties of the Spanish Inquisition.

One suspects that a convincing explanation of any one conflict will always bring in many factors. Such 'multi-factor' explanations accept the position of the hero in Dostoyevsky's (1868–9) *Notes from the Underground*, who complained that 'any primary cause I have immediately drags another in tow, and that one is even more primary, and so on *ad infinitum*' (1999: 19). For example, the English civil war of the 1640s can be explained in terms of religious change, the financial strains imposed on the Crown, the personality of Charles I, events in Scotland and Ireland, as well as restlessness within parliament over the possibility of a Catholic succession. In contrast, a social scientist would try to establish a hierarchy among such causes, and consider the question of whether the explanation applies in more than one case. Both approaches would like to identify factors whose removal from the causal chain would alter the outcome (Gaddis 2002: 55). For historians this could be an event or an individual (like the personality of Charles I). The social scientist, in contrast, must find a factor that matters in more than one case: a factor which has general causal significance.

To be able to say that a factor—such as state collapse or ethnic diversity—was the root cause of a conflict, we also need to test and eliminate rival explanations. This is hard to do when we have just one case. In contrast, 'large N' studies allow for the hierarchical reordering of causal factors because they include many observations of conflict from which one can test the explanatory significance of a given variable. Of the many potential causes of civil wars, the level of democracy, state weakness, ethnic diversity, the availability of natural resources, the size of a state, and the degree of inequality are usually investigated. The attempt is to tease out from this array of potentially relevant factors the one with the greatest significance. Hence the value placed on the quality of 'parsimony' in some social science explanations, which basically means 'a useful research project ... that explains a lot with a little' (Gaddis 2002: 55).

The distinction between a structural and a conventional historical approach can be clarified further by considering what is meant by 'coming before' in each explanation. Conventionally, the statement that the re-election of Abraham Lincoln as American President in 1860 led to the American civil war, suggests that there was something irreversible about what happened after 1860. A narrative account of the American civil war will incorporate some idea of a temporal sequence in the narration of events. Yet when we need to consider the influence of factors not covered by the strict sequence of experienced events, we bring in structural explanations. These factors also 'come before' and enter into events they precede: indeed they are the 'preconditions' of political events, but do not change from day to day (Koselleck 2004: 106–7). Structural factors could include demographic change, systems of rule, the economic relationship between ethnic groups, or indeed the resource base of a society. Since these provide the circumstances which shape political conflict, they may explain why some societies remain vulnerable to violent conflict over the long-term.

Indeed there is a difference between understanding civil war as an event and as a condition that some societies are vulnerable to. For example, it is only because the American civil war was exceptional—constituting a dramatic break-down of the United States's constitutional order—that we can debate its causes (what produced the event?) and its consequences. It constituted a tract of time (between 1861 and 1865), with a clear beginning and end, in which the exceptional violence of the contest over the Union did not become a permanent condition. In contrast, structural theories of recurrent conflicts, where civil war, as in Mozambique or Angola, was part of a series of conflicts, assume the violence symptomizes a general vulnerability to conflict rather than one exceptional event. It matters less what actually led to the fighting in 1975 and 1976 and more what the relatively permanent aspects of the social environment were that could have sustained the endless cycles of war.

Since in some societies the constellations of friend and foe can also become entrenched, even after the original source of conflict has disappeared, structural factors might also be able to answer the question of whether recurrent conflicts have an objective cause (ibid: 107). Consider Angola. With its vast terrain, long porous borders, and small population, Angola seems a good example of how an insurgency might be relatively easy to sustain in a certain physical environment. One army patrol that the travel writer Ryszard Kapuściński was travelling with in 1975 was the sole unit in a land one-third the size of Poland! We also need to explain why the conflict extended into the 2000s, after the departures of the Cubans and the South Africans who had aided the rival sides early on. In 1973, in terms of their contribution to the country's GNP, the main export products were oil (30 per cent), coffee (21 per cent), diamonds (21 per cent), and iron ore (6 per cent) (Kapuściński 2001: 133). Between 1969 and 1973 the value of Angola's exports, notably of oil, had doubled. The existence of plentiful natural riches (to which we could add cotton, corn, and fruit products) in a subsistence economy where hunger and poverty were widespread, raises the question of whether the fighting was not so much for the control of the state, but for the control of resources. Conflict was recurrent not only in having the capacity of being 'waged into infinity' (ibid.: 14) but also in stretching far back into the past. Apparently documents from the Portuguese state archives prove that in the course of 350 years 'there were barely five during which the Portuguese did not conduct war in one place or another in Angola' (ibid.: 138).

Although some scholars still see historical legacies of imperialism and slavery at work in Africa's many civil wars, the literature reviewed in this section explains the vulnerability of the new states to endemic conflict differently. Factors usually considered important, such as the strength of the state, its resource base, the size of the terrain, etc., have less to do with changeable aspects of politics (citizenship, legitimacy, leadership and power, etc.), and are structural (or environmental) in nature. When it comes to Angola, research had already demonstrated a general correlation between dependence on natural resources and the occurrence of civil war, so two questions were (1) whether the availability of natural resources made the Angolan conflict more likely to happen, and (2) whether, once started, dependence on such resources made it last longer. Perhaps war became endemic because the government had plentiful profits from oil to finance its war efforts, while the rebel organization, UNITA, led by Jonah Savimbi could rely on diamond mines to do the same. As the factor with potentially the greatest significance the resource argument could explain all the questions above.

Part of the appeal of statistical 'large N' studies of such cases is that they have the ability to test common-sense assumptions about conflict. For example, it is commonly assumed that ethnic and religious diversity make countries more prone to civil war, and that conflicts could be predicted to break out in areas with the strongest ethnic or political grievances. The same argument could be made about Angola since the 1970s. A statistical test of these expectations, for the period between 1946 and 1999, was carried out by Fearon and Laitin (2003). They argued that internal wars were more likely to occur in mountainous, impoverished, politically unstable regions that favour insurgency or guerrilla warfare, such as Afghanistan, Somalia, and Lebanon, rather than in culturally divided societies per se. Rather than ideology and identity being important, the conditions which favoured such insurgencies were extreme poverty, political instability (in new or failing states), rough terrain (enabling rebels to hide easily), and the availability of external finance (ibid.: 75).

Since it is one of the most cited studies in the field, Fearon and Laitin's 2003 article on this issue is summarized in the box below. Most of the post-1945 civil wars have been produced in poor countries, by the increasing contradiction between new political and economic aspirations—often fed by the example of other countries—and the relatively oppressive governments with which people are confronted (Luard 1972: 14). This gap might provide a natural reason for people to feel grievances, and possibly rebel against this situation. Yet the gap is felt everywhere in the developing world, whereas civil war is not universal. Fearon and Laitin (2003: 75) argue that what matters more are the conditions that allow people to rebel: civil wars, in failed states, reflect permanent 'conditions that favour insurgency – in particular state weakness marked by poverty, a large population and instability'. These conclusions build on the general statistical finding that civil wars are strongly associated with low GDP (Fearon 2004, Rotberg 2004). Fearon and Laitin's work challenges common-sense assumptions: grievances, they argue, should be seen as the product of civil wars, not their cause. Their methods of elimination, and the hierarchical reordering of causal factors, result in state weakness being identified as the strongest predictive factor for civil war in general. They eliminate 'grievance' factors, such as ethnic diversity and the low level of democracy. In terms of the hierarchical reordering of causal factors, mountainous terrain and large populations make civil war more likely, because they make state control more difficult. Such factors both allow for conflicts to emerge (the onset question), and help make them intractable (the duration question).

'Ethnicity, Insurgency, and Civil War'

Research question: Can the alleged spike in civil wars and insurgencies since 1989 be explained by ethnic and/or cultural divisions between groups?

Data source: Relies on data for the period 1945 and 1999 on the 161 countries that had a population of at least half a million in 1990. In this period 127 civil wars occurred, but there have been only 25 wars between states. Two-thirds of the civil conflicts are considered insurgencies by the authors.

Findings: The article concludes that the prevalence of civil wars after the Cold War is mainly the result of a steady accumulation of protracted conflicts since the 1950s and 1960s, rather than a sudden change associated with a new, post-Cold War, international system. Since 1945 civil wars broke out at a rate of about 2.31 per year. There was no consistent pattern; the rate of civil war was neither increasing nor decreasing. The study also argues that more ethnically or religiously diverse countries have not been more likely to experience significant civil violence in this period, compared to other countries.

(continued)

(continued)

> **Explanation**: The factors that explain which countries have been
> vulnerable to civil war are not connected to the diversity of the popu-
> lation. Rather, factors which can explain the occurrence of the civil war
> are conditions which facilitate insurgency. These include: poverty
> (which marks financially and bureaucratically weak states and also
> favours rebel recruitment), political instability, rough terrain, and
> large populations. It is also possible to argue for the role of decolon-
> ization in the occurrence of the civil wars. However, the authors argue
> that financially, organizationally and politically weak central govern-
> ments encourage insurgency, because they are more prone to weak
> local policing or inept and corrupt counterinsurgency practices.
> (Fearon and Laitin 2003)

Although Fearon and Laitin say little about motivation, another 'large
N' study by Paul Collier and Anke Hoeffler (2000) does so. These
economists also find a strong statistical correlation between low GDP
and civil war, but explain the proliferation of insurgencies in terms of
the participants' direct economic costs and benefits. The key factors,
they argue, are the actors' quest for private gains, and the opportunities that civil war provides, notably in the shape of 'predation of the
rents from primary commodity exports' (ibid.: 26). Unlike in the
'security dilemma', those that come together in civil war do so, not
out of fear, but as a response to opportunity. In terms of the elimination of rival theories, poverty does objectively matter—the higher the
GDP, the greater the opportunity costs of rebellion. Yet 'grievance',
defined as dissatisfaction caused by ethnic or religious differences,
political repression, or unequal economic distribution, does not.
Grievances matter only inasmuch as they might help sustain civil
wars once they have broken out: 'greed-rebellions need to generate
grievance for military cohesion, grievance rebellions might be driven
to predation to raise finance' (ibid.: 26).

How should we evaluate the structural approach? Some common-
sense assumptions about conflicts—such as their roots in poverty or
cultural differences—have been problematized by scholars working
with 'large N' methods. Some major revisions of structural theories of

what causes civil war have also been done by people working with similar methods. For example, Cederman, Gledistch, and Buhaugh (2013) argue that grievances, especially stemming from inequalities between ethnic groups, matter much more than others had suggested. The downside of the structural approach is that 'large N' methods do not allow scholars to get into the minds of the societies they are studying. When the standard school curriculum included fascism or the Spanish civil war, the ideas at stake in conflicts were not unfamiliar to the students. Now the focus of civil war studies is on parts of the world very remote from our experience, and where the ideological framework within which such conflicts take place is not easily identified. For example, Collier, Hoeffler, and Rohner do not explain the motivations of those who take arms against a state in terms of ideas, identities, or culture: they have a rationalist understanding of human behaviour. The discussion of why men and women rebel is structured around a polarity: one pole (grievance) is reduced to the other (greed). Acknowledging that this may be simplistic, the authors later refined their theory to make it even more structural and less about motivation. They subsequently wrote that 'where rebellion is feasible it will occur: motivation is indeterminate, being supplied by whatever agenda happens to be adopted by the first social entrepreneur to occupy a viable niche' (Collier, Hoeffler, and Rohner 2009: 24). This takes structuralism very far indeed: insurgencies occur where they are feasible and we know they are feasible because they occurred. Perhaps it would simply be better to say that there are a lot of greedy people out there.

Eckstein argued that structural approaches to revolution had limited explanatory value (1965: 149). They established (at best) structural parameters within which violence is more or less likely, but cannot actually establish causality (Kissane and Sitter 2013: 47). The problem is that instead of focusing on the events which lead to the outbreak of the fighting, such theories try to relate the variation in civil war to countries' longer-term social, economic, and institutional features. This means that instead of going into detailed analysis of the various micro-processes which cause civil war, these studies usually hang their analyses on the two tail-ends of the causal chain: initial structural conditions on the one hand, and outcomes (violence or non-violence) on the other. What connects material attributes to the onset of civil wars in these theories are (rationalist) stipulations regarding human motivations, which are employed to substitute for the complex causal processes behind civil wars, which this literature is unable or unwilling to specify (Ringmar 1996: 36).

Moreover, the stress on structural factors obscures the role of the state and its policies. As with the plague in Thucydides, civil war happens to states like an illness happens to a person. Yet the state can also produce the structural and environmental conditions which eventually weaken it. In Sri Lanka for example, ethnic categories were constructed by elites in the struggle against British rule. Later on, once they became enmeshed in majority rule and the political dominance of the Sinhalese, they ceased to be something constructed, and were therefore less subject to manipulation (Rampton 2011). The current conflict in Kenya's Rift Valley is not simply ethnic, but about land. The link between land and power originated with the colonial state, and has been reproduced by state policies after independence. The Rwandan conflict of the early 1990s did not naturally occur because of ethnic divisions. It was as much the consequence of a decision to introduce a democratic system at a time when the Hutus were in a position to burn the house down. In these cases, it was the actions of the state that turned the 'objective factors' into the causes of conflict.

The process of testing and eliminating rival theories statistically rests on the assumption that a root cause of conflict can be found. The logic is attractive because, once you know the root of a problem, it can be removed. At their most ambitious, such methods could turn social science into a preventive science and prevent future conflict. Yet there is no example in history of civil war being stopped in this way. How can one predict whether the current polarization in Turkey will lead to civil violence among Turks themselves? Most of the fatalities of the 2013 Gezi Park protests were members of the Alevi community.

Cengiz Hortoğlu, the head of the Anatolian Bektaş Federation, compared Gezi to an earthquake, standing on a social fault-line in contemporary Turkey. The Alevis, although Muslims, have been discriminated against since the foundation of the Republic in 1923, and have much to fear from the Muslim-majority spirit of the AKP. If present governing practices continue, the danger is that the fault-line will be opened, and its energy will be discharged throughout society (*Zaman* 1 June 2014). Although such a danger exists, how can one make an objective prediction about when this could happen? The Alevi grievances could be compared to an inflating balloon. Can we identify a point when—at a measurable pressure—the strain is too much and, with a loud bang, the balloon bursts?

Any general theory of the causes of conflict rests on the core assumption that the same causes must have the same effects, or will probably do so. The problem is that, unlike an earthquake or balloon, in human societies the balloon is actually thinking about itself (Lukacs 2012: 12). The literature I have just summarized believes the roots of civil war lie in objective social conditions: the world of ideas and actors simply mirrors this more important material level of reality (Kissane and Sitter 2013: 47–53). Yet things are not so simple. The situation (for Alevis, or anyone else) becomes intolerable when people decide it is so, and what goes on in people's minds—their sense of self and their memories—becomes an activating element in itself, converting an objective division into an actual conflict (Lukacs 2012: 12). One could say that structural approaches can only investigate the *underlying* factors which make societies prone to violence, but are weaker when it comes to identifying *catalytic* factors (Brown 1996: 13). By catalyst we mean something that converts the possibility of conflict into actual strife, and especially those processes through which political conflict becomes violent conflict, and low-level violence escalates to civil war proportions. To return to Eckstein's analogy of the cigarette lighter, it still took the physical act of ignition to produce the flame, even if this flame could not have been produced without the internal structure of the lighter.

Ultimately, the structural turn reflects the old faith of the European Enlightenment that the application of the correct scientific method could make social science a predictive tool, enabling us to control human nature and prevent violence. It is hardly surprising that studies of this kind would be funded by government or research agencies. Yet 'root cause' approaches are not better guides when it comes to establishing peace. They begin with a checklist of potentially relevant causal factors, and then reorder them hierarchically for each case. Yet the importance of such factors varies over time during any conflict. A temporal approach, studying a conflict over time, may actually be better at identifying how issues and objectives change during its course. It is also more useful in terms of identifying ripe moments for resolution (Hughes 2007: 109). Political scientist James Hughes's (2007) study of the alteration between conventional nationalist ideas and radical Islamism in the Chechen case, shows that how an issue is 'reframed'—from being about the desire for a territorial state to religious jihad—altered the views of the outside powers about whether the issue was negotiable. In order to judge what is driving conflicts, their dynamic nature needs to be accepted. The next section considers a range of theories that do so.

Process-based theories

Process-based theories are not new. When most universities taught courses on revolution, special attention was given to big cases, such as the French Revolution, linked to ideas of social transformation, or those like the Iranian revolution of 1979, which left their mark on the international relations of the era. As with the structural theories of civil war, some scholars did use comparative historical analysis of a small number of cases ('small N' studies) to identify 'preconditions' for revolution, and this work on crises and state break-down has been extended to more recent civil wars (Goldstone 2008). Others, however, attempted 'a natural history of revolutions', which they thought of as events or processes that went through regular patterns and cycles. The struggle between moderates and radicals within a revolutionary movement was a key theme. This natural history approach is very similar to the work on civil war discussed in this section.

In 'Does Modernisation Breed Revolution?' Charles Tilly argued that structural theories fell wide of the mark, because they missed out on 'the extent to which violence was a contingent outcome of interaction among contenders and government' (1973: 439). Forty years later, process-based approaches are regaining favour in the study of civil war. One review of four recent studies identified a significant '(re)turn to case-study methods' in the study of conflict, and concluded: 'it is not quantities but *interactions* that matter' (Tarrow 2007: 587, 596). Perhaps the key insight is that processes of radicalization and polarization themselves shape the outcomes of conflict, taking them beyond the issues which initially caused the conflict. If so, one can never study causes without paying attention to how the causers interpret them. For example, the conflict in Northern Ireland originated in a civil rights movement in the late 1960s. As it was met with a Unionist back-lash and clashes began between the IRA and the British army, within a few years the conflict had escalated into a protracted nationalist rebellion dedicated to the achievement of a united Ireland. A 30-year conflict ensued, in a small society that had had one of the lowest levels of crime in Western Europe before 1969.

Process-based approaches understand causes and causality differently. In place of the search for the one factor that matters, the assumption is that different causal factors matter together. In order to understand the relationships between actors, their organizations, and their ideas, we have to trace how these relationships develop over time. This means that an explanation of civil war must be embedded in a historical narrative. Process-based theories are also better at explaining 'the dogs that don't bark': societies which are objectively conflict-prone, but in which no violent conflict ensues. Eckstein proposes that we distinguish between situations with 'revolutionary potential' and the actual occurrence of civil war, suggesting that the latter may be a small subset of the former (1965: 153). Elite behaviour is a critical factor, converting many situations of crisis into something much worse. For example, many historians of Nazism explain its emergence in terms of long-term historical traditions in German political culture, or as a consequence of a deep crisis of capitalism in the 1920s. Yet the ability of Adolf Hitler to adroitly manipulate a democratic state, and use its laws to establish a dictatorship, was decisive.

The outbreak of civil war is usually the consequence of decisions made by pivotal actors, however constrained they are by structural factors. Consider the Irish civil war of 1922–3. Before independence in 1921, Irish nationalism was known for its ability to gloss over internal differences in order to maintain unity against the British government and the unionists who wanted to remain within the United Kingdom. Yet after the partition of Ireland in 1920 the British offer of dominion status to 26 Irish counties in 1921 led to a split within the nationalist movement Sinn Féin, and civil war among the nationalists followed within seven months (Kissane 2005). Political divisions, more than anything else, explain the internal split. Had the 1921 Treaty been more or less generous it might have been received consensually. The 'pro-treaty' camp was led by Michael Collins, while Eamon de Valera's opposition to the Treaty afterwards gave immense status to the anti-treaty IRA who were in control of most localities. Had the two men not become rivals, a war of this kind might not have happened. A different type of war (against the Northern Unionists or a continuance of conflict with Britain) might have ensued.

On the other hand, one can usefully distinguish between the factors that explain why civil war starts in the first place and those factors that make conflicts intractable. Structural factors *are* relevant to the second issue. The Irish civil war began in June 1922, and ended on 30 April 1923. Hence it proved far less intractable than many civil wars discussed in this book. The civil war had begun in a classic insurgent pattern; after being quickly defeated in conventional fighting in August 1922, the anti-treaty IRA started a guerrilla war—hoping to undermine the Dublin government and lose it popular support. As it was strong in exactly the same areas where the guerrilla campaign against British rule had been strongest before 1922, its Chief of Staff, Liam Lynch, was confident of success. Yet the IRA were soon confined to the most remote and mountainous areas of the new state, and lost popular support. The Dublin government, backed by the public— hence with access to local sources of information—was familiar with the IRA's tactics and hideouts. Given that the government had the military support of the British government, the moral support of the Catholic Church, and the financial support of the Irish banks, the objective conditions making for a long-term insurgency in such a small country were not present. Lynch had acted on a misdiagnosis of the objective situation when he turned his back on compromise in September 1922 (Kissane 2005: 9). Generally, one cannot diagnose the conflict potential of such situations without reference to structural factors.

The contrast with the structural approach is between seeing a civil war as something that 'develops', and thinking of it as something that simply 'happens', with all sorts of unforeseeable consequences (Brubaker 1996: 19). The process-based approaches are certainly better suited to the dynamic and unpredictable nature of conflicts, and the way the substance of any civil war is defined, not by objective conditions alone, but by the way relationships between actors evolve. Julián Casanova's (2012) *España Partido en Dos* (Spain divided in two) poses the question of how that complex but fragmented society could become divided into just two armed camps so quickly in 1936. The crucial event, Casanova argues, was the military coup and uprising against the Republic that began on 17 July 1936. This split the army and security forces, and prepared the stage for an armed struggle between supporters of the coup and those of the popular revolution and the Republic. The thousand-day war that followed was both a profound and shocking experience; the two extreme positions on each side— those of the communists and the fascists—became more influential as the war went on. Yet the social and cultural ties connecting Spaniards to each other were also torn in two. In the course of the war more than

6,800 religious personnel, including 13 bishops, were assassinated, numerous churches were sacked or burnt, and many graveyards were desecrated. After the military intervention these events also hardened hearts on the issue of the Republic.

In explaining why such conflicts escalate we must thus pay attention to the meanings given to actions by actors. Their interests and identities are not fixed by the material world, but emerge in an unpredictable way through processes of conflict and interaction (Kissane and Sitter 2013: 43–7). Concepts of state, identity, and especially community guide the moral evaluation of conflicts, providing answers to the questions of what kinds of actions and ideas are considered appropriate or necessary in a given historical situation (Hughes 2007: 203). In Spain the anticlerical violence, which had no historical precedent in the peninsula, blocked any possibility of pardon or reconciliation. The Catholic Church felt saved by the nationalist forces and gave its blessing to the military intervention as soon as the first shot was fired. The Catholic Church subsequently became a prop in the harsh and vengeful regime established by the victors in 1939, to the point of hero-worship of the leader of the Nationalist forces, General Francisco Franco, who had emerged as the dominant figure during the war.

Ultimately, when it comes to the causes of civil war, neither side of the structure–process dichotomy should eclipse the other. Dichotomies cease to be useful when they distort rather than illuminate complex realities. The objective conditions in a given society *do* matter. Just as we should not have causes without causers, there is no point in thinking that actors create the conditions for conflict at will, or that their relationships are not affected by structural realities. If we think of causes only in terms of the way relationships between actors evolve, this reinforces the delusional belief of altruistic outsiders that every conflict is essentially no more than a misunderstanding. Does anyone believe that peace between Palestinians and Israel could be established without the right of return, the ending of settlements, economic development in the Occupied territories, or without reference to all the other structural legacies of a hundred-year-old conflict? The question is how these approaches can be combined. The next section tries to do so for Algeria, employing both structural and process-based methods to explain why the 1990s became such a dark decade for what was once a model state for the Arab world.

The case of Algeria

Since the vulnerability of many post-colonial states to civil conflict is at issue in much of the recent literature on the causes of civil war, the Algerian experience is worthy of reflection. The country was colonized by France after 1830, and became independent in 1962. That year a 95 per cent majority voted in favour of independence from France in a referendum, and Algeria soon became a developmental socialist model for the Arab world. Problems began when the country went into deep economic and political crises in the late 1980s. Then, in a premonition of the Arab Spring, in 1992 a thwarted democratic transition led to a vicious civil war in which radical Islamists fought the forces of the secular state during the 'black decade' of the 1990s.

This vicious conflict was not foreseen. In the early 1990s some Islamic leaders had appeared open to the idea of a marriage between Islam and democracy (Volpi 2003: 47). Yet, consensus on the need for reform soon evaporated. When the military cancelled the national elections that the reformist Islamic Salvation Front (FIS) was poised to win in January 1992, fighting ensued. The authorities' suppression of the FIS then ensured that the ground-swell of public opinion in favour of Islam would not have an institutional voice. Authority consequently shifted rapidly to radical Islamic groups, such as the *Groupements Islamiques Armées*, who believed revolutionary and drastic methods were needed to acquire state power (ibid.: 621). Their thinking was heavily influenced by the conflict then taking place in Afghanistan. The military presented the conflict to the outside world as one between Western secular democracy and Islamic fundamentalism and eventually pacified the country.

What is remarkable is how quickly the public sphere became a battle-ground in the 1990s between two symbolically charged and mutually exclusive (Islamic and secular) visions of society. A political debate in the 1980s about how to marry reformist Islam to Algerian democracy had been ultimately supplanted by a culturalist debate about the proper basis for a just political order (Volpi 2003: 7). It seems that the underlying cultural fault-lines in Algeria were such that they could be easily manipulated. Once the democratic space was closed down, those actors that were able to use prevailing myths and understandings of social order had a decisive advantage (ibid.: 9). These myths were culturally coded, and the violence that was unleashed against musicians, intellectuals, journalists, and women by the Islamists was usually intended to carry a cultural message. It posed the question of whether—in its first 30 years of independence—Algeria had really overcome the cultural and geographic fault-lines that had been aggravated by the encounter with French colonial rule. As early as 1965 Ryszard Kapuściński predicted that it would be difficult for the post-colonial state to overcome these. He wrote of Algiers:

> In the small space of this beautiful but congested city intersected two great conflicts of the contemporary world. The first was the one between Christianity and Islam (expressed here in the clash between colonizing France and colonized Algeria). The second, which acquired a sharpness of focus immediately after the independence and departure of the French, was a conflict at the very heart of Islam, between its open, dialectical—I would even venture to say 'Mediterranean' current—and its other, inward looking one, born of a sense of uncertainty and confusion vis-a-vis the contemporary world, guided by fundamentalists who take advantage of modern technology and organizational principles yet at the same time deem the defence of faith and custom against modernity as the condition of their own existence, their sole identity (Kapuściński 2007: 226).

Throughout the twentieth century, French governments allowed the *colons* (or *pied noir* settler class) in Algeria to frustrate their attempts to include native Algerians in the running of the country. Before 1945 there was no opening of a political space that could have allowed an indigenous democratic tradition to develop. The absence of such a tradition made for a risky transition.

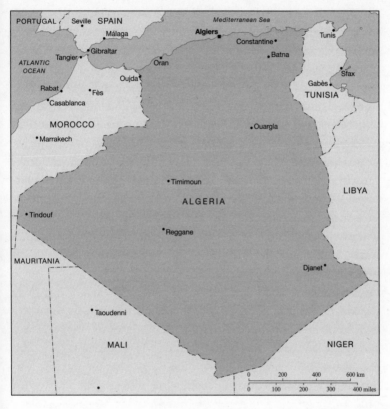

Map 4 Algeria

The violence of the 1990s has left behind a troubled legacy: just as the French gave themselves a blanket amnesty for those crimes they committed between 1954 and 1962, Algeria has reacted to the trauma of the civil war with blanket amnesties. The state legally blocks any attempt to investigate the acts that were carried out in the civil war. The historian James Le Seur poses the question of whether the state will now continue to move forward in history without ever looking back, as Algeria had done after 1962 (Le Seur 2010: 195–207). Algerian society had been highly militarized during the French period, with a memory of brutal colonial conquest. Then the country's violent separation from France led to hundreds of thousands of deaths and there was much violence against civilians between 1957 and 1962. Neighbouring Tunisia had also been deeply influenced by French culture, yet its experience of independence has largely been peaceful.

How might the tragic fate of Algeria illuminate the debate about the causes of civil wars, especially those which have taken place in post-colonial states? A natural tendency is to blame the earlier experience of French colonialism. Scholars like the linguist Jean Piaget and the anthropologist Claude Lévi-Strauss suggested that societies had 'an inner wisdom', or an intrinsic equilibrium, which should be left undisturbed (Gardner 1976: 226). A structured society should lessen the chance of a major break-down in order. Yet in states such as Algeria, by the end of the period of colonial rule in 1962 this inner equilibrium was long gone. After the annulled election in 1992, a war was fought to decide who would exercise power over whom, but this was also a war fought to change the identity of the state. It thus involved a struggle to impose identities on others, a process that had been ongoing since independence in 1962. Indeed, this struggle was also a feature of the French colonial period. Hence the dark decade of the 1990s may have had its roots further back than independence in 1962, to the arrival of the French in 1830—if not before, to the Ottoman period.

International historian John Lewis Gaddis calls the imposition of a new prayer book on the Scottish Church a point in the emergence of the English civil war of the 1640s when an equilibrium that once existed ceased to exist as a result of the conflict he was trying to explain (2002: 99). Yet the conflict in Algeria began 30 years after the end of French rule, and was the product, not of the loss of some traditional equilibrium, but more of frustration with the actual experience of self-rule. Consistent with Fearon and Laitin's (2003) approach, Algeria had become 'a weak state' by 1992: the large degree of legitimacy the state had enjoyed under the FLN since 1962, was gradually eroded by the state's poor economic performance. By the late 1980s the waste of oil resources, military rule, massive corruption, population explosion, and serious conflict over the nature of national identity, had led to disillusionment with the fruits of independence, particularly among the young. The 'greed and grievance' model could also be applied, because the existence of a surplus of unemployed young men made things escalate rapidly. The army's repression of the FIS, which had been working politically for decades, gave the initiative to the hard-line Islamists, who shielded themselves from public opinion and often used the war as a means to acquire wealth.

We must also be specific about the type of state we are referring to. In Algeria we are faced not only with the problems of a post-colonial state, but those of a socialist state based on oil wealth entering into an uncertain transition. The FLN regime was unable to use its oil wealth to appease enough sectors of society, and was facing the consequences of a demographic explosion that has tripled the population since 1962. The transition to independence formed the historical backdrop: the immediate context was one in which Islam was making a resurgence in a socialist state that had long denied it a central role. Decades of socialist politics had created distinct elite strata that were privileged within the state apparatus, tied by their material interests to this specific type of state, and who had a lot to fear, culturally and materially, from an Islamic resurgence. Hence when its economic base collapsed, their position was threatened on more than one level. Thus the dual transition—from authoritarian to democratic politics, and from socialist economy to neo-liberalism, needs to be stressed.

Nonetheless, it was the annulling of a general election that led to civil war in 1992. The attempt at democratic reform made the difference with other states in the region, which did not democratize in the 1990s and remained stable. Algeria's score on the Freedom House Index—a global measure of political freedom—showed decreased repression and more democracy from 1988 to 1991, when the first democratic elections took place (Tetsas 2010: 109–11). The regime had employed a consistent tactic of relaxing repression during economic crises, which usually brought a rise in protest. This tactic then went badly wrong in the 1990s, producing more polarization than was in evidence before 1991. The cancelled elections showed what Eckstein called a 'behavioural' factor at work (1965: 148): this conflict reflected not an absolute drop in living standards, but rising expectations for change being suddenly reversed. Indeed, it was this political collapse that made the availability of a large pool of angry unemployed young men a danger for the state.

'Toward a Democratic Civil Peace? Democracy, Political Change, and Civil War, 1816–1992'

Research questions: Does regime change—especially a transition to democracy—put a society at greater risk of civil war? This research tests three hypotheses: (1) that semi-democracies are more likely to experience civil war than either democracies or autocracies; (2) that institutionally consistent democracies and stark autocracies are equally unlikely to experience civil war; (3) that countries that have undergone a recent political transition are more likely to experience civil war than countries whose political system has been stable.

Data sources: Hundreds of transitions from the period between 1816 and 1992 are studied. For statistical data on violence, the article relates to the Correlates of War project database. Other potentially important factors for the occurrence of the civil war have been controlled for. Those factors include: proximity of independence, civil war or international war in neighbouring country, economic development, and ethnic homogeneity. Consolidated regimes (authoritarian or democratic) are not affected by these variables, and are thus more durable.

(continued)

(continued)

> **Findings**: Regimes that score in the middle range on the democracy–autocracy index have a significantly higher probability of civil war than either democracies or autocracies. There is no significant difference between the risk of civil war in harsh autocracies and in strong democracies (hypothesis 2). Regime change strongly increases the probability of civil war in the short run (hypothesis 3). The authors suggest that there is a relationship between democracy and civil war (hypothesis 1). There is a greater risk of violence during a transition, but in the long run democracies are better at securing peace.
>
> **Explanation**: The higher risk of civil war during a transition is explained by the coincidence of two factors: relaxation of repression (a factor which keeps very authoritarian systems stable), and increased openness (a characteristic of stable democracies). During a democratic transition creating opposition does not bring much costs, while the political system loses its stability, at least temporarily.
>
>   (Hegre et al. 2001)

There is a general theory of civil war which takes such behavioural factors into account. The box above summarizes a collective study of over 100 regime changes and their consequences between 1816 and 1993. Its conclusion is that when an authoritarian regime relaxes its repressive hold on society, and attempts to liberalize its political system, allowing for political mobilization, the risk of collective violence greatly increases. The study also found strong statistical support for the argument that states undergoing a transition or regime change are far more likely to experience civil war. In contrast, at the two poles of the transition process established democracies are open enough to accommodate protest; authoritarian systems are strong enough to repress it. The risk of violent conflict exists in between because transitional or 'institutionally inconsistent' regimes send out mixed signals or do not have enough time to develop institutions which could channel grievances in a peaceful direction and contain violence (Hegre et al. 2001). 'Institutionally inconsistent' regimes send out mixed signals and have insufficient time in which to develop strong institutions which can channel grievances and contain conflict (Hegre et al. 2001). This was the case in Algeria.

That there are serious risks with democratic transitions has been borne out by the general record of the Arab Spring, which has become a winter everywhere except Tunisia, a country which also experienced polarization over its identity between 2012 and 2014. In contrast to early hopes that democracy and Islam could be reconciled, the consequence of the Muslim Brotherhood President Morsi's exposition in Egypt in July 2013 might be that Islamic politicians will conclude that since not even the self-styled liberals and secularists have played by the rules, it is now time to revert to the old game of authoritarian politics and survival of the fittest, where political power falls to the strongest or the most violent. This is what happened in Algeria in 1992. Since the politics matters so much, it is very difficult to predict what the consequences of such transitions will be in advance. The political scientist Frederic Volpi (2003: 7–11) argues that the success or failure of a transition like Algeria's depends on processes of learning within the transitions, and on changing relationships. Indeed even the natural sciences cannot be completely precise when it comes to predicting events. For example, after the Oklahoma tornado in 2014 weather forecasters had to confess that they were able to predict weather patterns, but not the cloud or tornados these patterns produced nearer the ground. The same applies to the risk posed by regime change.

One consequence of the Arab Spring will be to bring back regime analysis and political variables to the study of civil war. As the recent history of South Sudan suggests, the creation of any new state can be an incentive to unbridled political competition. Moreover, the contrast between genuinely post-colonial cases and the relatively peaceful collapse of the Soviet Union suggests that the extent to which politics becomes institutionalized or structured before independence is a critical factor, especially if independence has been achieved by force. Without such a structure, the political competition that follows is unlikely to remain formalized. This might be the explanation of why countries like Algeria that experienced so much violence before independence have had long-term problems with political violence since.

Another factor is that the management of decolonization was quite different in the 1990s: the elite networks, the institutional choices, and the foreign policies of the successor states seem to reflect Soviet influence. We see less of a break. Perhaps the further away from World War II, the more experienced the most powerful actors have been in the game of conflict-management and state-building. This experience has left us with fewer civil wars than we might otherwise have seen.

The Algerian conflict is also a good example of how any theory of civil war will be incomplete without a proper consideration of standard variables such as institutions, interests, and power (Checkel 2011: 17). Yet economic grievances could be added to Hegre et al.'s. theory of what can go wrong. An Algerian political scientist, Abdelaziz Tetsas, argued that conflict became more likely because a state with a small taxation base found it hard to defend itself, while the opportunity costs of rebellion were also low, making it easy for the Islamists to find recruits (2010: 107–9, 117). Another refinement of the Hegre et al. model has been made by Paul Collier. He asks whether democratization is riskier in low-income countries, especially at the early stages. He posits a threshold effect where states having a per capita income greater than US\$7 per day are able to prevent the conflicts which democracy brings. One cannot say that the risk is really less at \$8 a day or more at \$6 a day but Collier found that the relationship holds at a general level (2010: 1–48).

It might not be useful to think of the risks involved in state strength and state weakness in binary terms. Algeria after all had strong repressive capacity, a sign of a strong state. States, like other organisms, depend for their survival on the maintenance of a complex life-support system. The different aspects of this system need to remain in balance with one another, and with the external environment: when one element fails, the whole system suffers, as in Libya and Syria. As with organisms, it may be that the adaptability of regimes depends on how they balance the integrative and disintegrative forces in the world. Those that survive are those that have been required to adapt often, but not too frequently, to changes in their external environment. Syria seemed to have lost this capacity three years ago. Consider the observation of the natural world made by the Roman philosopher Boethius, who in the sixth century AD wrote *The Consolation of Philosophy* under stay of execution:

> Moreover, each living thing is kept in being by what is suited to it, whereas hostile elements destroy it. Hard objects such as stones cling most tenaciously to their component parts, and resist easy fragmentation, whereas fluid elements such as air and water readily yield to agents which separate them, but then rapidly coalesce with the parts from which they have been sundered; and as for fire, it escapes all division. [Boethius 1999: 64]

Analogously, perhaps there are hard aspects of the state, such as the size of its coercive apparatus, its fiscal base, and its physical infrastructure, which must be maintained intact during crises, very much like a rock holding fast in a stream, or like those parts of the human body which must be maintained at all times to prevent death. The softer aspects of the state combine with other social actors, and are necessary for peaceful existence. In this vein, the sociologist Michael Mann (1995) distinguishes between the despotic and infrastructural power of the state, the latter referring to its ability to achieve its objectives by working with other actors. The weakness of the Algerian state was its inability to base its rule on something other than coercion. The attempted transition did coincide with a sudden fall in GDP. Yet what brought the frustration with the system to boiling point was the attempt to manipulate and eventually cancel those elections, and what guaranteed that the conflict would be violent was the brutal clamp-down on political space by the army. To go back to *The Consolation of Philosophy*, once the flexible aspects of the state's survival strategy—the attempt to give itself electoral legitimacy—back-fired, the state came to rely on its despotic power, the consequences of which we have seen. Perhaps it would be more accurate to say that the FLN regime was lacking in legitimacy rather than that it was weak.

Structural theories of cases like Algeria do investigate something basic: the vulnerability of many new states to repeated crises. Moreover, the fact that there are so many states in the first place reflects the diffusion of the nation-state model, a structural process. There are two obvious things to say about their vulnerability to conflict: (1) none of the European empires survived the twentieth century in a multinational form, and (2) the nation states which replaced them have also struggled to establish their legitimacy. Furthermore, these unresolved legitimacy crises are made worse by another structural process: the global spread of capitalist markets. Perhaps structures—such as the post-colonial states—are 'emergent properties' that are the product of past actions giving them causal status in any society. States set the parameters for action and carry meanings which inform the terms of any conflict about them. Structural theories of the kind developed by Fearon and Laitin and others simply do not tell us enough about where these structures came from, who built and captured them, or for what purpose. If the construction of such states had meaning during decolonization, their subsequent failures will also be understood in terms that motivated the independence movements.

This understanding of the state as 'an emergent property' may help reconcile the two poles in the understanding of causality. On the one hand, the 'large N' work aims to provide foundational knowledge, which looks for causal relationships that are so strong and predictable that the details of specific cases are ignored in favour of one attribute linking them. On the other hand, we can see that varying combinations of oil wealth, political system, religion, and military power have had decisive importance in explaining the different outcomes of the Arab Spring. The point is that the variables associated with state weakness are there in every case but with enough dissimilarity to make causal claims about the different outcomes, based on this vague concept, dubious. The material world actually operates in a way that falls between these two poles of explanation; for example, the structural similarity of atoms throughout the physical environment does not make uncertainty any less central a principle of physics.

The Algerian case also brings back the question of how past conflicts produce later wars. The historian of Spain, Pierre Vilar, asks us to consider the connection between the indecisive political revolution which took place in Spain between 28 September 1868 and 3 January 1874, and the attempt to establish a republic between 1931 and 1936 (2011: 37–9). Both lasted exactly the same amount of time, but while the former ended in failure, the latter resulted in disastrous civil war. What connected these events, and could the last civil war be explained without reference to Spain's long nineteenth century of conflict and instability? Vilar argues that those who attribute the military intervention against the Republic in 1936 only to the turmoils of the Republic in 1931 should remember that both those turmoils, and the disaster which followed, had been emerging for over a century. In order to make his conception of causality more concrete, he states that in the 80 years either side of 1900, Spain existed on a loose cord between its present and its past. (The term *cuerda* could be translated as cord, rope, or string.) The civil war in the 1930s was different from the indecisive conflicts of the past, but connected to them by these cords.

Unlike the structuralist theories summarized at the beginning of this chapter—which treat processes as simple reflections of structures—historians start from the reverse position. When faced with the structural residues of the past—whether the remains of old settlements or battlefields—their task is to reconstruct the processes which produced them. This is what Vilar attempts to do when he identifies the three cords that stretched back into the Spanish past, but proved decisive in 1936. These were imperial decline, the spirit of the dominant Castellano classes, and the nature of the Spanish state (a nation state or merely the repository of ancient historical divisions?) (Vilar 2011: 37–40). One could compare their legacy to a volcano, but to a quiet volcano, which had been there for a long time, and took time to explode. Likewise, when considering the state that fell victim to civil war in Algeria in 1992, those processes which produced that state, rooted in its colonial origins and its attempt at socialist transformation, are crucial. Had French (and before then Ottoman) colonial rule not unsettled the traditional society, leading to the subsequent demographic explosion, the large numbers of unemployed men—which serves as a structural variable in the Collier and Hoeffler model—might not have been present in 1992.

Conclusion

Just as Yugoslavia did in the 1990s, the Arab Spring will shape the study of civil war in important ways. The trigger for change across a whole region was the suicide of just one desperate Tunisian man, Tarek al-Tayeb Mohamed Bouazizi, in 2010. The way the winds of change easily crossed borders reminds me of David Abulafia's human history of the Mediterranean (2014): a sea which never had one settled population, and in which all relationships were, perforce, temporary. During the early stages of the Arab Spring, fresh claims were made for the sweep of globalization, the universal appeal of democracy, and the rapid nature of technological change today. The world seemed less structured and state-centric than it was. One suggestion was that social media had so accelerated the revolutionary process that taking state power would require less time, Tahrir Square in Egypt being the celebrated example. Yet this has proven to be an illusion. Struggles for state power, violent and non-violent, continue, and in Egypt the state remained intact, ultimately to negate the revolution. When the outcomes of the Arab Spring become clearer, attention will return to the behaviour of the state, its character prior to these events, the resources it retained, and the nature of its legitimacy. The state is the one structure that still matters. So while the winds of change cross borders easily, the political outcomes seem very dependent on prior regime type; notably how oil, militaries, and traditional legitimacy combine. Even the unity of the Mediterranean world—the theme of Abulafia's history—was shattered by the rise of the nation state in the twentieth century.

On the question of defining civil war, many people would object to the application of this concept to Algeria in the 1990s. Much of the violence was gratuitous terrorism and had no military logic. Nor was it necessarily directed at the state and its forces. Yet there was a vertical aspect even to the forms of horizontal, and essentially cultural, violence, which darkened a decade that also produced the Salman Rushdie fatwa and the Taliban. The question of who would rule over whom was linked to a struggle to define the nation, an aspect of many civil wars. In *The Divided Self* (1960) the psychiatrist R. D. Laing suggested that the self could be compared to a revolving vase with two facial images painted on different sides. A secure self rotated such that one never saw only one image. Indeed a person, and a state, can normally combine many selves. In the 1990s the Algerian state lost the ability to hold on to two images of itself. What happened was so horrible that it could be compared to a psychotic episode. As in Laing (1960: 39–61), a state of ontological insecurity existed when there was a struggle between an allegedly artificial and an authentic self—represented by Islam.

What then does the break-down of Algerian society in 1992 tell us about human divisiveness? There is a sense in which the cancelled election was only the occasion for the civil war. The grievances were there, the state was in economic crisis, and there was a youth bubble. Would it have made a difference had the election been cancelled, held three years earlier, or three years later? The concept of state weakness is a very abstract way of stating the various problems the Algerian state faced. No less vague is the idea that a state can be 'vulnerable' to civil war over a non-defined period of time. A state can only be judged vulnerable or weak in this sense if its history is taken into account. Volpi sees the cultural violence as a manifestation of Carl Schmitt's thesis that the affirmation of a community in opposition to another is the essence of politics (2003: 9). Yet the Algerian polarities were not new. During the anti-colonial war against France between 1956 and 1962, the FLN had also presented political issues as a battle of opposites. The result was a political culture that placed little value on dialogue, pluralism, or constructive dissent (Evans and Phillips 2007: 298). As conflict unfolded in the early 1990s, both sides claimed to be the real trustees of the revolution, and the other side was accused of betraying its values. In other words, the past was key to the form of divisiveness that emerged. Not only does democracy generally need time; there was little in the historical formation of Algeria to suggest that its introduction would not be divisive.

5

CONSEQUENCES

It is no pleasant task to review the literature on the consequences of civil war. Thucydides considered them worse than the effects of plague, natural disaster, or foreign invasion. For the social and psychological traumas left behind by such conflicts seemed 'peculiarly resistant to therapeutic redress' (Ober 2007: 173). Research by economists suggests that many societies can find themselves in a 'conflict trap' long after the violence of a civil war has abated. To the loss of revenue must be added the moral harm this concept implies. Perhaps the ultimate consequences take the form of an emotional wound carried within the body politic for generations. As the Roman historian Lucan remarked: the wounds inflicted at the hands of fellow citizens tend to sink deep (Lucan 1992: 4). Thucydides was only the first thinker to suggest that civil war brought out the worst in human nature. For this Hobbesian apprehension still lies behind our current fear of state collapse, and with it our willingness to support humanitarian intervention, so that people may be spared the consequences. This chapter begins with a survey of the typical consequences of civil war, before discussing concepts—such as the conflict trap and state collapse—which have been developed for the contemporary era.

Consequences

The consequences of civil war seem no different from those of international wars: terrible loss of life, shattered economies, uprooted populations, scars left on the body politic for generations. Americans would find this no surprise: their civil war was twice as deadly—in terms of the loss of American lives—as World War II, and was fought among a much smaller population (Regan 2009: 123). The casualties alone can be staggering. Sixteen million killed in civil wars which have taken place in the last 50 years (ibid.: 1); more than 200,000 killed in Syria in the last four years, and over 75,000 people killed in Mexico's 'Drug Wars' since 2008.

The victims, increasingly, are found in some of the poorest places on earth. Between 1950 and 2000, civil wars killing half a million people or more occurred in Angola, Nigeria, Afghanistan, Sudan, Mozambique, Cambodia, Angola, Indonesia, and Rwanda (Tilly 2002). In terms of ratio to overall population, almost 1 million were killed in Rwanda from a population of 7 million; between 900,000 and 1 million were killed in Mozambique out of a population of 15 million; and in Angola more than half a million were killed from a smaller population. The tendency of modern states to carry out murderous campaigns against their own citizens—what Rummel calls 'Death by Government'—through ethnic cleansing, genocide, and 'politicide'/the mass killing of one's political opponents, accelerates during such wars. Examples from the past include China, Nazi Germany, and Stalin's Russia. Yet large-scale politicides—if not genocides—also took place during the 1980s in Afghanistan, Uganda, El Salvador, Iran, Syria, Sri Lanka, Ethiopia, and Iraq (Tilly 2002).

Civil war itself has no monopoly on human suffering. The forced march, the concentration camp, the mass rally, or the atomic bomb, all stand as suitable symbols for the history of the past century. Yet if there is one experience which can stand as symbol of the suffering brought by civil war, it is population displacement. Think of Syria: in the next five years Lebanon alone may see its population rise by a fifth to a quarter due to the number of displaced Syrians. Turkey has already received way more than a million refugees, many of whom plan to settle there. The Jordanian state is taking—from a potential refugee population of 7–9 million people—more than its social services are able to cope with. When it comes to the refugee question the consequences of civil war extend across physical boundaries (separating states), temporal boundaries (separating generations), and legal boundaries (dividing combatants from non-combatants).

Refugees living without hope can also be a source of further conflict. The existence of literally millions of Afghans in Pakistani and Iranian refugee camps between 1978 and 1992 created a unique opportunity for political education and military training that prepared another generation of combatants for combat when the Russians left (Harpviken and Lischer 2013). More than half of all rebel groups in combat since 1945 have had transnational connections (Salehyan 2009). A recent study showed that the tactics, ideas, and resources of rebel groups in Chechnya, Kurdistan, Rwanda, Uganda, and Sudan were decisively changed by such linkages (Checkel 2013). Exile and displacement are two issues that touch the humanitarian imagination. The US and NATO intervention in 1999 in Kosovo was clearly provoked by images of hundreds of thousands of Kosovan Albanians escaping the assaults by Serbian forces that year. Yet this conflict spilled over into another state. Unable to force the issue in their home country, armed groups often take advantage of the availability of sanctuary across the border to revitalize their campaign. The way in which Albanian nationalists who had cut their teeth in the Kosovan conflict in 1999 turned their attention to neighbouring Macedonia, which experienced a short armed conflict in 2001, is a good example (Lund 2005: 238).

The spectre of population displacement seems to follow civil wars wherever they occur. A complicating factor in the current conflict in the Democratic Republic of Congo is its contiguity with Rwanda, and the fact that many exiled Tutsis used this territory in the past as a base for attacking Rwandan troops. Indeed, those African states from which the largest number of migrants emanated in the 1990s (Liberia, Burundi, Eritrea, Somalia, Angola, and Sierra Leone) had all experienced civil war (Lucas 2006: 341). In economic terms this can be a form of resource depletion, when those possessing capital take flight, rather than staying and investing in the country. If the emigration is only of those with the least stake in the fighting, it could leave the country more polarized.

In emotional terms, exile is a forced departure from a national homeland, a departure which carries the same emotional register as human loss in general. The Russian poet Joseph Brodsky (1999: 29), who lived most of his life in the United States, compared exile to being in a time capsule, moving—not earthward, but outward, in time and space—while remaining stuck in retrospection. Consider the departure of perhaps more than 100,000 Greek leftists and Macedonian Greeks behind the Iron Curtain after their civil war defeat in 1949. Initially, some of these people continued to believe in the possibilities of socialism in Greece. The collapse of the Soviet Union in 1989 made theirs one of double exile. Mayme Sevander's *They Took My Father* is a memoir about a Finnish family that emigrated to the United States after the civil war of 1918 (Sevander and Hertzel: 2004). Socialists in White Finland had become effectively second-class citizens because of the war, and her father chose to move to Minnesota, where Mayme was born in 1923. Yet rather than accept American capitalism, her father, a labour activist, decided to return to the Soviet autonomous Republic of Karelia in 1934, home to many exiled Finnish communists since 1918. This was to be Mayme's home until she died in 2003. Yet the Republic, which first provided Finnish language schools, Finnish newspapers, even a Finnish orchestra, proved no 'socialist paradise'. Her father perished in the Stalinist purges that followed. Mayme herself survived, and would eventually revisit North America in the later stages of the Cold War. Given the better material conditions she saw, she was asked whether her father had made the right choice in 1934. Her reply was that she recognized the superiority of democratic capitalism, but would make the same choices all over again.

Mayme Sevander's life was shaped not just by the experience of a civil war but by the two (Finnish and Soviet) regimes established at the end of a civil war. Indeed, any assessment of the consequences of war must always take into account the regimes civil wars give rise to. There were approximately 350,000 deaths attributable to the Spanish civil war fought between 1936 and 1939. This war was so violent that Spain saw a 20 per cent rise in the 1935 death rate, each year, during the period 1937–9. The conflict ended in 1939, but because of continued political violence, hunger, disease, and imprisonment the death rate in Spain did not return to normal until 1943. Indeed the post-war recorded figure for deaths above the pre-war norm amount to 215,000 during the period 1940–2. Remarkably, there were as many deaths recorded in 1941 as there were at the height of the civil war. These were consequences, not so much of civil war, but of a victor's peace; of the absence of reconciliation under General Franco (Richards 2014: 82).

That the consequences of conflicts affect more than the generations that experienced the fighting is also borne out by research on public health. The box below shows the results of a study into the relationship, globally, between civil war and the general vulnerability to death and disease in the decades which followed. The authors relied on a World Health Organization dataset that focused on DALYs (disability adjusted life-years) and based their findings on detailed information on 23 major diseases and conditions for different categories of the population, distinguished by gender and by five age groups. The main finding was that while men were the most direct victims of violence, women and children were the long-term victims, particularly with respect to early death and disease. This research estimates that the health of another 8.01 million people were affected in 1999 as a result of the lingering effects of civil wars which occurred between 1991 and 1998. The health consequences of civil war lingered on to the next generation.

The 2003 World Bank Report *Breaking the Conflict Trap: Civil War and Development Policy* (Collier et al. 2003: 33–48) focused on the economic consequences of civil war. It suggests that it usually takes countries more than a decade to reverse the flight of capital, the diminution in the tax base, and the absence of inward investment, which occur during a civil war. In a typical civil war country, the percentage of private wealth held abroad rises to 20 per cent by the end of the conflict (ibid.: 15). On average, in the decade following a civil war,

---

'Civil Wars Kill and Maim People:
Long after the Shooting Stops'

Research Question: The paper attempts to fill a gap in the 'limited systematic research on the consequences of war for civilian populations'. The authors' hypothesis is that civil wars produce long-term damage to public health-care systems that extend well beyond the period of active warfare. These consequences manifest in specific diseases and conditions. Furthermore, the consequences affect women and children disproportionately.

Findings: This hypothesis is explored through a more general political–economic model of conditions affecting death and disability globally. The estimates show the additional burden of death and disability incurred in 1999, from the indirect and lingering effects of civil wars in the years 1991–7. The number of deaths and disabilities was approximately equal to that incurred directly and immediately from all wars in 1999. Indeed for all population categories, it is estimated that 8.01 million DALYs were lost in 1999 from civil wars during the period 1991–7.

Source of Data: The study relies on a World Health Organization dataset that focuses on DALYs. This contains detailed information on 23 major diseases and conditions for different categories of the population, distinguished by gender and by five age groups.

Argument: Among the long-term consequences of civil war, there is the higher incidence of death and disability due to particular infectious diseases and conditions in the different population subgroups. There is also some evidence, though weaker, that civil wars increase the risk of death and disability through the breakdown of norms and practices of social order, with a possible increase in homicide, transportation accidents, other injuries, and cervical cancer.

(Ghobarah, Huth, and Russett 2003)

---

between 9 and 20 per cent of private capital flees a country. The report also asked what the economic consequences of a general reduction in the incidence of civil war would be, at national, regional, and global levels. Since the level of national per capita income tends to be reduced by more than 2 per cent each year a country suffers from civil war, a natural assumption would be that the primary benefit of such a reduction would be at the national level (ibid.: 14). Yet costs resulting from massive migration, and the greater need to provide for public health, burden neighbouring countries. The endless circulation of light arms over a border, the spread of disease from a refugee to a host population, and the recruitment of young men into armed movements (as with al-Qaeda in Afghanistan, Iraq, and Somalia), pose similar problems for neighbouring countries. Among the economic costs at the global level is the income spent on international agencies, aid, and reconstruction, and sometimes military intervention. Over 90 per cent of the world's drug supply is produced in areas affected by civil war (ibid.: 2).

Population displacement, loss of faith in political leaders, reduced expenditure on health and education, as well as the effects of violence on social trust, also deplete levels of social capital. A series of interviews conducted with the current residents of Kosovo noted people's lament for the loss of the good neighbourly relations between Albanians and Serbs, social ties that had been much stronger before the war in 1999 than the image of an ethnically divided society suggests (Seifert 2015: 220–4). The consequence of seeing your neighbours being transformed into enemies, when it seems to have no basis in previous experience, is often a feeling of bewilderment (Kalyvas 2006: 82). Another social problem is how to demobilize large armies of young men, at a time when social tensions are running high and when the opportunities for violent crime are more extensive than normal. In neighbouring Bosnia-Herzegovina, Croatian and Serbian criminal and political networks that were formed during the collapse of Yugoslavia continue to have decisive influence on its politics (Kostovicova and Bojicic-Dzelilovic 2015: 220–33). Despite a peace agreement and a democratic transition, El Salvador shares with some of its neighbours some of the worst homicide rates in the world. Gangs had not been a dominant part of the society before the mid 1990s. Stimulated mainly by return migration from North American cities—where gang culture flourishes—the judicial system was unable to quell the wave of violence that came when the *Maras* (gangs) returned from the US. A similar problem in neighbouring Guatemala has resulted in the emergence of vigilantism on a large scale.

Part of 'the conflict trap' is that there may simply not be enough time to address the consequences of a civil war before another war returns. Between 1922 and 1974 Greece experienced no less than nine coups and counter-coups, three periods of dictatorship, and a major civil war, which began under the German occupation and ended in 1949. The first major episode in this chain of conflict—'the Asia Minor Disaster'—involved an unsuccessful attempt to retake lands in the west of Anatolia from the Turks between 1919 and 1922. After the displacement of around a million Greeks from Asia Minor and the Black Sea region to mainland Greece which followed, Greek society remained unsettled. Amidst the influx of refugees, women (and widows)—as well as orphans—were disproportionally prominent. Out of a total Greek population of around 6 million there were some 25,000 orphans (Clogg 2013: 101). Theo Angelopolous's film *The Weeping Meadow* begins with a shot of Greek refugees arriving in eastern Thrace from Odessa at the end of World War I. Among them is Eleni, the heroine of the film, an orphan who settles, with her new foster parents, in a village populated by migrants. Images of houses constructed in marshlands, of flooding, of villagers travelling on rafts, and of the emigrant ship leaving Thessalonica for America, evoke the underlying themes of displacement and uprootedness. By 1949, when the civil war ended, Eleni has lost her two sons to the conflict, and a husband to emigration, and returns to the original village in Thrace only to find that it has been destroyed by war.

The Weeping Meadow thus dramatizes the inability of people to re-establish basic social roles after 'the Asia Minor Disaster'. Only the local women survived these decades, often without sons, husbands, or homes. Whether the issue is sexual violence, or the problems of women raising families in communities with few men afterwards, gender roles are usually changed by civil war. While the immediate casualties are male, women and children usually constitute a majority of refugees and of displaced people. Returning to the Spanish case, in Catalonia—one of the most economically developed regions of the country—the infant mortality rate was 40 per cent higher throughout the 1940s than in 1935, before the Spanish civil war began. Average general life expectancy in Catalonia in 1941–5 was lower by four years than the pre-war level; the number of widows under 30 multiplied fivefold, compared to the number in 1930 (Richards 2014:82).

Maria Barbal's (2010) novel *Stone in a Landslide* tells the life story of Conxa, who was born in the Catalan Pyrenees, and leaves home at the age of 13. She finds her life changed by the maelstrom of the Spanish civil war, when she loses her husband Jaume, a Republican, to the conflict. She then endures the bitterness and silent animosity of village life under Franco. Such was the atmosphere of hatred, suspicion, and vengeance in many Spanish villages in the 1950s, that many young people emigrated to the large cities or abroad to escape from it. The unfamiliar surroundings of Barcelona provide the backdrop to Conxa's old age, after she had moved south with her family. Barcelona may have been a beautiful city, but it was only one stop from the cemetery. When, in the evening, a story from up north begins to be told, there is no one to tell it to, 'and it annoys everyone that I want to turn an evening in Barcelona into some remarkable event on a forgotten mountain' (Barbal 2010: 125). The book title's image of a stone in a landslide is one of endurance, and lack of bitterness. Like Brodsky's time capsule however, it also suggests randomness. For random suffering is not chosen. The consequence is often a life that has lost its shape. One could compare how a civil war makes an individual's life shapeless to what happens in the fairy tale *The Snow Queen*: when you look into the mirror it breaks, and the many fragments pierce people.

The conflict trap

The consequences of civil war are not always purely destructive. In *Battle Cry of Freedom: The Civil War Era*, the historian James McPherson showed how the American civil war accelerated patterns of state financing and administration beyond the rate they would have expanded had peace existed (1988: 859). Increased powers of taxation, of military conscription, more judicial oversight, and monetary control accrued to the federal government during and after the war. Rather than being the antithesis of political development, bills like the Freedmen's Bureau Bill, passed in 1865, and intended to deal with the emancipation of 4 million slaves, represented a new extension of the powers of the federal government into the areas of social welfare and labour relations (ibid.: 842).

The United States recovered from its civil war in ways that few countries today show any sign of doing. The strength of American institutions prior to the civil war was significant: after 1865 the federal system continued to operate, even in the defeated Confederate states, much as it had done in the 1850s. Poorer countries lack both the impetus towards economic recovery and a coherent set of political institutions. Paul Collier et al.'s *Breaking the Conflict Trap* (2003) argues that those countries now most at risk of civil war—largely very poor countries with a history of past conflict—are also those most likely to continue to suffer from child poverty, human rights abuses, inflated military expenditures, infrastructural damage, capital flight, civilian deaths, refugees, and the destruction of social norms over the longer term.

These consequences keep the state weak, and vulnerable to predatory neighbours. The most disastrous contemporary example is the Democratic Republic of Congo, where no less than seven states have intervened in the fighting. This process began after the genocide in neighbouring Rwanda in 1994 when the Tutsi government pursued Hutu forces across the border into the Eastern Congo, thus igniting existing tensions between the Congolese population and the local Tutsi minority. The consequence has been to fragment the Congolese state further, since the outside powers—both in order to pursue military objectives and to exploit natural resources—have a vested interest in maintaining this situation of state weakness. The Congo's colonial transport infrastructure has almost completely collapsed, and the Republic has gone beyond the point where the reconstruction of either a unified state, or a unified nation, is possible (Hall 2010: 4).

The concept of a conflict trap may be understood in two ways. As with a 'poverty trap', later generations may be stuck with certain economic and social problems because of conflicts fought by their parents' generation. Collier et al. add that civil war leads to such traps because most of the fighters—including those who go on to dominate politics after 'peace' has been established—might be unaffected by the economic and social consequences affecting the general society (2003: 4). Hence recovery from conflict is not a major objective for them. The existence of such conflict traps has the potential to bifurcate the world into two broad categories: societies that have grown beyond civil war, and those where a combination of underdevelopment and conflict will exist for the foreseeable future. *Breaking the Conflict Trap* groups countries into four economic categories: (1) highly developed states exposed to little risk of civil war, (2) countries on a developmental path which will take them to a place beyond risk, (3) low-income countries already affected by civil war, and (4) economically marginalized countries now at peace, but very vulnerable to civil war as a result of their poverty (ibid.: 101–3, 108). The report concludes that the core challenge must be to bring the latter into the mainstream of development. Where peace is recent however, the challenge is more to stabilize peace in the first decade after the peace agreement has been signed (ibid: 104).

Another aspect of the conflict trap is that the consequences will be passed on to the next generation, in the form of more violence. A country that has recently experienced a civil war is four or five times more likely to suffer a recurrence of fighting, than a society with no civil war in its recent past (ibid.: 83). One simple explanation is that a prior history of violence against civilians—especially between ethnic groups—makes it very difficult for either side to believe in peaceful coexistence in the future. 'The second round' of fighting could simply be the natural expression of the accumulated fears and hatreds of the past. Statistical studies show that a country where civil war seems to be drawing to a close runs a 44 per cent risk of conflict recurring after a termination of hostilities (ibid.: 83). The nature and legitimacy of the regimes established after the initial conflicts is probably the critical factor. On the other hand, a certain degree of war-weariness in places like Angola, Mozambique, and Northern Ireland has given the post-conflict regimes time in which to build more effective and inclusive institutions.

When civil wars have a political logic, they may be a catalyst for social development. In the United States issues like slavery and seces-sion were at stake, and the civil war changed the nature of the population's identity. To illustrate with a linguistic example, before 1861 'the United States' were used as a plural noun ('the United States are a Republic'); the war marked a transition to a singular noun (McPherson 1988: 859). Yet other conflicts have shown little evidence of this potential for change. A group of Latin American scholars compared the impact of violent conflict on popular identification with the state and nation since the 1990s in Colombia, El Salvador, and Mexico (Centeno et al. 2013). René Girard's study of ancient myths (1995) suggests that foundational violence is at the heart of most social orders. He argues that for a successful myth of social order to be constructed, the community must identify some section of society to be sacrificed or scapegoated. Colombia, El Salvador, and Mexico seemed good candidates for this type of analysis, since an official 'us and them' rhetoric was promoted against Colombia's FARC paramili-taries, El Salvador's gangs, and Mexican drug syndicates. Yet in no case did the conflicts strengthen popular identification with state or nation: rather, in all three, institutions were so weak that popular support for the state in implementing hard law and order policies was low.

Our traditional image of civil war has been a sporting one: the purpose of the participants—as in the United States—was to win the war and gain state power. Making the analogy with the war on terror, David Keen (2012) stresses the advantages that may accrue from wars that cannot be won, and are perpetuated by elites for economic and political reasons. He argues for a recognition of the hidden purpose of civil conflict. Civil wars need not be, as in the United States, political crises amenable to decisive resolution, or simply break-downs of social order. Increasingly they are systems of violence. These systems may originate in political divisions, but are perpetuated by a complex web of interests. Colombia, for example, had experienced an intense bout of armed conflict, *la violencia*, between 1948 and 1958. In the 1980s the country went through a sharp intensification of violence that has lasted for decades. In his study of its political economy, the political scientist Nazih Richani describes a 'system of violence', predicated on the state's inability to mediate the main conflicts of the society, and on the absence of an actor strong enough to dominate politics. What made this negative equilibrium a stable 'system' was the fact that the actors in contention had adapted themselves to a condition of war, and saw it as the best alternative, given the higher costs, for them, of peace (Richani 2002: 3–4). The 'systems' approach holds two cautionary lessons. If civil wars are not driven by political differences, a formal compromise will not produce peace. On the other hand, if they are allowed to run their course, the expectation that a strong Leviathan will emerge to create a new social and political order may not be realistic either. It may take the intervention of an outside actor to break the negative equilibrium.

Material and moral harm

That moral damage results from civil war is undeniable. Consider the language the Africanist René le Marchand (2013: 319) uses to describe the ongoing wars in the Democratic Republic of Congo. He writes of civil war 'injecting' a strong element of distrust into social relations, 'tearing to bits' the fragile social ties that had once 'sustained' social life, and of violence that has 'created hatreds' where none existed and 'unleashed predatory instincts' on a large scale. A conflict that was a product of a failed state has 'sown the seeds' for another in the future. This naturalistic language suggest that the roots of a healthy society become spoiled by civil war, but also that the corrupted roots then contaminate those which might return vitality to a society. This language is of corruption, of vitality polluted, as if the well-springs of social existence are corrupted at their source. The consequence is a demoralized country, one unable to find the energy to recover before the corruption Le Marchand speaks of extends further into the society. Thus to the material damage we must add this moral stain.

Le Marchand was not the first to use naturalistic images, or to imply that impulses towards both corruption and renewal exist after civil war. In 'Last Stop', a poem written in 1944 as Greece's civil war divisions were taking shape, the poet George Seferis juxtaposed fertile images of trees casting their branches in virgin forests—branches which will rivet themselves in the earth and sprout again—with the more permanent image of a country chopped up and burning like a pine tree. Seferis's image is one of stunted growth (1995: 156). The literary scholar Vayos Liapis sees echoes in it of the work of the classical tragedian Aeschylus, for whom evil was self-perpetuating and self-renewing (2014: 22). In Aeschylus, the destructive force of this pattern could be halted only by the universal mechanism of retribution (ibid.: 22). Just as violence begets further violence, evil requires additional evil to keep the destruction within limits.

The 'shoots' Le Marchand speaks of flourish of their own accord. Liapis argues that Seferis's poetic response to the Greek civil war was to visualize it as a widespread disease, a monster feeding off its own polluted blood, and an evil with the potential for endless recurrence (ibid.: 23). After civil war, many societies are left with an evil seedling, an apt phrase for the moral and emotional meanings of the conflict trap. It is not that economists, who show that capital flight makes future conflict over limited resources more likely, are wrong. Rather, it is that since a society at civil war is also at war with itself, the damage it must recover from must be understood holistically. The task in contemporary Iraq could be one of reconstruction and state-building. It is also a more intuitive one of preventing the legacy of sectarian killing being passed on to the next generation. Hence governments and international agencies find themselves in a race of time against the natural tendency for these shoots to reappear.

The metaphor of a tunnel is often used for the psychology of the conflict trap. International wars last on average only six months, and people are more aware of their beginnings and potential ends. One reason civil war is more demoralizing is that when members of a society are deprived of such a vista toward the future, their attention turns inward. *The Civil Wars* by the Roman historian Appian focuses on the succession of civil wars which led to the establishment of the Roman Empire in the last century BC. These were conveyed, stylistically, to heighten the sense of an ever-darkening polity. What produced the tunnel effect was that the different episodes were not related to each other. Nor was there an attempt to find underlying common causes. Rather the events were ordered by Appian to show the decline—from 133 BC onwards—of a once peaceful and law-abiding polity into the chaos of civil war and eventually the establishment of an empire (Appian 1996: Introduction).

The Israeli novelist and peace activist David Grossman (2008: 59–69), concerned with the decline of the Israeli polity today, uses the tunnel metaphor to show how hard it is to remain human during intractable conflicts. The psychological problem he sees in Israel is that all events and relationships are continually related to the main conflict between Israelis and Palestinians. For Grossman this is dehumanizing. Evidence elsewhere also shows that people continue to construct the tunnel long after the violence has ended, because they retain the habit of relating all aspects of life to the earlier conflict. The boundaries between war and peace thus remain blurred. Commenting on how much progress had been made in Northern Ireland since peace was agreed in 1998, the journalist Gerry Moriarty still remarked:

> At all levels of society there can be a studied wariness of the other; an instinctive need to be able to place people in their correct political or religious boxes; an attention to surnames, where one went to school, or who is or isn't wearing the Remembrance Day poppy, an ear to the Catholic-pronounced *haitch* or the Protestant aitch. [*Irish Times* 17 November 2012]

For Thucydides, the civil conflict which took place in Corcyra during the wider war between Athens and the Peloponnesian Leagues was devastating in both its material and moral effects. It took on a whirlpool-like character, and an essentially *moral* distemper followed the descent of the *polis* into murderous factionalism (Ober 2007: 173). The ultimate victim was not the individual, but the social fabric itself, undone by leaders who succeeded in destroying the *polis* through their ambitions. Stasis to him meant the collapse of *everything* that had once united the *polis*, including human decency, patriotism, and individual nobility.

This raises the ultimate psychological question, of how people who have lived through societal collapses of this kind relate to the world afterwards. The Greek civil war led to the displacement of at least 700,000 people. For some, the experience was an initial exile—from Asia Minor and the Black Sea region after 1922—and then double exile from the regime established after the civil war in 1949. Seferis himself lost his childhood home in the Gulf of Smyrna (a largely Greek city before 1923), and spent much of his life outside Greece in diplomatic service. He had been left a house in the Gulf of Smyrna (now Izmir in Turkey) by his grandmother in her will. Its loss coincided with the fall of Smyrna to the Turkish nationalist forces in August 1922. Later, Seferis complained of the number and quality of the temporary quarters he and his wife had to live in during the war years. Such accommodation he compared to putting on borrowed clothes (Liapis 2014: section 5).

Few today are aware that the Ukrainians established an independent republic in 1917. This republic was then engulfed in a series of international and internal conflicts unleashed by the Bolshevik revolution, and became absorbed in the Soviet Union in 1921. Most of us think of the Spanish civil war as the emblematic civil war of twentieth-century Europe. Yet the mixture of banditry, revolution, ethnic conflict, famine, land agitation, and outside interventions which destroyed the Ukrainian Republic was more representative of what was to come in the rest of the world (Yekelchyh 2007). One reason for our ignorance of the Ukrainian disaster is that Spain survived as a state but the Ukrainian Republic did not. Its fate poses the ultimate question about the consequences of civil war: what it is like to have lived in a community and state that has disappeared? How does one live with no chance of return? Must one always be wearing borrowed clothes?

Ancient philosophers such as Plato, Aristotle, and Lucretius wondered whether the identities of human beings can meaningfully be said to remain the same after going through such drastic changes. What consolation can these philosophers provide for people permanently deprived of those 'here and now' aspects of social existence which anchored them in the world? Broadly speaking three possible answers were outlined. (1) Plato (428/9–348/7 BC) argued that there is a changeless realm, like the ideal realm of geometrical objects, which is beyond the ever-changing material world, and one's essential self—one's psyche or soul—resides in this changeless realm, and thereby ensures personal immortality. The loss of a state might mean a loss of the self rooted in a specific place, but not of the soul. (2) Aristotle (428/7–348/7 BC) also thought that there was a changeless dimension within every material object, which allows material objects, including human beings, to remain the same in spite of changing, although this may not ensure personal immortality. A continual self was possible, despite great changes. (3) The materialist atomists such as Lucretius (90–52 BC) argued, however, that both change and stability in material objects are the product of changeless material atoms, coming together and pulling apart. People—or at least their material bodies—are temporary configurations of this sort. From this perspective, the self—no less than atoms and states—can emerge and disappear with the flux of time (Barresi and Martin 2006: 4).

Consequences such as death, demoralization, and displacement are part of the human condition, and may have no specific remedies. In the end there may be an unbridgeable gap between the ancient Greeks and Romans, who saw civil war from a moral perspective, and the modern social scientist, who is more likely to think that moral consequences can be ameliorated by tangible changes in living conditions (Regan

CONSEQUENCES

2009: 130). Yet both traditions believe that the worst consequences of civil war stem from the collapse of that which held a society together. Today's social scientists are still Hobbesian when they take the state to be the source of this unity, and the factor accepted as the key to ameliorating the consequences of civil war. Since Hobbes remains so influential, the next section considers one of its central tenets: the view that the worst consequences of civil war flow from state collapse.

State failure and state collapse

Thus far we have not asked the question of what it is about civil war, as a distinct form of conflict, that produces the consequences we fear. For centuries civil war has been associated with extreme violence and brutality, connotations it shares with anarchy, sedition, and terrorism. Writing soon after the Yugoslav wars, the historian Mark Mazower (2001: 150) blamed the violence not on Balkan culture or inherited ethnic divisions but on civil war as a form of conflict which is fought out 'amid a total breakdown of social and political institutions'. Yet what is it about state collapse that produces these consequences? Two related claims should be considered: that civil wars bring out the worst in human nature, and that this deterioration happens most often under conditions of state failure and state collapse.

State collapse began to be seen as the worst aspect of civil war in the specific context of the 1990s. The capacities of many African states have been continually weakening since then. Domestically, decades of single-party rule had damaged them economically. Externally, the decline in outside aid following the end of the Cold War, and the rise in world oil prices, made finance even scarcer (Hall 2010: 5). The result is a vicious circle. Consider the huge state of Nigeria, whose potential for economic development had once been strong. Its oil revenues have been spent to benefit a small elite or for immediate gratification, despite the existence of an ideology of state development once shared by most Nigerians (Hall 2010: 7). Originally strong enough to thwart the secession of Biafra between 1967 and

1970, it now lacks effective control over much of its territory and is facing a lethal Islamic insurgency in the northern provinces. Nigeria is now commonly classified as a failed state.

The language of fragile, weak, and collapsed states also reflected the new security fears which have gained ground since the 1990s. Large states or superpowers no longer presented the main threat to global security. Rather, these emanate from groups that could profit from weakened states in places as far afield as Kenya, Mali, Nigeria, Pakistan, the Yemen, and the Philippines during the war on terror. In Africa particularly, the death throes of the Central African Republic, Democratic Republic of Congo, Eritrea, Libya, Somalia, Sudan, and Timor Leste gave rise to fears of this kind. The situation in the Middle East and North Africa has kept these fears alive. In Arab countries, characterized by low levels of basic education and of infrastructure, dependence on oil, and repressive state apparatuses (Hall 2010: 2), the fear is of radical Islamists taking control should the state further weaken. Thus far, four states have been brought to the point of state collapse as part of the Arab Spring: Iraq, Libya, Syria, and the Yemen.

Hobbes wove 'contumely', 'factions', 'sedition', 'civil warres', and 'warre' together into one vision of catastrophy. The Hobbesian paradigm seems appropriate for a world of weak, failing, or collapsing states. Its continued relevance is suggested by the recent appearance of new concepts for old fears. The term 'strong state' is now typically used for a polity that fulfils the basic functions of the state, with sufficient capacity or legitimacy to fend off challengers. A 'weak state' is one that fails to fulfil these functions: though violence may not be about to engulf it, its weakness could be seen as the first step in the process of disintegration. A 'failed state' exists on the border of anarchy, where the state has lost the monopoly of violence over its territory. Finally, a 'collapsed state' is an extreme version of a 'failed state' (Rotberg 2004: 9): there is a complete lack of central authority, and the state itself has become a mere geographical expression, even if it remains recognized in international law (ibid.: 1–51). The growth of international trade, civil society, and the mass media—the bulwarks of liberal values—has not rendered fears of state collapse out of date. Quite the contrary; the way the media continually reinforce the link between violent conflict and humanitarian disaster keeps this perspective at the forefront of our consciousness.

If Hobbes was right to believe that the state rested on the calculation of individuals to come together so that the life of all would be more secure for all, the loss of this protective capacity has to have negative consequences. On the one hand, the absence of a firm legal basis for rights and security intensifies competition for everyone. On the other, state collapse also raises the question of who should take over—an issue on which people will naturally differ. Hobbes is also famous for proposing a solution: a new Covenant entered into out of fear for the purpose of protection. His stress on the importance of a strong central authority for the preservation of peace is very relevant to what has happened to Iraq since Saddam Hussein was overthrown in 2003. Tony Blair, the former British prime minister, reflected that the primary lesson to be learnt from the US-led invasion of Iraq is that dismantling a state apparatus is dangerous during an occupation. Once 'the lid' is taken off a repressive system, a variety of social and territorial rivalries brewing underneath the surface will reappear (*Northern Echo* 18 June 2014).

The lid analogy suggests that even if violent conflict is not normal, a weakening of central authority can quickly bring it to the surface. Research by Fearon and Laitin on the incidence of violent conflict on the African continent between 1960 and 1979 estimated that neighbours of different groups interacted a total of 38,000 times in this period, but these interactions produced only 20 instances of actual communal violence. Hence, 'for any randomly chosen but neighbouring pair of ethnic groups, on average only 5 in 10,000 had a recorded conflict in any year (Laitin 2007: 10–11). It follows that if there is nothing natural about 'ethnic conflict', only an 'X factor'-type change could produce it. Laitin at least concluded that 'the culprit' is again the 'weak state': a state unable to provide basic services to the population, unable to keep the peace in its peripheries, and unable to distinguish between law-abiders and law-breakers (ibid.: 21). Yet how can we identify a state at risk of such developments? Objective indicators, such as whether a state is newly created, whether the state is in economic crisis or has undergone a recent transition to democracy could be a guide. Yet as the American sociologist Jack Goldstone (2008: 25) warns, state failure results, not just from shifts in some index—per capita income, for example—but from shifts in the perceptions and incentives embodied in institutional arrangements, 'such that people *suddenly* shift their behaviour and allegiances to those institutions'. These shifts are hard to predict.

The Yugoslav case suggests that Goldstone was right to argue that a state can collapse because of a *sudden* shift in popular perception. The novelist Gertrude Stein showed how easily a sturdy structure, such as a language, could be exposed by altering something simple, in her case word order in a sentence (Lehrer 2012: 147). In politics this 'something simple' is the protective skein of the state. The security-dilemma perspective on the collapse of Yugoslavia was an alternative to the standard way of explaining the wars which occurred between 1991 and 1995 as the product of group divisions which preceded the war, and were only awaiting violent expression (Kalyvas 2006: 65). It suggests that the polarization between the ethnic groups was the consequence of the weakening of state authority, not its cause.

Christian, Freudian, and Hobbesian perspectives on political violence are at one in seeing civilization as a very thin edifice. Once it is removed, horrible consequences will follow. Their basic premise is that humans are naturally violent, and are likely to express their violence unless controlled (Kalyvas 2006: 55). Terrible consequences can follow the collapse of the state. The question is what these human dispositions waiting to express themselves actually are. Are they universal, or specific to some cultures? Do men act on them, rather than women? In Yugoslavia the collapse of the state presented an opportunity for a range of criminals, paramilitaries, and politicians. In large parts of Bosnia-Herzegovina, the ethnic cleansing of villages was done not by neighbours, but by outsiders coming to the villages and

Map 5 The break-up of Yugoslavia

forcing people to take sides. When a state weakens, civil war can be the product of a more sinister motive than fear: predation or greed (Kasfir 2004: 53–76). Indeed, both fear and the desire to covet and acquire the possessions of others have the same sources in state collapse and anarchy (ibid.). The suggestion that fear drove events forward conjures up the image of a society literally destroying itself. Yet in Yugoslavia, the process also involved the 'asset stripping' of the state by groups of criminal, paramilitary, and political elites. Is human nature an appropriate name for these diverse motivations? Hobbes himself thought competition, diffidence (based on fear), and the desire for glory to be the principal causes of conflict (Hobbes 1985 [1651]: 185). Seferis's 'The Last Stop', written in October 1944, is quoted in the preface to this book. The poem—which begins 'Man frays easily in wars'—expresses disillusionment with the sight of human nature fraying under the stress of war, but also suggests no attribute is more fundamental than another. The traits of human nature he depicts are plural, not uniform, and before attributing the worst consequences of state collapse to something so general, a discussion of some different contexts is needed to add some sociological nuance to the Hobbesian outlook.

Should Hobbes be our guide?

The Hobbesian paradigm continues to cast a long shadow over us because of the images of conflict the media continually exposes us to. According to the late American novelist Saul Bellow (1993: ix), public consciousness today is like a large virgin territory just opening itself to settlement and exploitation. The way the media constantly rushes to invade this consciousness he compares to the Oklahoma gold rush. It invades our consciousness through the proliferation of images of conflict, crises, and disasters. The result is that, with no effort on our part, we keep track of the latest crises in the lives of celebrities, civil war in Syria, the travails of the Eurozone, rates of violence in Egypt, health scares among royals, and terrorism in Kenya as if these were all manifestations of a general global crisis! In this invasion the most dramatic crisis states (such as the Congo) are presented as paradigmatic for a global experience of conflict which actually takes many shapes and forms.

No doubt terrible consequences can flow from state collapse; many civil wars become humanitarian disasters and interventions are necessary. Nonetheless, some nuance should be brought to the debate about the consequences of civil war. First, one needs to make a distinction between conflicts that can be compared to humanitarian disasters, and those which cannot. In ancient Greek the concept of crisis implied decision: under the pressure of time a stark situation requires decisive action, and actors must take one of two courses of action (Koselleck 2002: 237). Hence the resolution of the crisis is implicit in the definition itself. It is in this sense that the historian John Bell wrote of *The Crisis in Costa Rica* (1971), where a short civil war was fought in 1948 over the issue of electoral fraud. After the decisive victory of the forces led by the Social Democrat José Figueres that year, a series of dramatic decisions were made concerning the future constitutional order, including the abolition of the army. The result was the most stable democracy in Latin America. This crisis was very different from what the Italian Marxist Antonio Gramsci referred to as an 'organic crisis': a situation endangering the state, and putting into question the future existence of the social order (1975: 174–276). Such crises produce consequences of a completely different nature.

Secondly, civil wars in weak states do not always result in anarchy. The literature posits a continuum ranging from state weakness to state failure, with the end point being state collapse (Rotberg 2004: 4). The continuum approach does allow one to ask specific questions: is the danger the worse the further along the continuum a society travels; at what point along it will the cross-over to collective violence take place; is the threshold passed with the emergence of groups as quasi-state actors, with the potential to perform some of the functions of the state, as in Yugoslavia? Yet although ideas of descent, decay, and disintegration permeate this literature, the movement to the end of this continuum, anarchy, is extremely rare. Political scientist Robert Rotberg suggests that the concept of anarchy represents only the end point of the process of state collapse, which he rightly describes as 'a rare and extreme version of state weakness' (2004: 1–51).

A third point is that the zero-sum conception of the state we can trace to Hobbes allows for no grey zone between a properly functioning state and a situation of near-anarchy. Yet these exist in many places. Zimbabwe, for example, remains an intact if disastrous state. Its economy may have collapsed, the rule of law has been weakened, and its external legitimacy is under attack, yet Robert Mugabe has still been able to exploit both nationalism and land hunger to keep the regime in place (Hall 2010: 2). Haiti, in contrast, collapsed in the absence of violence. Stathis Kalyvas makes the point that theories which explain violence in terms of break-down, collapse, and by implication, anarchy, usually mischaracterize as states of break-down places where both order and disorder coexist (2006: 70–3). Colombia, for example, suffered for decades because the FARC guerrillas were able to finance a rural insurgency through kidnapping and drug-running. State collapse could be the outcome of a degrading Hobbesian process, where people begin to turn to their own sectional leaders for the provision of security. Yet the situation may also improve. That Colombia survived decades of insurgency without controlling most of its habitable territory suggests that Western notions of the state—based on absolutist notions of authority—have limited application there.

The study of international politics cannot proceed without the concept of the state: when we look at the map the state is the basic organizing principle. Yet the struggles of the new state may reflect a more fundamental problem: that of building states on the basis of divided or non-existent nations. This is the fourth problem with this approach: it is not weak states but divided nations that matter. The concept of state weakness was developed in the face of clear evidence of state *and* nation-building failures in Africa, the Middle East, and parts of Latin America. Yet the ethnic or secessionist conflicts that have recently arisen may be no different in this respect to what happened in much of Eastern and Central Europe between 1918 and 1945. The explosive potential of nationalist politics has been attributed to the destabilizing force of the principle of self-determination—which can mean that every putative nation is entitled to its own state—or to the fact that the world is so culturally diverse that huge amounts of force and violence will be needed if political and cultural boundaries are to become congruent (Kedourie 1960, Gellner 1983: 1, Conor 1980: 226–8). Either way the difficulty of finding a successful formula for nation-building has made the task of constructing viable states enormously difficult.

The state has a clarity and integrity in political theory which it does not have in reality. States are always rising and failing, struggle to become more than they are, and continually looking for new ways to deal with the threats posed by their external environments. If so, it may not be useful to think of the peaceful norm as being the strong state. If we conceive of state collapse as decay at the level of the nation state, the specific question is what aspects of 'stateness' matter most during wars: institutional capacity, the rule of law, state legitimacy, or the state's roots in society? It may be strange to consider the United States from this perspective. Yet for four years large swathes of its territory were under the control of the Confederacy, and some border states—such as North Carolina—saw little effective government for most of that period. Nonetheless, no generalized Hobbesian state of anarchy emerged, although life in some states became extremely brutalized. The Union was able to marshal far more resources; but besides coercive strength, American statehood also rested on its institutional capacity, external legitimacy, and not least, its economic dynamism. Crucially, when it came to the aftermath, both sides subscribed to a common idea of the state, and fought the war as if it was a 'War Between Two Sovereigns'.

In contrast, the conflict which began in Mozambique in 1976 conforms to the vista of a vicious spiral leading to total societal collapse. The civil war lasted until 1992, four times longer than the American civil war. More than 900,000 people were killed in one of the poorest countries on earth. As the Frelimo government lost authority, the situation on the ground progressively worsened; the insurgent army Renamo abused human rights on a massive scale. There was a period of near-anarchy: 5 million people became refugees, famine and economic collapse took place, Renamo relied on the forced conscription of soldiers, and economic and sexual slavery were widespread. Yet these disastrous consequences cannot simply be blamed on the collapse of the state. When was a strong Mozambican state ever in existence for it to collapse? If there had been little 'stateness' in Mozambique before 1975, how can such a disastrous descent into anarchy be explained mainly by the collapse of the state? Who is to say that the problem was one of inherited state weakness, and not the over-ambitious use of state power on the part of Frelimo, which employed a set of Soviet-style policies that had been equally disastrous elsewhere? The basic problem with the Hobbesian paradigm—when exported beyond early modern Britain—is that the state is not a constant, but a conceptual variable.

Yet Hobbes made the state not only the main source of coercion in society but its central organizing principle. Of the things tending to dissolve the Commonwealth, he argued that the division of the sovereign power was one: for 'what is to divide the Power of a Commonwealth but to dissolve it; for Powers divided mutually destroy each other' (Hobbes 1985 [1651]: 368). His dramatic stress on the absolute centrality of the state reminds me of Spain's reactionary Bourbon monarch Ferdinand VII, who died in 1833 and compared himself to the cork in the bottle of beer: once it was pulled, the liquid would foam out everywhere (Hughes 2004: 71). As we have seen, this zero-sum conception remains influential; it suggests that the more of the state the better, the less of the state the greater the chance of anarchy. Yet this zero-sum conception may limit the application of Hobbes' paradigm to other parts of the world.

In reality, if state strength was that important, and weak states the main source of violence, the world would have experienced much more violence and conflict than it has. What about strong states like Israel as a possible explanation for conflict? Cannot the conflict which began in Algeria in 1992 be blamed, not on the weakness of its economy, but on the strength of its repressive military apparatus? Moreover, there is no central state organ, the loss of which will necessarily kill off the state. Each state may have its own operating procedures, and may survive even if certain basic functions become impaired. Consider the Irish civil war of 1922–3. By June 1922—after four years of revolution—much of the Irish countryside was sliding into a state of lawlessness. Since the truce agreed with the British government in July 1921, the IRA had been in control of the larger part of the future state's territory. This situation continued up to July 1922, and might have encouraged widespread lawlessness and criminal opportunism. When the civil war began on 28 June the new police force and army existed only in embryo. What followed was a bitter war, of such dimensions that it certainly affected the exercise or structure of authority (Kissane 2005: 2–3). Yet no Hobbesian free-fall developed. Rather the impact of the civil war was to reinforce the conservative cast of southern Irish society, which in turn strengthened the state.

The state does not produce or prevent outcomes monotonically, as sound impacts on our hearing. With sound, increases and decreases have a direct and unmediated impact on the listener. In politics, increases and decreases in the coercive capacity of states cannot shape outcomes in this way. A contrast between Ireland and the Spanish civil war would suggest that what really makes a civil war 'zero-sum' is not the absence of state authority, but the lack of agreement on the basic foundations of social order. Much has been written about the religious violence during the Spanish civil war, when supporters of the Republic killed as many as 7,000 religious personnel, and carried out sacrilegious acts such as disinterring their bodies. By desecrating churches, the republicans were themselves performing a religious rite; they were, as mentioned earlier revealing a religious sensibility of their own. They were also attacking the authority structures within which priests and monks (like landlords) were embedded (Graham 2005: 27). The Spanish Republic obviously lacked a consensus about the nature of the social order.

Harry Eckstein (1965: 153) reflected that the literature on 'internal war' paid insufficient attention to forces that might countervail those pushing a society to the brink. In the real world events occur not only because the forces leading toward violent conflict are strong; those tending to inhibit or obstruct violence are also weak. The absence or presence of state authority matters, but it may also be that the overall sum of authority in some societies is spread so diffusely as not to allow an easy monopoly by the state. One alternative source of authority is religion. The Commander-in-Chief of the Irish Army, Michael Collins, a supporter of the Anglo-Irish Treaty, was killed in an ambush in Cork on 22 August 1922 by those opposed to the Treaty. When news of his death reached Kilmainham jail in Dublin— temporary home to thousands of anti-treaty prisoners—their response was to go down on their knees and pray for his soul. This shows that just because the state (meaning here a centralized set of institutions with strong coercive power) collapses, the society need not collapse too. In Yugoslavia in contrast both state *and* society collapsed. State collapse created an opportunity for mass predation, ethnic cleansing, and sexual violence, but not all societies take this opportunity. In contrast, the collapse of state authority in Northern Ireland between 1969 and 1972 led to around 60,000 people fleeing their homes, but did not lead to sexual violence. If we want to understand consequences, we must ask under what circumstances society itself, in addition to the state, collapses during civil wars.

State collapse is an improbable outcome of state weakness for the simple reason that some degree of inertia characterizes most social orders (Gardner 1976: 215, 226). Since societal collapse may be even rarer than state collapse, the alternative to Hobbes is to think socio-logically about the state. Eckstein defined internal war as a kind of social force, exercised in the process of political competition but departing from previously shared social norms (1964: 12). The contrast between Ireland and Spain shows us that state collapse does not always take a society outside social norms. In southern Ireland the collapsed (British) state could be compared to a scaffold, the removal of which left the basic building structure of a conservative Catholic society intact. What matters is whether the collapse of the state also destroys social relations. The moral philosopher Alasdair MacIntyre made the point with respect to Hobbes:

> To use the word social is to be reminded of one of the oddest of Hobbes' confusions, that he appears not to have distinguished the state and society, to make political authority not dependent on the prior existence of, but constitutive of social life. There are of course situations where the disappearance of the state's power of repression may lead to the rise of anarchic violence. But there are and have been plenty of situations where an orderly life continues without such a power being present. [MacIntyre 1971: 134]

Hobbes' unacknowledged presence in this literature does reflect a genuine anxiety in Western capitals about the fact that many post-colonial states—notably in Africa—are worse off now than they were in the 1960s. Nonetheless, the language that is applied to them is Darwinian, and the substance and meanings of conflicts are derived primarily from their structural relationship to the developed world. One sign is that the conceptual language becomes one of success and failure. In Jared Diamond's *Collapse: How Societies Choose to Fail or Succeed* (2006), the terms 'rise' and 'fall' (as applied to states) are used analogously to those of success and failure. 'Collapse' becomes the fate of those who lost out in an almost competitive challenge. In the seventeenth century, Hobbes—writing in an increasingly commercialized society—also took competition to be the basic social relation. Impatient as it is with anything short of success, the gaze of much of the literature will not dwell on the many 'grey areas' between success and failure that remain the social reality in most parts of the world.

Ultimately, the Hobbesian approach is both biased against human beings and biased in favour of states. It suggests that where states are strong, men and women rely on the better side of their nature; where states are weak, secular forms of evil flourish. In 'Retreating from the Brink' the American political scientist Scott Strauss (2012) stresses the value of looking at negative cases, where the same probability of escalating conflict existed as in 'positive' cases (such as Rwanda), but no genocide occurred. The sources of restraint he identified were moral aversion to using violence against one's neighbours, established traditions of cooperation between groups, and the dependence of elites on the support of minority groups. It could be objected that restraint is an ethical category, which only traditional societies will uphold. The more sinister 'all-out' attitude towards victory at all costs had not existed in the century which produced the American civil war and may not have existed in Ireland in 1922. The Americans in 1861 and the Irish in 1922 had not witnessed Hiroshima and Nagasaki, or the Holocaust. As wars became more devastating in the twentieth century, this brought out a darker corner of evil inside human beings; there was no longer a built-in sense of restraint. Yet this shift in the moral compass should not blind us to the definite dangers of state strength. Just consider the statistics on 'Death by Government' in the twentieth century, collected by the American political scientist Rudolph Rummel (1994). The greatest killers were precisely states involved in war. When the case is made for stronger states—in the interests of freedom, development, or security—it still makes sense to ask who is making that case, and on behalf of whom.

Indeed, a 'realist' tradition within modern political philosophy predicted that the modern state (weak or strong) would remain in a condition of suppressed civil war. Hobbes' *Leviathan* may have emerged because it was better able to protect peoples' lives, but this state was only a 'mortal God'. Since it was based on a rationalist contract, commanding obedience in return for protection, it could always relapse into civil war, 'its native state' (Koselleck 1988: 32). Carl Schmitt agreed with Hobbes that the basic role of the modern state was to prevent civil war. Yet if 'friend/enemy' distinctions remain basic to international politics, what would stop a state from domesticating such distinctions during crises, by finding an internal enemy within, and thus taking the first step towards civil war? During the European Enlightenment the hope was that a more rational form of state would eliminate such conflicts. The French philosopher Jean Jacques Rousseau imagined a benign social contract based on the *volunté générale* (the general will). Koselleck commented, 'in that "miraculous state" in which no one rules yet everyone obeys and is at the same time free, the revolution becomes sovereign' (1988: 163). While Rousseau maintained otherwise, Koselleck (ibid.) suggested that Rousseau's new morality of politics would result only in a total state, 'the permanent revolution in the guise of legality'. These perspectives have not become obsolete. The new external environment created by globalization may have created a new context for states to deal with. The question of who can speak with the authority of the state remains decisive nonetheless.

Conclusion

Any assessment of the consequences of a civil war also raises issues of definition. When civil war is defined in exceptional terms the evaluation of consequences is much easier. The Spanish historian Santos Juliá (2010) argued that nothing that has happened in Spain since 1936 is comprehensible without the civil war. It was a total war, and Franco's vindictive regime kept the divide alive for generations. In contrast, Spain's internal wars of the previous century, which did not produce clear winners and losers, had consequences of no such proportions. Likewise in societies whose recent experience has been one of perpetual conflict, consequences are not necessarily the result of an exceptional event we can call civil war, and are harder to identify. The civil wars themselves could be a symptom of an underlying syndrome (implied by the idea of a conflict trap). The consequences—capital flight, corruption, hopelessness, underdevelopment, weak institutions, the violent struggles for resources, massive migration—might have emerged anyway. And since these consequences also carry a risk of conflict, it becomes harder to distinguish causes from consequences. Civil war acquires, as Koselleck put it, the image of a society senselessly circling upon itself.

For no other topic in this book has the concept of the state been asked to explain so much as with consequences. Concepts like state weakness, state failure, and state collapse now stand as metaphors for the most tragic experiences of some countries in the developing world. No doubt weak institutions and high levels of poverty do make it harder for poor countries to recover from conflict. But these concepts are often used as metaphorical, not analytical, concepts. Many of these concepts came with globalization, and could be used to classify the majority of the world's states as crisis or weak states. Yet few of the 130-plus new states created in the twentieth century have actually collapsed. A far greater number could be considered states in which areas of order and disorder have coexisted in a durable way for long periods of time. The overuse of these concepts must be related to the desire for more and more external intervention in civil wars. Some concepts—like 'development in reverse'—have within them a time horizon. By suggesting that civil wars are the antithesis of development they overlook the possibility that it could in fact be the very processes of state-building and economic development themselves that generate violence. Other concepts, such as the concept of state weakness, encourage people to believe that the state is a passive victim of civil war, and that such wars should be seen by outsiders as akin to natural disasters. However appropriate the language may be as a way of dramatizing the sufferings of ordinary people, whether we call a state strong or weak does not make the question of whose interest would be served by having a stronger state any less decisive. The politics cannot be avoided: for all the talk of state weakness the state itself is the object of struggle in most of these wars (Ferguson 2003: 10). These conflicts may challenge the state's principles and result in regime change. The territory of the state may be at issue if the challengers want some form of autonomy or partition. Or there may be a pattern of challenge or response with no tangible difference made to the state's legitimacy or territorial basis (ibid.: 11).

The burden placed on state weakness as an explanatory concept could be reduced were we to accept that these conflicts are often cases of a failure of nation-building, as much as a failure of state-building. When the new interest in civil wars and reconstruction emerged in the 1990s, war-torn areas were seen mainly through the prism of the state and the earlier literature on nation-building was largely forgotten about. Success or failure was seen in terms of state capacity, the most important areas being the provision of security, macro-economic policy, and institutional reform. Others continued to explain everything in terms of ethnicity and nationalism. The danger with the latter is that much as ethnicity is constructed by political actors, scholars see ethnic and territorial factors as the natural basis of solidarity in conflict. Nonetheless, nationalist scholarship has been right to pose the question of whether states need a usable past in order to build a common future, or at least to suggest that state-building involves cultural activity. Holsti defined 'wars of the third kind' as wars fought over the definition of the political community (1996: 19–41). A legitimate state, in addition to doing what states normally have to do in terms of public policy, is also one where there is a shared idea of the state. Yet the task of constructing such an idea is especially complicated after civil war (Kissane 2015: 1–16). While narratives of international war are usually unifying, those of civil wars divide.

On the sources of human divisiveness, the 'state collapse' perspective assumes much about human nature. The Hobbesian vision resonates with a general conservative belief that human nature abhors a vacuum, and will deteriorate in the absence of central authority. Perhaps it is no surprise that it emerged out of a Christian culture, which assumed that a flawed human being will never escape its imperfections. Admittedly, fear of disintegration, insecurity, and loss is probably hardwired into human beings. Indeed, the connection made between state collapse and the vicissitudes of human nature goes back 3,000 years, and has recently resurfaced in Yugoslavia, where the worst consequence was the complete collapse of social relations in a once-integrated community. What have we learnt about the connection between state collapse and human nature from that particular conflict? It was only when they ended up refugees in Western Europe that questions like 'Are you a Muslim, Croat, or Serb?' became normal in social introductions for the citizens of former Yugoslavia. The essential catalyst was certainly the collapse of the state; what drove so many people into different communities— eventually into rival states—was fear. Yet no one factor was paramount: memories of the Chetnick-Ustashi massacres in the 1940s, mass military training in the Yugoslav National Army, and the elite's exploitation of people's fears through the media also mattered. Indeed if this conflict disclosed something about the divisive tendencies in human nature, it was not something we can take to be universal. Hobbes is only one source of insight. Rather, Yugoslavia tells us that Thucydides was right: people approach war the wrong way round; action comes first, and it is only when they have already suffered that people begin to think (1972: 82).

6

RECOVERY

The subject of this chapter is both old and new. The question of how a society can recover from violent conflict is a contemporary policy issue but it raises questions of ethics, memory, and forgiveness that are as old as mankind. When, in the aftermath of civil war, the task of reconstruction forces people to reveal their vision of the good society, their thoughts can be guided by pessimism. Hobbes, for one, recommended a strong state, resting mainly on obedience and fear. Only recently—after the defeat of Nazi Germany in 1945—have the victors understood the task as one of reconstructing a whole society in a positive way. So successful was the subsequent reconstruction of Western Europe that a veritable tool-kit now exists for this purpose. Few topics have generated a literature of such diversity.

Part of the appeal of the subject is the prospect of a society coming out of conflict undergoing a moral transformation. Yet dark perspectives on this process also exist. Sigmund Freud's reading of the Oedipus myth in ancient Greece, as a story about the origins of human civilization, suggests that repression may be needed to establish social order after conflict (Smith 2013: 182–3). For Freud this Greek legend located the origins of social order in a very violent series of events: the rebellion of the sons against the father, the father's murder, the son's competition for the father's wives, and the subsequent repression of fratricide through the internalization of guilt. This account does not assume a good side to human nature. The post-conflict order is premised on suppression: of the sons' desire to sleep with the mother. Mankind thus acquired a social order and a basis for law only through the institution of the incest taboo (ibid: 183).

Not everyone agrees that violent conflict and repression need be permanent aspects of human society. Where, if not here, should faith be placed in 'the better angels of our nature' (Pinker 2011)? Many argue that reconciliation, not reconstruction, should be the goal of societies moving out of conflict. The current popularity of this belief reflects the important role now played by ideas and discourses associated with globalization in this field. In economics, globalization has been facilitated by narratives which present austerity as the only option for countries in crisis. Just as economic options are narrowed down, global ideas of how to recover from conflict also supply criteria: democracy, transitional justice, reconciliation, coming to terms with the past, according to which societies coming out of conflict are evaluated. This chapter is structured around two of the most basic concepts of this new vocabulary: reconstruction and reconciliation. By the end the reader will either agree with Freud, or retain their faith in 'the better angels of our nature'.

An age of reconstruction

The term 'reconstruction' entered the political lexicon after the American civil war. Initially, it referred to the ambition of the radical Republicans to transform the defeated Confederate states in the image of the North. Later, it became used in history books to refer to a period of time between 1863 and 1877 in which a series of messy compromises diluted the radical promise of reconstruction. The reconstructive moment was one that made people reveal their vision of the good society (MacIntyre 1971: 132). Yet the radical Republican plans for the defeated South were not realized. A botched set of compromises followed.

The sociologist Karl Mannheim (1998 [1940], English trans. 1946) was the first to call the twentieth century 'an age of reconstruction'. Given our stress on scientific solutions to political problems, the growth of bureaucratic policy-making, urban planning, and the associated dangers of social and biological engineering, he had good reason. The nineteenth century had been marked by a belief in the limited state, but the twentieth century, in contrast, saw the promotion of the state as the central organizing and mobilizing institution in society. Some revolutionary societies, such as the Soviet Union after 1917, became state-dominated, but others, such as Portugal before the 1970s, projected an image of the state rooted in a very traditional Catholic society.

The events of the past century may have destroyed the socialist hopes of those who believed that the state's greater role in the economy would produce greater freedom and equality. Nonetheless, our instinctive reaction to wars—as to disasters of all kinds—is to look to states and international organizations for solutions. Why so? World War II provided the first, crucial threshold of experience. Europe after 1945 clearly needed rebuilding in a physical and moral sense; the horrors of Nazism had represented—if not the end of European civilization—certainly as sharp a break as one could imagine. A programme of de-Nazification was accompanied by economic reconstruction. Yet the treatment of Germany after 1945 was also not vindictive. It was thought that the failure of the victorious powers to settle World War I on terms that were conducive to peace had been a major cause of World War II. The priority, after all, was to prevent future conflict. The scale of the war had changed attitudes to what the state could practically do. Under the aegis of the United States, post-war reconstruction proved largely successful in bringing stability, and eventually prosperity, to states like France, West Germany, and Italy.

For today's generation the end of the Cold War has been the second threshold of experience. The affiliation of a war-torn country to either of the blocs during the Cold War had been the determining factor in foreign policies towards them. One sign of a political dealignment after 1989 was the tendency to encourage peace based not on victory but on drawn military outcomes, and inclusive negotiations. Since the end of the Cold War, international supervision has played a key role in peace processes in places as diverse as the Balkans, Central America,

Southern Africa, and the Middle East. Once peace was agreed, reconstruction became the responsibility of a host of international institutions, such as the World Bank. International agencies, such as the UN, have overseen successful peace negotiations in a range of war-torn countries, from Mozambique in Southern Africa, to El Salvador in Central America, to Bosnia-Herzegovina in the Balkans. A cynic could see in the recent flourishing of reconstruction thought the global reassertion—via international organizations—of Western models of social and political development over the Third World once its anticolonial movements had run out of steam. Yet globalization itself has mattered, primarily by changing attitudes to violent conflict. The recent growth of the mass media, and of a transnational civil society which monitors human rights abuses, has raised awareness of overseas conflicts to an unprecedented degree. To make a contrast with the situation during the early Cold War, the Greek civil war—which ended in 1949—also involved massive violence, the displacement of over 700,000 people, and the abduction of some 20,000 children who were subsequently sent behind the Iron Curtain or to America (van Boeschoten 2015: 97). Although it led to a humanitarian disaster, the involvement of powers such as Britain and the United States was dictated primarily by Cold War considerations. Half a century later, intervention in the Balkans after the Yugoslav collapse took place in a very different climate of international opinion.

Yet the thought and practice of reconstruction remains shaped by the initial post-war moment. Reconstruction first flourished precisely at a time when Europe itself had become exhausted by conflict; its pragmatic spirit stood in sharp contrast to the ideological zeal of the 1930s (Müller 2011). The historian of ideas Jan-Werner Müller has shown that 'reconstruction thought' was directed towards finding a middle ground in politics (2011: 125–71). On both sides of the Iron Curtain, states became legitimized primarily by economic success and effective management. In Western Europe, consensus was promoted both as a precondition for democratic politics and as an attribute of leadership. In stark contrast to the recent experiences of dictatorship, war, and genocide, only a 'disciplined democracy'—sticking to strict legal limits on the exercise of popular sovereignty—was now desired. Institutional devices such as constitutional courts were created to allow for a balance between the top-down and the bottom-up aspects of government (Müller 2011: 126–70). After 1989 stability returned as the main criterion by which reconstruction projects were evaluated. This concept had entered the political vocabulary originally from the field of technology—engineering in particular—and has guided policy-making in post-1945 Europe. Just as institutional changes such as the creation of constitutional courts had 'disciplined' European democracies after 1945, the debate today over institutional choices after civil war is couched in the same language of democratic stability and good governance. For example, given the preference for consensus, rather than partisanship, the effectiveness of various electoral systems is to be judged in terms of their moderating influence (Reilly 2008).

One indicator of the change is that the number of 'blue helmet' UN peacekeeping operations jumped from a figure of 5 in the late 1980s to 15 in 1990, and has not fallen since then (*The Economist* 9–15 November 2013). What led to this new activism by the UN in particular? First, globalization has placed great expectations about what should be done when such conflicts come to an end. It was once possible for a society simply to lick its wounds after civil war, and recover in isolation. This has changed. Indeed, if there have been three ripe moments for reconstruction projects in the last century—1918, 1945, and 1989—they exist on a continuum of more and more international influence. The historian Charles Maier (1981: 348) once commented, perceptively, that successful systems of political equilibrium must remain isolated, or become truly international in scope. Autarchic impositions of political order—such as Franco's Spain after 1939— are now seen as ethically problematic, and reconciliation and democracy were only achieved in Spain as part of its accession to the European Union. In cases of really protracted conflict—Central America, Southern Africa, ex-Yugoslavia, and Northern Ireland—it seems that only a fully internationalized model can bring peace.

Secondly, 90 per cent of all wars in the post-Cold War era were internal wars, often taking place in weak or collapsing states, which meant that outside intervention could not always be resisted. The ability of the global mass media to raise public consciousness of the plight of so many millions of people also meant that states and their international organizations would have found it difficult to resist pressure to intervene, even if they had wanted to. The coming to power of Mikhail Gorbachev—and the resulting non-use of the Russian veto—ended the earlier paralysis of the UN Council during the Cold War (Berdal and Economides 2007: 2). The ethical case for intervention became especially strong after the experience of genocidal conflicts in Cambodia in the 1970s and Yugoslavia and Rwanda in the 1990s. Major interventions in those countries took place after 1989, and also in Timor Leste, Haiti, Kosovo, and Sierra Leone.

Thirdly, since 1989 a succession of successful peace agreements—in Central America, Nepal, Mozambique, Northern Ireland—have encouraged people to believe that even the most intractable conflicts could be resolved through negotiation. Before 1989 it was unusual for violent conflicts within states to be ended through negotiations; even less so for the international community to encourage the 'drawn outcomes' these negotiations typically require. Appendix 1 presents information on the external dimension—usually involving the UN—on 34 relatively successful peace agreements signed in the past three decades. The information is taken from the Peace Accords Matrix maintained by the Kroc Institute for International Peace Studies at the University of Notre Dame. This matrix codes all comprehensive peace agreements and their components since 1989. What Appendix 1 clearly shows is that the end of the Cold War brought with it a new ethics of intervention. Table 3.1 in Chapter 3 had listed the 29 longest-lasting internal conflicts since 1945. When we cross-tabulate this list with the agreements detailed in Appendix 1 it is noteworthy that many of the world's most intractable conflicts, as listed in Table 3.1, have resulted in a comprehensive peace agreement being signed since 1989. The big exceptions were Kashmir, Israel/Palestine, and the Kurdish conflicts in Iran and Turkey.

Appendix 1 lists 34 agreements: one from 1989, 21 from the 1990s, and 11 since 2000 (India's Bodo Accord was negotiated between 1993 and 2005). It clearly shows that external involvement in both the negotiation and implementation of peace processes after civil wars has become common. This external involvement is usually by the United Nations but the importance of the external factor clearly varies, from the mere support of outside donors in Djibouti after 2001, to the existence of a UN-controlled transitional authority in Cambodia after 1991. In all 34 cases bar four (Dijbouti's 1998 Peace and National Reconciliation accord, India's 2005 Bodo Accord, Lebanon's 1989 Taif Accord, and Senegal's 2004 General Peace Agreement), there was significant external involvement. In 30 cases, this involvement involved either a role for the UN in the verification of what was agreed, the deployment of a UN or regional security force, or provisions for the review of the agreement by external parties. The agreements in Burundi (2000), Sierra Leone (1997), and in the Sudan (2005) combined all three kinds of external involvement. In three of the cases (Cambodia 1991, Croatia 1995, and Timor Leste 1999) a UN transitional authority was also established.

Since ending conflicts by negotiation is now more common, what are the factors making for successful negotiations? For political scientist Barbara Walter (1999, 2002), such are the risks involved in entering negotiations—and so great is the need to extract real concessions—that another form of 'security dilemma' exists when civil wars come to an end. The parties are being asked to lay down their arms without knowing much about the intentions of their adversaries, or whether outside actors will insist on the enforcement of an agreement. Hence any successful peace process should have enforceable and credible security guarantees for each side, the provision of which usually requires international involvement (Walter 1999: 160, 340).

In *Elusive Peace: Negotiating an End to Civil Wars* the political scientist William Zartman identified another key problem as being that of asymmetry: a recognized government usually holds a variety of cards that its opponents cannot bring to the negotiating table (1995: 3–4). When two states conclude an inter-state war, neither state need lose in legitimacy or status. When a government negotiates with a challenger in an internal conflict, it has to risk a loss in legitimacy, and of popular support. For an insurgent group that has drawn on the maximum of human commitment from its supporters during a conflict, its leaders must be able to justify this suffering with a compromise that will inevitably fall short of its core demands. Being less experienced in conventional politics, they also face the risk of being outmanoeuvred in the negotiations. How then can peace be achieved? Although asymmetry is a problem, the existence of 'a mutually hurting stalemate' can encourage each side to enter into talks (ibid.: 11, 18). Peace can be achieved if all groups feel they will be better off by abandoning war, and when both the elites and the population at large believe a return to the *status quo ante bellum* is neither possible nor desirable. This is what happened in Mozambique, Sudan, and Northern Ireland.

The history of human conflict does not show conflicts in different times and places to be essentially different. Arguably however, democratic states have a wider set of tools which they can apply to the resolution of internal conflict. In the 1990s reconstruction and peacebuilding became informed by the 'liberal peace theory': the belief that market liberalization, democratization, and the protection of human rights were universal preconditions for durable peace. The confidence with which these ideas were applied to a range of war-torn countries shows how the end of the Cold War allowed the West to recover its intellectual self-confidence, however temporarily. It matters that the victors in World War II were seen as democratic states and that their subsequent economic and social success was related to their being democracies. When it comes to the evaluation of this interventionism it is important to note that these interventions usually have a dual transition in mind: both from war to peace and from authoritarian to democratic politics.

The influence of the liberal peace theory also reflects the interests and power of the United States and the concept of 'reconstruction' still bears the imprimatur of American power. During the US-led invasions of Iraq in 2003 and of Afghanistan in 2002 the goals of the Western coalition were defined as occupation, pacification, and then stabilization—followed by reconstruction. Very soon after the coalition established its military bases, the emphasis moved from security issues, to state-building, to reconstruction, and lastly to democratization. As a presumption in favour of intervention grew—and the right of states to their territorial integrity was increasingly waived—the concept of reconstruction became more ambitious. It could now include peace-building, demobilization, institutional reform, economic development, democratization, human security, transitional justice, rebuilding community relations, reconciliation, coming to terms with the past, and rebuilding identity. These concepts would have been completely unfamiliar to a person studying political science in the 1980s. Were a state to devise policies for each area—and needed to draw on appropriate expertise from outside—the project would be enough to employ a whole medium-sized university.

One consequence of this interventionism has been conceptual change of the kind that readers of this book will by now find familiar. Consider the concept of human security. This concept originally stressed the need to be free from physical harm, during and after conflict. In 1994, however, the UN Development Programme added four more dimensions: health security, environmental security, community security, and political security (UNDP 1994: 22–34). Such conceptual change might simply reflect the way interventions themselves grow in scope. When the eight-year British military command in Helmand province came to an end in April 2014, the cost was estimated to have been 25 billion pounds sterling, if not much more (*London Evening Standard* 2 April 2014). The initial aim of depriving al-Qaeda of a training base there had been supplanted by a commitment to a counter-insurgency against the Taliban, an effort to quell the production of opium, and military support for a vaguely defined humanitarian effort—to which words like governance, state-building, and reconstruction were applied. As the purposes of intervention changed, so has the language used to describe it.

Nonetheless, state-building still provides the core agenda in these endeavours. The first steps are usually to build institutions that provide security, to reform those that existed in a democratic direction, and to construct an institutional basis for macro-economic stabilization. The Institute of State Effectiveness, based in Washington DC, tries to guide policy-makers in their attempt at 'fixing failed states', and was welcomed for providing a new paradigm, with real impact on the ground. It identified ten critical functions that could satisfy citizens and meet states' international obligations (Ghani, Lockhart, and Carnahan 2006: 111). Some of these functions—securing the monopoly of violence, providing the rule of law, public administration, managing public finances, and protecting the market—were absolutely necessary. Others—investing in education, delineating the rights and duties of citizens, conducting the state's international relations properly, and exploiting a country's natural, industrial, and intellectual assets—are secondary.

The scale of the external intervention the UN now undertakes, and the extended scope of reconstruction, also requires a strong administrative centre. Indeed, if there is a core assumption to intervention and reconstruction it is Hobbesian: war-torn countries need a strong state that functions rather like a protective skein in order to protect their populations from future violence. Once removed by civil war or by state collapse, society must again be covered by such a skein, an undertaking that requires intervention (Hampson 1996: 3, 12). What gives these reconstruction projects coherence is, first, the existence of a *political* authority with sufficient resources to direct change (such as a state) and, secondly, a political and social coalition legitimate enough to direct that potential for change (Cramer 2006: 277). In the absence of these two conditions, state-building requires the involvement of outside actors. This external dimension makes these projects something different from the traditional models of state formation. The Western conception of the state had been shaped by the history of the most successful states; these evolved over centuries, and had such economic and military success that they were able to draw huge resources from their populations. The exchange of resources was largely endogenous, even if stimulated by wars with other states. State-building after civil war in poor countries requires outside aid, and is always an uphill struggle (Zartman 1994: 273). In such countries, reconstruction projects can serve the immediate interests of both internal and external actors, since both have a vested interest in strengthening top-down forms of authority, especially when the task is the restoration of security. Yet as we proceed to the evaluation of these projects, the question is also whether both the domestic and external actors share an interest in the long-term transformation of these societies.

The evaluation of peace-building missions and reconstruction projects

The end of the Cold War thus coincided with a massive increase of peace activism in the UN Security Council. Between 1987 and 1994 the Council quadrupled the number of resolutions it issued, tripled the peacekeeping operations it authorized, and multiplied by a factor of seven the number of economic sanctions it imposed each year (Doyle 2006: 6). In the period between 1987 and 1994, the peacekeeping budget of the UN alone skyrocketed from US$230 million to US$3.6 billion (ibid.). Between 1989 and 1999, a total of 14 major peace-building operations were launched in territories that had recently experienced civil conflicts. One name of the World Bank is 'The World Bank: International Bank for Reconstruction and Development'. In the period between June 1990 and June 2002, it gave major loans to the value of more than US$37,000 million specifically to assist projects associated with law, justice, and public administration. These exceeded the combined figures for major loans on education and health in the same period (The World Bank Group 2002).

How effective have such reconstructive projects been? At first glance, the record of UN peace-building missions has been very positive. Michael W. Doyle's (2006) study of UN peace-making argues that the international community—and the UN in particular—can assist, at least in the reconstruction of peace. Another international relations scholar, Edward Newman, argues that, of the factors accounting for the apparently declining rates of civil war he sees for the period since 1989, interventionism has been one factor contributing to more peace, in the sense of less civil war (Newman 2009). Yet this achievement should not be understood in a purely military sense. Bringing conflicts to an end may be less important than the effort spent on maintaining peace and consolidating the promise of peace agreements.

Since it is a given that many conflicts will reoccur, it is not enough to have completed a transition from war to peace: to evaluate outcomes we also have to define what is meant by lasting peace. A simple cessation to violence is only an initial step. Of a total of 419 internal wars which ended between 1949 and 2009—in the sense that hostilities ceased for one year—the reality is that in the majority of these cases the peace did not last. These endings can be grouped into four categories: those that ended with peace agreements, those ending in victory, those ending with ceasefires, and those that ended by other means. Although those which ended in peace agreements had a better record than the others, the majority of wars in each category reoccurred (Wallerstein 2011: 30). It actually made little difference whether they ended in a military victory for one side, or in a negotiated peace.

So likely is the reoccurrence of conflict that peace has to be defined as being something other than a state of non-violence. One alternative idea is that of conflict resolution. A transition to non-violence, or the achievement of an agreed institutional framework for peace, are insufficient bases for this. Conflict resolution implies that the underlying issues have been resolved; that the parties will tolerate each other's existence and commit to pursuing their goals peacefully. These three elements also require a nurturing environment in which peace can grow over time. Of the factors that can sustain this nurturing environment, the level of international support for the peace agreement, the desire of the warring parties for the agreement, and a peace agreement sufficiently well-designed for the parties to remain loyal to it are usually crucial (Hampson 1996: 3).

So while one task for political science has been to identify the factors which made negotiations more or less likely to succeed, another has been to explain why peace agreements either stick or unravel. Some 'realist' scholars believe the critical factor is whether the security needs of the warring sides are addressed during and after the negotiations (Walter 1999, 2002). For others (Stedman 1997), the danger to peace comes most often from 'spoilers'—that is, splinter groups who may or may not have been included in the negotiations but later find it in their interests to defect from the terms of the peace. A considerable literature has also emerged on whether such agreements should allow the warring parties to share executive power. A high-quality peace agreement requires exactly this inclusive means of self-government (Hampson 1996: 21), because if they are not included in government, the parties are more likely to spoil the settlement.

When evaluating the long-term outcomes of peacekeeping missions and reconstruction projects, much also depends on the paradigm one brings to the evaluation. Consider the record in Mozambique since peace was agreed in 1992. The country still has the distinction of being one of the poorest democracies in the world. The 1992 peace agreement remains in place, both armies have been demobilized, and there are democratic elections every few years. If the business of evaluation were that of deciding on success and failure in terms of specific policy goals—such as the demobilization of armies— Mozambique has been an outstanding success. From a realist perspective, the resolution of conflicts means addressing the security dilemma endemic to all civil wars, and the primary tasks of peace-makers should be to impose order and to establish security. The aim should always be to find a balance between security and freedom, on the assumption that the former is always desirable, while freedom without security may not be. From this realist perspective Mozambique has ostensibly been a success.

In contrast to the emphasis on force and security in the realist position, liberals will see in reconstruction a process of socialization whereby local actors come to share the values and norms of the external agencies, who project their 'soft power' through institutional building, education, and negotiation. Since Mozambique has competitive elections and a functioning parliament, many believe this approach has worked in Mozambique. Yet Cramer calls it 'a gangster democracy'—remaining poor, becoming more corrupt, consolidating another one-party state in Africa (2006: 245–79, 269). Frelimo, which has been in power since independence in 1975, has won all the elections since 1992. Indeed, the degree of electoral competitiveness has decreased; the main opposition party, Renamo, which began the civil war in 1976, shows little sign of gaining power at the national level.

A third, Marxist, approach would evaluate both politics and peace-making from the perspective of capitalist development. Reconstruction can be presented as a top-down technocratic exercise, which runs the danger of actually disrupting the organic processes of primitive accumulation, necessary for the creation of a strong state and a viable capitalist economy. In Mozambique, the decentralized state-building enterprise, and the informal ways the two sides share power and resources, creates a range of opportunities for corruption and local domination by elites. The current political conflict between Frelimo and Renamo can be represented by the participants as a real struggle, a profound historical antagonism, like that during the civil war. It could also be called a struggle between two parties established for the purpose of running the same socio-economic system to their mutual benefit. The changes since 1992 simply reflect the way the contradictory interests of the different groups within the country continue to carve out a role for themselves within the structural constraints of the international system that were present when the civil war began in 1976 (Debord 1995: 36).

Appendix 2 details the specific contents of 34 peace agreements signed since 1989. Column by column these are divided into four categories, reflecting the different priorities of the four main theoretical approaches to peace outlined with respect to Mozambique. The details were again taken from the Notre Dame Peace Accords Matrix. The force and security column reflect the realists' emphasis on security, the political and administrative reforms column relates to the liberal approach, while the much less frequent social and economic changes column is for the Marxist paradigm. The purpose of representing these peace agreements in tabular form in Appendix 2 is to make the differences between the approaches more concrete, and to show that they do not result in equally extensive policies in practice. I have added a (fourth) separate reconciliation column to extend the coverage to the question of whether attempts to reconcile the fighting groups have been planned.

Of the four columns, the provisions for political and administrative reform are usually the most detailed. This is not a surprise: the liberal will approach the task of building peace with the greatest expectations. Reflecting the dominance of this approach, of the 34 agreements almost all contain commitments to human and/or minority rights, 20 commit the parties to the agreement to some form of decentralization of power, while 16 agreements provide for transitional governments. Both the liberal and the realist approaches to peace have resulted in very specific policies, laws, and measures. When it comes to security, almost all these agreements have provisions on the disarmament, demobilization, and reintegration of combatants. Commitments to the goal of reconciliation are increasingly common, but as with the provisions for more social and economic equality, they tend to be vaguer than the first two categories. To make a simple contrast, security provisions are ubiquitous, while only a handful of the 34 agreements have detailed provisions for the investigation of human rights abuses or reconciliation. The most common means of the latter is the establishment of a dispute resolution committee. Thus while a large theoretical body of literature has developed out of the belief that peace requires reconciliation, this is not reflected in the actual contents of the agreements signed since 1989. Commitments to social and economic development are also common but tend not to be detailed. They do not figure at all in 9 of these 34 agreements.

Of course these four approaches are not mutually exclusive: just under half of the 34 make specific commitments in all four areas. The most ambitious and detailed agreements were signed in Burundi, Guatemala, Indonesia (Aceh conflict), Nepal, South Africa, the Sudan, and Northern Ireland. The geographical range shows that a holistic approach to peace has emerged in most regions of the world. Nonetheless, the realists vie with the liberals for supremacy. In *At Wars' End* political scientist Roland Paris (2004) advocates a middle way between the two influential approaches, recommending a specific sequence of peace-building: 'institutionalization before liberalization'. This suggests that in the short term, liberal values may have to be secondary to those of security, strong government, and the rule of law, but given gradual institutional development and extended international commitment, these societies may, over time, eventually become strong enough to withstand the shocks of market reform and democratization. This approach is now being tried in the Balkans, where states like Bosnia-Herzegovina have been placed under a form of international governorship until they can develop in a more harmonious way.

What about the success or otherwise of these agreements? The realist approaches peace with the least expectations and in this sense success is common. If we require, in addition to order and security, that peace agreements enable a substantive transformation of society—in a liberal or egalitarian direction—most of the systematic evaluations of the UN reconstruction projects suggest that we are likely to be disappointed. Paris's *At War's End* (2004) studied the effects of those UN peace-building missions deployed between 1989 and 1998, in Namibia, Nicaragua, Angola, Cambodia, El Salvador, Mozambique, Liberia, Rwanda, Bosnia, Croatia, and Guatemala. His cases were all peace missions intended to be liberalizing, both politically and economically. Yet in all of them, but Namibia—which did not experience a civil war anyway—no such outcomes materialized. The reforms either destabilized society, or reignited the fighting (Paris 2004: 56). A more separate and more provisional analysis is given of three later interventions, namely Kosovo, Timor Leste, and Sierra Leone.

Paris was examining a domestic variant of the liberal peace theory that democracies do not go to war against each other. This domestic variant maintained that the application of free market economics and democratic rule would lead societies beyond conflict. Hence the two cardinal features of successful Western democracies (democratic elections and market economics), when combined, would prevent future conflict erupting. Ultimately Paris questions whether reconstruction projects should be guided by the liberal peace theory. He makes the analytical distinction between the two types of transition mentioned above: a movement from war to peace, and a transition from authoritarian to democratic politics. Yet he questions whether these transitions actually complement each other. If the belief that they should is peculiar to our age it is worth pointing out that the regime trends did indeed suggest some connection. One study by the political scientist Nancy Bermeo found that of all the 73 democracies that were founded after 1945, over half emerged in the immediate aftermath of a war, or as a means of bringing a war to an end (Bermeo 2003: 159). Another study suggested that nearly 40 per cent of all civil wars which took place between 1945 and 1993 resulted in an improvement of the level of democracy (Wantchekon 2004: 17). Three dramatic examples were El Salvador, Mozambique, and Nicaragua. Other authors (Olson 1993, Wantchekon 2004, Weingast 1997) have argued that, even in the very poorest of countries, democracy could be the quickest route out of anarchy and poverty, since economic development required institutions—such as courts, an independent judiciary, the rule of law—that are also associated with successful democracy.

The 'democratic peace theory' consists of a set of propositions that tries to explain why democratic states generally do not go to war against each other. Before the 1990s few thought this theory had an internal application. It is true that, historically, some countries that have gone through the maelstrom of civil war later became durable democracies: Costa Rica, Switzerland, and the United States are three examples. Only since 1989 however, has it been generally believed that peace after an internal war needed democracy, and that more democracy would solid-ify the peace. The problem is that what seems attractive in theory does not seem to have worked in practice. Another recent comparative study (by Zürcher et al. 2013), explored the relationship between peace-building and democratization. It is the most recent assessment of UN peace-building after internal wars. The cases chosen were Afghanistan, Bosnia, Timor Leste, Haiti, Kosovo, Macedonia, Mozambique, Namibia, Rwanda, and Tajikistan. Going back to the distinction between a transi-tion from war to peace and one from authoritarianism to democracy, this research actually found little relationship between intervention, peace-building, and any substantive political transformation of these societies. While the UN has been effective in securing peace, the regime outcomes were largely negative. This proved to be the case irrespective of the nature of the prior conflict, the logic of the initial peace settlement, the amount and source of aid donated, the relations with neighbouring countries, and the amount of resources at the disposal of the peace-building mission (ibid.: 132).

The authors recorded their scepticism about the ability of outside agencies to transform war-torn societies. Perhaps the very idea of post-civil war democracy is flawed. The factor that influenced out-comes most was political relationships: local power-holders have had sufficient resources, support, and skill to thwart genuine democratic reforms, when democracy is perceived as being too costly for them. Their interests may coincide with the outside actors when it comes to the provision of security, but they do not coincide on democratization. Moreover, the local population is also unlikely to consider democracy equally important to security or economic development (ibid.: 133). Hence, if we want to know whether these interventions prevented the violence which provoked the civil wars, the evidence is positive. If we ask whether peace means the transformation of these societies, the findings are negative.

Since the 9/11 terrorist attacks, an emphasis on security has replaced that on democracy promotion and peace-building. A more sceptical body of literature on reconstruction has also emerged. It takes two forms: (1) literature which assesses success and failure in terms of the implementation, (or not), of key symbolic targets of reconstruction programmes, and (2) literature which may be interested in the practical evaluation of specific programmes, but also compares reconstruction projects to other collective enterprises, such as revolution, urban planning, or agricultural reform (Cramer 2006: 245–78). Some literature of the first kind has already been discussed. The economist Christopher Cramer works within the second tradition. He compares how Mozambique has, since 1992, served as 'a blank slate' onto which outside agencies projected their fantasies about post-conflict development, with the way, after independence in 1975, Frelimo fantasized about using top-down socialist programmes to deliver the country from the legacies of colonialism within a decade (2006: 259–72).

Interestingly, the language of 'fresh starts', 'security vacuums', 'collapsed states', and 'ground zero' seems to accompany most interventions (ibid.: 255). The technocratic appeal of the concept of reconstruction is boosted by these blank slate, or *tabula rasa*, images of societies. Indeed there is a hint of social engineering in the concept: decisions are made following a technical type of analysis. Since reconstruction implies political and social transformations—not just military ones—the very concept might also be misleading about the kinds of change which it can produce and about how much change can actually follow intervention. One reason is that there is never a blank slate. Since what existed prior to the civil war produced a civil war, the totality of the past cannot be reconstructed. Yet societies are still *re*constructed, and the outcome will show great continuity with the pre-conflict society.

For example, the American historian Eric Foner wrote of reconstruction as America's unfinished revolution (2002), because after the American civil war the southern states exploited the long-established federal system to continue discrimination against black people under the notorious Jim Crow laws. The struggle was intense: involving the lynching, hanging, drowning, and shooting of black Americans on a large scale (Cramer 2006: 251). It also lasted a long time: the CIA would continue to monitor the activities of the Ku Klux Klan well after World War II. Since the past had forced its ugly divisions into the future, Foner was not writing about 'post-conflict reconstruction'. Rather, the operation of the federal system showed remarkable continuity—even in terms of the officials employed in government posts at the state level—with the *ante-bellum* era.

Another reason why the concept of post-civil war democracy is flawed is that, rather than being 'post-conflict' technical operations, reconstruction projects are also war-embedded in important ways. In his study of the Kurdish conflict in south-eastern Turkey, the social geographer Joost Jongerden shows that the official policies on the resettlement of literally millions of displaced rural dwellers in the 1980s and 1990s were not only consistent with military objectives, but they showed continuity with the urbanizing preferences of the architects of the early Republic in the 1920s and 1930s (2015: 153–61)! These preferences included a desire to raise the standard of 'civilization' to Western (urban) standards, in a region where the state had relied heavily on techniques of population control in its efforts to build a homogeneous nation state after 1923 (Üngör: 2011).

Peacemakers will always face the question of how much of the past should be carried forward into the future. In the American case, a formal shift in the nature of citizenship was accompanied by a realignment of interests among Northern and Southern elites that evinced profound continuities with the *ante-bellum* era (Cramer 2006: 250). The degree of continuity undermined reconstruction. The botched history of its Reconstruction Era suggests that decisions emerge, not from technical analysis, but out of an ideological battleground in which different blueprints compete for hegemony. Far from being technocratic, the aftermaths of conflict are fundamentally political moments, in which the term reconstruction is used, primarily, as a rhetorical and legitimizing term to promote specific social and political orders (Reinisch 2006: 231). When such projects are successfully promoted in a society, the coalitions behind them can produce enormous change, as in Europe after 1945. In the United States, the comparable coalition was flimsy, and the radical Republican vision of reconstruction was quickly swamped in a mire of political compromise between old elites and renewed racist violence in the South.

The liberal peace approach could be condemned as a form of Western imperialism, involving the promotion of a set of values which outside powers have used in order to rebuild nation states in the self-image of the Western liberal state (Cramer 2006: 257). Just as with the various market reforms after civil war—which seldom differ from standard structural adjustment policies—generic terms like democratization, state-building, and reconstruction have been used to justify interventions as if the ideas that were relevant to one society must be relevant to all. In Iraq, the disastrous result of intervention and reconstruction has been to unleash a series of brutal conflicts which will extend themselves to generations of Iraqis who had no experience of Saddam's regime. Ultimately however, when UN-sponsored reconstruction projects themselves become the subject of historical enquiry, they will no doubt represent not a single theoretical model but a mixed array of local and international elements, reflecting different calculations of how the balance between freedom and security was drawn. The lesson learnt will surely be that a 'one size fits all' model will not work. Just as there are many causes of civil war, reconstruction projects are likely to differ in their characteristics and influences (ibid.: 277).

The moral philosopher Alasdair MacIntyre saw in Hobbes' *Leviathan* an early example of what is now a general tendency to think of reconstruction in mechanical terms:

> The method is that of resolving any complex situation into its logically primitive, simple elements and then using the simple elements to show how the complex situation could be reconstructed. In doing this we shall have shown how the situation is in fact constructed. This is the method Hobbes took Galileo to have employed in the study of physical nature. In the case of physical nature, of course, the theoretical reconstruction of complexity out of simplicity has no moral function, but in the case of human society the rectification of our understanding may provide a rectification of how we conceive our place in society and of our beliefs as to how we ought to live. [MacIntyre 1971: 132]

The danger MacIntyre warned of was that of simplifying the complexity of social orders, and assuming that social orders can be reconstructed piece by piece, with each element considered in isolation, as with a machine. Cramer (2006: 272–6) compares the North American case with the consequences of the invasion of Iraq. In America, state power was modified, in the sense that the end to large-scale violence between two regular armies resulted in the devolution of violence to localized acts of intimidation and repression. In post-Saddam Iraq, the destruction of the Baathist state apparatus has released a million young men into society, with few economic prospects, and the ability to use weapons (ibid.: 276). There was thus, in both cases, a connection between the change in state power and the increasingly fragmented and localized patterns of sectarian violence, which in the case of Iraq lasted up to the invasion of the north of the country by ISIS in the summer of 2014. Since then a full-scale war has been raging.

State formation may be a better concept than state-building or reconstruction for these processes, for the latter terms imply a technical exercise in which some steps follow logically from the other in a planned sequence. The reality is that successful state-building is not just about getting the essentials—state capacity or security—right, in a mechanical way. The state may gain initial support if the citizens identify with the state as the provider of public goods. Yet this support may not outlast a serious crisis. After civil wars, where state collapse was driven not only by institutional decline, but by the collapse of the legitimacy of the central authority, the situation cannot be fixed only by institutional restabilization (Lemay-Hebert 2009: 28). Legitimacy is the most important thing (Lake 2010). Its restoration depends both on input from society (a sense of common identity and of legitimate rule among the population) and on 'output' factors (effectiveness of the state in dealing with problems). Ultimately, 'it is in the realm of ideas and sentiments that the fate of states is primarily determined' (Lemay-Hebert 2009: 24). The next section considers a process, reconciliation, which requires input from society, and may be an essential requirement if that sense of cohesion and belonging is ever to be restored.

Reconstruction and reconciliation

There is something specific to civil war that makes the idea of reconciliation appealing. After an international war the opposing sides return home to different countries; after civil war they must learn to coexist within the state's borders. The challenge of coexistence is obviously much greater. While the two armies can hold on to different narratives of what had happened after an international war, a new basis for unity must be found after a civil war. Civil war usually leaves behind a deeply divided nation. Olusegun Obasanjo was a Nigerian general who commanded the third Marine Commando Division of the Nigerian army during the Biafran secessionist war of 1967–70. Obasanjo believed that in order to prosecute this war effectively—in a way compatible with future reconciliation—the war had to be prosecuted humanely. Civil war was the most difficult war to prosecute: during an international war 'you fight simply to destroy' but in a civil war 'you are fighting to unite, to build, to integrate' (Stern 1993: 69–81). The term 'reconciliation' has become synonymous with this desire to build, to integrate, and to unite.

Reconciliation is seen by some as the ultimate goal of reconstruction for two further reasons. First, there is the abundant evidence of the price societies can pay if the aftermath of a civil war is dominated by those who only want to punish the losers. The horrific massacres of Tamils during the final victory of the Sri Lankan army in May 2009 show the terrible price the losers can pay when the victors have no desire for reconciliation. Secondly, the exclusion of the losers from the political system after a civil war makes it difficult to see integration and reconciliation happening, except perhaps in the long term. This has recently been the case in Eritrea, Ethiopia, and Uganda, countries still struggling with the legacies of conflict. In North America, too, the limits of reconstruction in the area of race relations became apparent over time, as the civil rights movement emerged in the 1960s to challenge the many segregationist policies that the victors of the civil war did little to challenge. Reconstruction without reconciliation proved a huge missed opportunity.

In order to grasp the desire for reconciliation in 'post-conflict' societies, again we have to distinguish between two types of transition: those from violent conflict to peace, and transitions from divided societies to integrated ones. The distinction is often expressed in terms of 'negative' and 'positive' peace. Consider the question of whether peace remains 'fragile' in Northern Ireland (Kaufmann 2012: 204). A return to large-scale violence is unlikely; the 1998 peace agreement is no longer challenged by any major party, and there is a degree of support for the power-sharing institutions among the public, which was not there for about a decade after it was signed. Things have cooled down. Yet fragility could also be what is felt when what is still a very divided society begins to address the legacy of conflict; when mechanisms of transitional justice force them to address the meanings of the conflict they have experienced. The process is fragile because the relationships are fragile, and because the national allegiances of the two groups differ. Thus far, nationalist and unionist parties have been sharing power; on the issues of flags, parades, and marching they continue to differ. As the anniversaries of many important events in twentieth-century Irish history approach, they have agreed to use public funds to allow both sides to commemorate their events. Yet these will not be joint commemorations.

There is a fundamental difference between reconstructing the state and reconstructing a nation. It is precisely because he accomplished both that the death of Nelson Mandela in December 2013 was accompanied by such fond recollections, effusive praise, and political approval. More than any other leader, Mandela personified the values needed to make a transition from war to peace. These values may be personal (freedom from bitterness), ethical (commitment to peace), or political (success at nation-building). Mandela has been identified with all of them. This may partially be a function of representation: few doubt the media's tendency to offer light entertainment in place of analysis, honing in on one man from a distant country to reassure us that all is for the best in this, the best of all possible worlds. Yet Mandela was in reality 'the great unifier', and thus 'the great reconciler'. His example, South Africa's in general, gave to the world the hope that human beings can be transformed by political leaders, even in the most unpromising of situations. It encourages us to believe that we can approach the task of building peace after civil war with at least a degree of hope.

Reconstruction could be a time-constrained process, aimed only at 'the restoration of the condition of the assets and infrastructure, to the same or similar state in which they were found before the outbreak of hostilities' (Etzioni 2007: 127). In societies with greater expectations, some hope for a wholesale societal transformation which prevents relapse to armed conflict (Richmond 2011, Roberts 2011). A good example of a frugal approach to peace was that of independent Ireland, where the mood following the civil war which ended in April 1923—after the series of violent conflicts going back to 1916— was for consolidation, not for social transformation. Those aspects of society that had traditionally provided stability were relied upon to do so again: the Catholic faith, land reform, and the British legal and administrative system. The Irish response to conflict was not unique. Note our general reliance on medical language—getting back on your feet, healing, recovery—when we consider how societies recover from internal shocks. This language suggests that returning to the past is the way towards recovery from conflict. Discussing only recovery from physical ailments, the philosopher Hans Gadamer noted that the ancient concept of healing involved trying to restore an equilibrium that has been disturbed (1996: 36–7). As with doctors and their patients, the process does not involve making something new, but is principally concerned with 'supporting those factors that help sustain equilibrium'.

In contrast, in South Africa the establishment of a Truth and Justice Commission by the ANC, at the end of the Apartheid regime, is an example of a society building high expectations for peace. There was a transition from one stage (the Apartheid system) to another and the result was a new South African identity. Thus the approach to healing the wounds of the past was transformative rather than restorative. No doubt a myth was constructed out of its experience. When the legislation establishing the Commission was passed, it ruled out criminal trials when the tribunal was running. However, the family of the murdered ANC activist Steve Biko were not happy with that, and brought a criminal case against his killers. They lost the case, to some extent because the court ruled that a positive verdict might disturb the peace (May 2012: 88–98). Yet this verdict has not diminished the appeal to our moral sensibilities of wrong-doers being openly confronted by their victims.

In life there is no simple answer to the question of whether happiness requires great or low expectations but one source of the former when it comes to peace-building is undoubtedly globalization. That so many peace processes across the globe are seen as comparable, is testimony to the way certain concepts and practices have become standardized, irrespective of the contexts which gave rise to them. To use the web analogy made for the city of London again, a small and unpredicted change in one corner of the world, like South Africa's establishment of a Truth and Reconciliation Commission, has had reverberations throughout a host of peace processes. It not only brings new hopes for truth and reconciliation in other countries, but in places like Colombia, Mozambique, Rwanda, new ways of making this goal accord with local traditions have also emerged.

Another sign of these great expectations at work is the emergence of transitional justice as an expanding body of legal doctrines and practices for societies in transition out of conflict. Consider the broad remit of the Transitional Justice Institute, founded at the University of Ulster in 2003, five years after the Belfast Peace Agreement was signed. Transitional justice scholars generally work on legal issues involved in the transition from conflict to peace, and have an interest in the moral and legal dilemmas that arise when dealing with the legacy of human rights abuses, and with the abusers in conflict situations. Yet the Institute is also interested, more broadly, in how law and legal institutions can assist transitions out of conflict. Its agenda, like our expectations of peace, has expanded. Work has begun on four other themes: dealing with the past; gender conflict and transition; Northern Ireland itself; and theories, methods, and evaluation.

Yet the proposition that societies must go through a process called reconciliation in order to properly recover from civil war has never been empirically established. Like reconstruction, perhaps reconciliation is only a social myth which puts a gloss on the substantive trade-offs that peace really entails. Yet even if the activity has no core scientific content, the question of whose visions of reconciliation come to be acted upon is decided by politics and the possession of resources—very real factors. The local elites possess some resources, the outsiders others; the outcome will reflect their respective bargaining power (Zürcher et al. 2013: 26). Moreover, the desire for reconciliation, the powerful grip of this idea in any society, stems from very real experiences of chaos, polarization, and violence. Memory of these experiences—not its claims to science—give the myth its power as a principle of reorganization. Those who accept this share a new morality, a commitment to the creation of a totally different type of society: what dissidents in Eastern Europe used to call 'a morality of the shaken'.

Is there a core agenda to this activity, comparable to that played by state-building during reconstruction? There seem to be a multitude of tasks—rebuilding the physical infrastructure, restoring the rule of law, providing retribution for the worst crimes committed during the war, repairing relationships, and restoring lost property—all relevant to the desire for reconciliation (May 2012: 19). Unlike other ideas that underpin a *jus post bellum*, like restitution or reparation, reconciliation is such an amorphous normative principle that it is unlikely to be instantiated in a set of rules of *jus post bellum* reconstruction (ibid.: 101–2). Perhaps there is no outcome, just a process—like that on the psychoanalyst's couch, where the purpose is simply to talk about the past. One alternative is to stop asking questions about ultimate outcomes and core agendas, and just talk about 'mopping up' after conflict. Mopping up would include any principles or practices which end war and help establish peace (ibid.: 3).

Yet if the rules and procedures are not made concrete, how can people orientate their behaviour towards the goal of reconciliation, or construct a pathway to guide societies through uncertain transitions (ibid.: 101)? A distinction between rebuilding and healing needs to be made. A large part of what people do after civil war—such as rebuilding roads and railways lines—provides a platform for further development. Without this work no reconciliation would be possible. The largely cultural and psychological work that addresses values and social relationships is more difficult to justify in terms of scientific methods, or evaluate in terms of objective indicators of progress. Like democracy itself, reconciliation can be considered a process that exists right now, or a future-oriented concept defined by its *telos* (direction or purpose). This *telos* can cover both rebuilding and healing, but as with the charisma of Nelson Mandela, it is the ethical and emotional imperatives that inspire great expectations about peace.

The distinction between rebuilding and healing can also be expressed in terms of objectivist versus subjectivist understandings of what true peace consists in. In 'I Too Have Kurdish Friends', Çigdem Artik describes her peace mission to the Turkish–Syrian border in the autumn of 2014, at a time when better fighting between ISIS and its Kurdish defenders was taking place in Kobani:

> Politics has become such a circus where stomping elephants are squashing ants. When politicians sit down at the negotiation table, the lives of people do not come into question for states. Individuals that are surrounded by the order, feel like they are mere objects in the face of events. While the weapons industry, wars over water and oil were commoditized, the system still contains fractures in itself: the people's will! In this respect, the resistance in Kobani and all over the world signifies the methods of reacquiring the subjectivity and the autonomy. Experiencing the combat area and witnessing actual events is also a sense of revolt against the 'reification' of events. [Artik 2014: 6]

If war brings its own epistemology, peace too requires its own system of knowledge and values, which for this writer means re-establishing the subjectivity and autonomy of individuals who are otherwise made to feel like objects in the face of events.

The medical language often used to describe civil war legacies gets to this distinction between rebuilding and healing. In the language of medicine a trauma refers to the impact of a sudden event on the body, leaving it less functional than before in some crucial respect. Applied to the area of psychotherapy the same event may have a long-term and incapacitating impact on the personality, leaving it mentally or emotionally damaged in some way. We could extend the analogy to the social and political realms, asking how the body politic has been damaged by events that will usually deplete both its economic resources and physical infrastructure. Like a broken limb it certainly needs rebuilding. Yet the body politic has also been damaged in the form of bitterness, distrust, and hatred, all of which deplete the social capital of any society (Sztompka 2014: 450–1). The most common word for the knotty tissue of biological, physical, psychological, and social tissues that make up this damaged body is that of a wound. Recovering from a wound involves something more than rebuilding: every aspect of that body politic has to be allowed to heal.

The medical analogy breaks down when we consider the actors that we rely on for leadership in this endeavour: politicians, not doctors, take the lead. They will run into very real and specific dilemmas when faced with the question of how to deal with the legacies of civil war. Mandela's genius was to combine political realism with reconciliation. He possessed political judgement of a kind that is rare. The first dilemma concerns whether the civil war should be brought to an end through negotiation or victory. That there is a dilemma here is evident from the box below, which summarizes some of the research

---

'The Consequences of Negotiated Settlements in Civil Wars, 1945–1993'

Research question: This paper investigates which is more effective in ending civil wars: negotiated settlements or military victories?

Data source: The research is based on a dataset on 91 civil wars, covering all civil wars from 1945 to 1993. The dataset was created by applying Licklider's own definitions of civil war to several other conflicts.

Findings: How a civil war ends impacts significantly on the reoccurrence of civil war. After military victories, 85 per cent of civil wars did not reoccur. After negotiated settlements civil war reoccurred in 50 per cent of the cases. There is also a difference between economic and political conflicts and identity conflicts. After one side won a military victory in an identity-based conflict, in 27 per cent of the cases some form of genocide followed. This did not happen when such conflicts ended through negotiation.

Explanation: Licklider notes that after a civil war the combatants have to face the problem of living together after the fighting. Compromise in such a setting is particularly difficult, because the stakes in civil wars are presumably more intense, and more difficult to resolve by negotiation than after inter-state wars. Negotiated settlements of civil wars are much more likely to break down than settlements based on military victories. Consequently, the long-term casualties of negotiated settlements are likely to be greater than those of military victory. Military victory, on the other hand, is likely to destroy the organizational structure of one side, making a resumption of the civil war much more difficult.

(Licklider 1995)

---

findings of the American political scientist Roy Licklider (1995). His findings show that negotiated ends to civil war do not generally lead to repression and victimization, and may be compatible with reconciliation. The problem is that about half of those negotiated agreements signed between 1945 and 1993 actually collapsed, and led to a resumption of violence. This is the first dilemma: there may be trade-off between the stability brought about by *force majeure*, and the more inclusive settlements that can lead to reconciliation.

The second dilemma concerns the issue of how soon democratic elections should be held. Elections could, in theory, generate popular support for the new political arrangements; if introduced straight away, they could give the losers a stake in the system and allow them to become the loyal opposition. Alternatively, if early elections bring back memories of the civil war, creating an atmosphere of instability, perhaps they should be postponed. From a realist perspective, if competitive elections take place when some form of security dilemma persists, the only outcome will be polarization. The logic of Roland Paris's 'institution-building before liberalization' is that a divided society should first acquire the capacity to withstand the shocks and volatility that competitive elections bring. Yet elections denied may also be justice denied, and enable one side to continue to dominate the state, thus precluding reconciliation.

The third and biggest dilemma to consider is whether discussion of the recent past should be encouraged. Should civil war atrocities be investigated, and should special legal procedures be employed to bring offenders to account? Both seem essential components of 'transitional justice'. The German response to the Holocaust has influenced thinking on this issue. Had the silence about this crime which existed in the 1940s and 1950s been allowed to continue, the democratic consciousness of today's Germany—its efforts to pursue an ethical role in world affairs—would not be what they are. Yet a strong tension may exist between the imperative of achieving elite cooperation on the one hand, and many things that follow from establishing the truth about the past on the other. A participant in a recent BBC documentary on the legacy of the partition of Cyprus in 1975 compared history to a knife (Margona 2014). A knife can cut a piece of bread into two. It can also be used to share the bread between many people. If the purpose is to share the bread, why, he asked, do we need the knife of history at all?

Consider the actions of the short-lived 1989–90 Greek coalition government which included representatives of the right-wing New Democracy Party and a left-wing coalition party, even some communists. This coalition made 'national reconciliation' official policy for the first time. Among other conciliatory measures, all discriminatory measures against the former partisan Democratic Army were repealed. Yet the government also ordered the incineration of perhaps 17 million police files on suspected left-wing sympathizers (van Boeschoten 2015: 105). In response to the question of whether the knife of history was needed for reconciliation the coalition government clearly decided that it was not. The incineration clearly makes research into the civil war, and especially into the 1950s when people were stigmatized and victimized for being on the left, especially difficult. Kalyvas calls this decision 'the most outrageous act of destruction of a country's collective memory' (1999: 11). Yet the files were incinerated in celebratory bonfires held all over Greece in the summer of 1989 celebrating national reconciliation and 'the true end of the civil war' (ibid.). Is it not the case that one of the most important healing powers we possess consists of our ability to sink into sleep each night and forget the stresses of the previous day? Not to be able to forget those stresses would be a major affliction (Gadamer 1996: 138). The coalition government could also have invoked the ancient Greek myths about Lethe, one of the five rivers of Hades, drinking from which was supposed to induce forgetfulness and oblivion. Some also believed that souls were made to drink from this river before being reincarnated, so that they would not remember their past lives. If the purpose is to start anew, why not drink from the river of forgetfulness?

Contrast this decision with the reunified German state's approach to the records of the former East German Stasi, which was established as the Ministry of State Security in order to spy on the population.

When communism began to collapse orders were given by the Stasi for its agents to cover their tracks by destroying its files. This was prevented when activists occupied its HQ in January 1990 and salvaged more than 600 million pieces of paper. At the local level too activists occupied Stasi buildings in order to prevent further destruction, and then used the media to publicize what had been happening within their walls. The intention was to make clear what the dictatorship meant in practice. At the individual level those whose lives had been damaged by informants and police surveillance could, by accessing the files, get part of their lives back, fill in the gaps about their pasts, and perhaps achieve some form of accountability.

Anthropologist Riki van Boeschoten remarked of the Greek incineration that 'the past could not be buried that easily' and contrasts Greece, unfavourably, with South Africa (2015: 105). The contrast with Germany also begs the question of whether a democratic future can be constructed by suppressing the past. Since the Eurozone crisis began in 2008 Greece has again become polarized between left and right, and the neo-Nazi Golden Dawn has been attracting hundreds of thousands of voters. Unlike in East Germany, those who collaborated with the Nazi occupiers during World War II, including the members of the notorious Security Battalions, were never purged from the Greek state. The British and American governments saw their usefulness during the early stages of the Cold War and encouraged them to penetrate the security services and the judiciary. The civil war defeat of the left five years later meant that those who had actually liberated the country from the Nazis in 1944 were denied victory. Today, in the words of a Greek communist veteran Manilos Glezos (now an MEP), 'the deposits remain, like malignant cells' (Vulliamy and Smith 2014). The Stasi example shows how coming to terms with the past can be a constructive policy, used in this case to strengthen the democratic credentials of the new system. Yet there is no instant release from the past in this case either. Those who have been spied upon will find that they have been betrayed by those close to them—family members, friends, or neighbours. Since these are basic social ties, how can they or their children re-establish them? Such revelations further corrupt the things that hold a society together, making recovery a task for subsequent generations. The 'malignant cells' Glezos described have not been disposed of; they have simply been put under the microscope.

In Germany a Federal Commission for the Stasi Records was established and there have been no less than 3 million requests for access. Usually however, a society that wants to avoid what happened to the Greek files will find itself running a race with time against the natural tendency for traces of the past to disappear. At least 3,650 people were killed during the Northern Irish conflict which began in 1969. The vast majority of the cases have not been resolved, although peace was agreed in 1998. One case that was concerned the killing of a Protestant, Billy Fox, a Senator in the Irish parliament, in Tircooney in the border county of Monaghan on 11 March 1974. This seemed an obvious case of the IRA killing a Protestant at a time of heightened tension along the Irish border. Four of its members were convicted and admitted their guilt. Yet 40 years later we still do not know why Fox was killed. Some IRA men said under questioning that it was an operation that went wrong. Fox had been dating Marjorie Coulson, daughter of a Protestant family mistakenly rumoured in the area to be hoarding arms for loyalist paramilitaries. He might just have called to their farm at the wrong time: he visited every night. Yet Fox's politics were suspected: he had been called 'a B-special' (a notorious branch of the Northern Irish police force) in the Irish parliament and been derided by Unionists as 'Bogside Billy' because of his involvement in peace talks in the (Catholic) Bogside area of Derry. The fact that there was a conviction does not establish the truth about what happened. Rather layer upon layer of interpretation has been added. Were Protestant paramilitaries operating across the border, and were later attacks, such as the bombing of Monaghan town (which took place during the trial) linked to his death? Fox's killing has been the subject of a documentary on Irish state radio which concluded, 'memory fades, but the essential truth remains' (Woods and Rocks 2006).

Many of those who were at the farm that night are dead or disabled by illness. The convicted men refuse to speak about what happened. Some of those involved were Fox's neighbours, but they are silent too. Koselleck (2004: 106) writes of 'a threshold of fragmentation' below which a conflict dissolves into a series of unrelated perhaps meaningless incidents. Will the truth about Norhern Ireland's remaining unsolved killings be easier to establish?

The German response to the Holocaust is not the norm; in any case it took generational change before that genocide was really confronted. In many countries the solution to past violence has simply been to keep the knife of history deep in the pocket until it loses its sharpness. The response of politicians, especially, to civil war is often to leave issues of truth and justice to a later generation. For example, the initial aim after the brutal Finnish civil war of 1918 was not forgiveness—or to restore relations through mechanisms of transitional justice—but to create institutional contexts in which political relationships between former 'Reds and Whites' could heal on their own. These institutions, such as parliaments, allowed for formalized encounters between former enemies, out of which trust emerged incrementally. Yet this was still 'reconciliation without truth' (Forsberg 2009). When it came to justice and a public acknowledgement of their suffering, the left had to accept second-class citizenship in the 1920s and 1930s, and remained culturally isolated for decades. It was only in the 1960s that the loser's position in the civil war became sympathetically voiced in public (Alapuro 2002: 176–7). Yet Finland had, by then, become a social democracy.

Perhaps societies with lesser expectations can also achieve some form of reconciliation. Some authors distinguish between a 'thick' reconciliation, which aims at achieving a total restoration of relationships, mutual forgiveness, and notions of a shared future, and a 'thin' reconciliation, involving a more open-ended and fragmented process, in which the divisions of the past may survive without leading to renewed violence (Eastmond and Stefansson 2010: 5). The sequence in Finland was to first aim for thin reconciliation in the 1920s and 1930s, before a thicker reconciliation took place (Alapuro 2015: 19). This is a pattern that has occurred generally after European civil wars since then (Kissane 2015: 281–6). Yet justice postponed was not justice denied; the Social Democrats—who had been on the losing side in 1918—have been a frequent presence in government since 1937, and were dominant after 1945. The critical factor has been the overall direction taken by the political system as a whole since 1918.

Societies' different expectations in this field could be understood in terms of the nature of any specific community that wants to atone for the past. For example, when it comes to historical redress for past wrongs, we should try to identify the reasons why a society might seek to account for past injustices through special legal procedures. Motivations range from the possibility that someone might still be benefiting from those injustices, to the idea that the wrongs are not past at all; someone might still be suffering from them (Vernon 2012: 13–14). The different motivations might reflect the existence of different political communities: for example, a society that conceives of itself as something continuous in time may have to change its identity by accounting openly for its past (ibid: 88–110). If so, it will resist the idea.

Certainly, past societies have reconciled experiences of conflict to their conceptions of themselves in different ways. To give some practical examples: in the United Kingdom history was used to construct a myth of legal continuity after the civil war, based on the argument that the 'Glorious Revolution' of 1688 was the rational terminus for the civil wars of the 1640s, a view which downplayed the role of radical republican and religious agitation (especially that of Scottish Presbyterians) in driving events forward in the 1640s. Alternatively, a political organization conceived as a project for the future may atone for the past in order to prevent its members from committing further injustices (Vernon 2012: 94–6). This was the motivation for the adoption of the Basic Law of the Federal Republic in Germany in 1948, a constitution symbolizing both the renunciation of the past (Nazism) and the embrace of a democratic future.

Politically, not every society is equally capable of opening itself to the past. The historian of Algeria, James Le Seur (2010: 195), quotes Nietzsche's remark that only a strong personality can really withstand history. When the state is weak, and lacking in legitimacy—as in Algeria—a general amnesty may be the only way of dealing with the past. No investigation or discussion of the many civil war massacres committed by both sides in the 1990s is legally permitted at present. This seems to preclude reconciliation, but has been justified in the name of stability. In Spain in the 1970s, it was felt that the imperative of establishing democracy justified a pact of forgetting/*olvido* about the civil war past. When Spaniards began to dismantle the Francoist regime, there was no legal prohibition of discussion of the civil war, but a greater value was placed on establishing elite consensus behind the transition to democracy (Vincent 2010). The Francoist Cortés (parliament), actually voted itself out of existence on 18 November 1976. The limitations of this transition were exposed by a 'second transition', which began in the 1990s under the government of José Zapatero (Field 2010), and the past returned to heat up political debate. Yet democracy had been secured by 1990, and even though many victims of Franco's regime have had no legal redress, a new reality was nonetheless created by this elite pact.

The Spanish experience suggests a distinct sequence; different priorities may exist at different stages in the recovery process. The literature on reconstruction often relies on a series of signposts—the first democratic elections for example—to mark progress towards peace. These initial hurdles matter. The provision of security, institutional reform, and economic development, *are* essential pillars of recovery without which recovery from conflict is impossible. Yet institution-building is only the first phase: psychological and cultural changes are also necessary if some form of reconciliation is to be achieved. Ten years after the 1998 Belfast peace agreement, the poet Seamus Heaney put it this way: Northern Ireland could walk forward only with 'a crippled trust' (Heaney 1990: 13). The long-term task is one of restoring damaged relationships. The initial phase of reconstruction involves practical tasks—such as physical rebuilding, providing security, and institutional reform—but the emotional and moral repair Heaney refers to requires work that is both cultural and psychological.

An implication of this sequence argument might be that only when the generation that experienced the civil war—and carries the bitterness within—dies, is release from conflict in a psychological sense really possible. The adage that 'time heals all wounds' might simply mean that questions of memory, forgiveness, and justice need time for this repair to take place. In Finland the first public step was initiated not by the political elite, but by the publication in 1966 of a trilogy of novels, *Under the Northern Star*, by Väinö Linna. His novels showed how fierce social and political tensions, especially over land, had been slowly building at the local level in the decade before the civil war. His sympathetic account of 'the Reds' grievances led to a re-evaluation of the civil war, and allowed the Finns to eventually incorporate this conflict into their sense of themselves (Alapuro 2002: 177).

Yet the adage could also mean that thick reconciliation is possible only for later generations, which means that the task of the generation that experienced the violence is to achieve coexistence, and only when this is established can one consider opening up the past. The Finnish sociologist Risto Alapuro noted something important about his country's experience. In the 1990s it became fashionable to say that the 1918 civil war demonstrated what *we*—the Finnish people or humanity—were really capable of (Alapuro 2010). The new focus was on the violence which took place, rather than the political issues which mattered to both sides after the Russian revolution. Earlier generations would have thought about the conflict in terms of left and right, but the society is no longer so class-based. This re-evaluation, and the rejection of the violence as inhumane, is not a reconciliation between the two poles of political life that were crystallized in 1917. It comes from a distance, not from those who experienced the civil war and its aftermath at close hand. As T. S. Eliot's *The Dry Salvages* put it: 'time is no healer: the patient is no longer there' (1974: 210).

One cannot extract a standard model of how to achieve reconciliation from such cases. Nor can one force great expectations on bitter and polarized countries. Since different experiences of conflict leave different legacies, and because 'dealing with the past' means various things in different cultures, societies will not converge on a specific set of principles and institutional practices with respect to reconciliation. Perhaps it is better to see reconciliation as an evolving project rather than an end state—moving on a continuum, stretching from non-violent coexistence to a shared society with a common vision of the future (Siani-Davies and Katsikas 2009: 560). In Greece, the discourse of reconciliation in the 1980s was linked to party politics and elite rivalries. Democratization did not see agreement on the rights and wrongs of the civil war, but did foster a culture in which violence was repudiated as an aspect of politics (ibid.). Instead of new beginnings, or establishing a 'post-conflict society', perhaps the real purpose of political leadership might be to transform memories of the past into a meaningful state in order for them to heal. Fossilized memories will only arrest development. Reconciliation becomes a question not of 'conflict transformation' or moving on in grim silence, but of managing the legacies of conflict in a constructive way.

True, it is only in the past two decades that social scientists have begun to study the issue of recovery from civil war in a systematic way. The long-term effects of many peace processes remain to be seen. Thus far however, the literature does nothing to support Hegel's claim that the wounds inflicted by history can be healed without leaving scars (Koselleck 1988: ix). Rather, the question of how much of the past can be brought into the future is unavoidable in the area of reconciliation too. One study of Central America (Peceny and Stanley 2001), found that liberal reconstruction worked in El Salvador and Guatemala (not Nicaragua), in the 1990s, only when it reconfigured existing institutions rather than designed them from scratch. In contrast, in Burundi after the civil war fought between 1993 and 2005, ambitious plans to achieve justice and reconciliation through new and special legal means floundered on the fact that the regular legal institutions were not strong enough to provide normal justice. Everyone is entitled to great expectations when it comes to justice and truth, but should some of the past not be confined to the past?

What should we make of the one undeniable fact that our firmest hope for reconciliation lies in generational change? If reconciliation can only be a long-term goal in reconstruction, the questions are: who is reconciled, to whom, and to what? The Jewish philosopher Martin Buber (1958) suggests that the most human relationships—conveyed by the term 'I–thou'—exist when love informs every relation. This 'I–thou' relationship does not normally exist with 'hes' and 'shes' that are only our neighbours. 'I–it' neighbourly relationships emerge when one moves back from he or she, to estimate feelings and qualities, to place someone in context, or to assess their usefulness to me (Vermes 1988: 45). These relationships resemble rather 'a point inscribed in a world grid of space and time' and require detachment as a precondition for any kind of love. This detachment is also necessary for reconciliation after civil war, but since it requires generational change as a preconditon, reconciliation reconstructs only an 'I–it' relation. Buber's categories are applicable to communities where the earlier intimacy of the people was of the 'I–thou' kind. After this intimate relation has been shattered by civil war, generational change and the emergence of new contexts allow for parity and reappraisal, but cannot produce other than an 'I–it' relation. In other words, civil war leaves a permanent wound within the body politic, a wound which will not allow a full reconciliation within the generation that experienced it.

Conclusion

The initial response to the conflict which took place in Kosovo in the 1990s was to believe that what had happened was so bad that no reconciliation would be possible. In the period between 1990 and 2000, almost 1.2 million Kosovan Albanians were displaced. When the conflict with the Serbs intensified between March and July 1999, between 10,000 and 13,000 Kosovan Albanians perished (Seifert 2015: 218–20). What do such legacies tell us about definitions of civil war? The Kosovan conflict was not primarily a war between citizens— fought for political ends—but a war over identity, which had the effect of destroying age-old traditions of neighbourliness and friend- ship in the region. In *The Republic* Plato commented that when Greeks fought non-Greeks this was seen as natural, but wars among Greeks who were naturally friends 'betrays a Greece that was sick and divided' (2012: 188). Certainly relations between Albanians and Serbs are now sick and divided. Neither was the conflict new: the struggle between the two groups had existed ever since Yugoslavia was founded. The problem that remains is not one of legitimacy; the world has, by and large, recognized the independence of Kosovo. What remains to be seen is whether partition is effectuated with respect to the remaining Serb enclaves. What has been damaged, perhaps permanently, is the social fabric or tissue. The ultimate consequence is that the willingness to live together, to be friends, no longer exists. Such legacies are those of an internal war: the wounds are felt internally. As the Roman historian Lucan put it, it is the wound left by the hand of a neighbour that will not be easily forgotten.

In 'Enemies of the Nation—A Nation of Enemies', an article on the legacy of the Greek civil war, the anthropologically inclined historian Riki van Boeschoten (2015: 96) takes issue with the importance nor- mally given to the state in the area of reconstruction. After civil war, reconstruction needs to take place in four arenas: the physical envir- onment and the economy, the formal institutional arena, national identity, and that of social relations (ibid.: 94–5). Of these four arenas the current literature prioritizes one—the formal institutional arena— even though restoring social relations at the local level is the most important task. No institution, however strong, can achieve reconcili- ation where people are not willing to rebuild their social relationships. Moreover, as the history of the European Union has shown, it is not easy to create a cohesive identity for an entity that lacks history. No state can be abstracted out of its surrounding culture, the web of meanings which can create feelings of both belonging and estrangement. For this reason the task of reconstruction is not purely a technocratic one: not only do the building-blocks lie in cultural and social realities, the choice of what traditions to base the identity of a state on is a political one, which will create new divisions. Hence the reconstruction of a state can involve the deconstruction of another. The late novelist Yoram Kaniuk, who had fought in the 1948 war from which Israel's founding generation emerged, made this point about Israel. Decades later, his disillusioned comment was that Israel had founded a state based on religion, 'rather than on the nation we have nearly become' (*The Guardian* 10 June 2013, Obituary).

Indeed there are few political scenarios more divisive than the aftermath of conflict. The fact that many prefer to victimize their opponents rather than seek reconciliation says something about human nature. Perhaps because the human temptation to dominate is so strong many think reconciliation a *prerequisite* for peace. Without such a sequence, the natural tendency will be for violence to reoccur (Long and Brecke 2003). Yet the sequence may be the other way round: that it is peace that is the precondition for reconciliation. Realists believe that security comes first and that no peace is possible in an atmosphere of fear. Marxists would add that it is an unfair distribution of resources rather than the absence of truth or justice that will make conflict reoccur. When security and prosperity are established, there will be so little at stake that elites simply will not be able to persuade enough people that more war is desirable. If both these positions are correct, to expect and aim for more than this in the immediate aftermath of civil war may actually make peace harder to establish. This is not only because the things involved in reconciliation—truth, justice, and changes in identity—take time. Nor is it because elites always matter. It is because too much should not be expected of human beings.

EPILOGUE: CIVIL WAR AND HUMAN DIVISIVENESS

Human divisiveness, the tendency for human beings to organize themselves into diverse and smaller communities, has always been a trait of mankind. Neither universal empires—such as Rome, which provided diverse peoples with citizenship rights—nor universal religions devoted to only one God—such as Islam—could suppress it. Nor have they been able to prevent its expression during civil war. More than religious schism, or the formation of new language groups, civil war is now the most troubling manifestation of this tendency. The problem it poses for those who believe in the essential unity of humanity has actually become stronger as the world becomes more globalized. Ethnic groups continue to argue for recognition on the grounds that they will contribute to the cultural stock of humanity, and universal norms like democracy, progress, or human rights, continue to justify rival positions in civil war. The altruistic expectation that more development will eventually produce less of this divisiveness is a forlorn hope. Hence it is appropriate that an epilogue to this book should ask what the literature on civil war tells us about this trait in humankind.

Two perspectives on human divisiveness

This literature could be said to consist in a set of theories that aim to explain the form of human divisiveness represented by the recent waves of civil war. It focuses on the period since 1945, and its historical remit is the new states created by decolonization. The sceptic will object that civil wars have occurred in all periods of recorded history—for all kinds of reasons—and that a proper consideration of this form of human divisiveness requires a longer-term perspective. Yet a discussion of the post-1945 context *can* shed light on the basic analytical question in this field. In the nineteenth century 'naturalists' saw war as a natural expression of the dark side of *human nature:* that inherent cultural and biological differences continually drive people into war. 'Situationalists', on the other hand, believed war an exceptional event, which flourished only in certain contexts.

The situationalist perspective on human conflict is largely correct in that it helps us explain more. Violent conflicts *are* usually the product of exceptional contexts. A constant—such as human nature—cannot explain how these contexts arise. Consider the current divisions between Shia and Sunni Muslims in Syria. Some perennial sources of human divisiveness—clannism, sectarianism, or religious resurgence—are relevant. Yet why have they come to matter now? The divisions have resulted from the unusual way in which a Shia minority group from the margins—the Alawites from the hills above Latakia—gained control of the secular and totalitarian Ba'ath party, and went on to suppress the majority of the Syrian population for decades. This system was the concrete product of the special military training and entitlements of this Shia minority group under French colonial rule (1920–45). Hence there is a very specific situational factor to this civil war (Ruthven 2013).

Other aspects of civil war are more open to the naturalist perspective. Unlike changes in voting behaviour, the spread of civil society, or population growth, civil wars are not produced developmentally: they are often the result of dramatic and unexpected crises, like mental break-downs. Hence, in addition to specifying the precise contexts from which they emerge, it is important to look at the experience they bring, and what these experiences disclose about human nature. Hence we can distinguish between two approaches: that of tracing the historical factors that make for conflicts, and studying what people experience when these wars begin (Kalyvas 2006: 3–5, 52–87). This distinction takes us back to Thucydides, for whom the initial causes of stasis were less important than what set in during its course (Price 2001: 32). He stressed how typical sources of solidarity in peacetime, like the family, can lead to bitter divisions during civil war. His was a vivid summary of the changes in behaviour brought about by internal war:

> Then, with the ordinary conventions of civilized life thrown into confusion, human nature, always ready to offend even where laws exist, showed itself proudly in its true colours, as something incapable of controlling passion, insubordinate to the idea of justice, the enemy to anything superior to itself; for, if it had not been for the pernicious power of envy, men would not have so exalted vengeance over innocence and profit above justice. Indeed, it is true that in these acts of revenge on others men may take it upon themselves to begin the process of repealing those laws of humanity which are there to give a hope of salvation to all who are in distress, instead of leaving those laws in existence, remembering that there may come a time when they, too, will be in danger and will need their protection. [Thucydides 1972: 245]

The fact that Thucydides' insights remain relevant shows that the problem of human divisiveness posed by civil war is not merely a contemporary one. In his discussion of the murder of the tryrant Hipparchus by Harmodious and Aristogiton, Thucydides traces their political motives back to those of homosexual jealousy (ibid.: 46, 443, 446). Since the murderers later became recruited into the myth of Greek democracy, as heroes, Koselleck (2002: 67) calls Thucydides' method one of 'unmasking', a strategy very suited to the task of illuminating what civil wars tell us about human divisiveness. We find the same method, underpinned by similar strategies of radical disillusionment, in the work of Hobbes, Goya, and even in Kalyvas's works (2006) on local violence during the Greek civil war of the 1940s.

This method of radical disillusionment is closely connected to the popular belief that such conflicts bring out something dark in human nature. This suggestion is present throughout 'Los Disastres de la Guerra', the series of Goya sketches about Spain's guerrilla war against Napoleon's army and its aftermath. On this book's cover the plate

'Esto es Peor' shows an enormous half human body on top of a tree. The torso suggests that violent conflict could so stretch a person's humanity as to turn a man into something other than human. Another sketch 'Con Razon ó sin ella' ('With Reason or Not'), shows two men being bayonetted or shot by three regular soldiers. The title, which is deliberately ambiguous, could mean that the soldiers alone or their victims had reason to fight and die. It might also mean that standards of human rationality simply do not apply. The diabolical expressions on people's faces—the prevalence of masks, ghosts, and witches in the prints—suggest an alternative reality in which there is no distinction to be made between good and evil, liberty and fear, or reality and hallucination.

Goya was sketching 'an inverted world'. Many have posed the question of how he was able to look forward into our own world from the vantage point of early nineteenth-century Spain. Indeed with reports from northern Syria of forced conversions on pain of torture, beheadings, rapes, and massacres of minorities, ISIS seems to have brought back to our television screens that part of human nature which Goya dramatized. In Thucydides, human nature was both residual and primordial: once violence begins, more divisive behaviour emerges naturally because people are predisposed to behave like this. Hobbes' method was both empirical and theoretical. Although his vision of civil war was certainly based on observations of the brutal 1640s, theoretically, his end product, the State, was already implied in the premise of civil conflict. This is because people were described as being subject to a sovereign authority to begin with. Only when that subjection loosened did the two elements in his view of human nature—*appetitus et fuge* (desire and fear)—give rise to civil war (Koselleck 1988: 24, 31). The French Enlightenment philosopher Denis Diderot differed in combining a benign view of human nature with a vision of man at perpetual civil war with himself. There was first a 'natural' man but when an 'artificial' man was admitted inside that man a civil war followed which has yet to end. The natural or the artificial man could prevail: in both cases the result will be human beings 'divided, tugged, tormented, stretched on the wheel' (Porter 2014: 104).

So not even the most pessimistic authors agree on what human nature means. Yet without clarity on this issue, establishing what civil war discloses about human divisiveness will be very difficult. When we turn to the empirical study of civil war, Carl Schmitt praised Hobbes' strategy of disillusionment, for Hobbes had shown that during such wars 'all legitimate and normative illusions with which men like to deceive themselves regarding political realities in periods of untroubled security vanish' (Schmitt 1996: 52). Schmitt also predicted that the fundamental correctness of Hobbes' 'protection obedience axiom' will be revealed when there arises, within a state, a situation where there are organized parties capable of according their members more protection than the state (ibid.). For many, Yugoslavia in the 1990s has confirmed this axiom. Hobbes' stress on the way people seek out their own kind primarily for protection and security was key. Only when the state loosened—a very Hobbesian fear—did the divisive behaviour come to the fore.

Nonetheless, the empirical study of such conflicts brings us no closer to specifying what exactly civil war discloses about human nature. One reason is that the divisive traits in human beings have no one source. In Yugoslavia, on top of fear there was also greed, lust, and the hunger for power among people at the top. Indeed precisely because conceptions of human nature are hard to make specific in explanatory accounts, art and literature may be a better source of insights into the divisiveness of civil war. In *Le Testament Français*, the novelist Andreï Makine describes the trip of Charlotte, a Russian-speaking Red Cross nurse, from France, to the Volga region where hundreds of thousands had died from famine, and on to Siberia at the height of the civil war in 1921 (1997: 57–63). As Charlotte set off 'she saw everything', including images of what hell must be like (ibid.: 58). One image was of a horse running wildly through the fields, with a sabre standing erect upon its back. The two halves of the rider's body had fallen to each side, onto the trampled grass. This sabre must have cut the rider in two, from shoulders to stomach, before becoming embedded in the saddle. Another image was of a group of peasants angrily pushing away a barge with long poles to prevent them landing. Those on the barge had typhus, and were dying of hunger. Once they lost their physical strength, they would eventually be unable to dock anywhere. Awaiting them was just the 'indifferent horizon' of the Caspian Sea. Only once, in the Ural mountains, did Charlotte see a group of people who seemed content during the civil war, sitting serenely on a bank scattered with dead leaves, outside a village which had been half destroyed by fire. As their pale faces shone with 'a blissful calm' in the mild autumn sun, the realization soon dawned on her that these were lunatics, freed from a mental asylum that had just burnt down.

Charlotte was also experiencing an inverted world, an idea that has its psychological and sociological equivalent in the concept of fragmentation. The concept was implicit in the earlier discussion of the consequences of decolonization. As the political map of the world fragmented into more and more nation states during and after World War II, the next step was often the fragmentation of the new states themselves into civil war. When a specific conflict begins, we can also think of how it may deteriorate. Based on observations of Angola, Chad, the Congo, India, Liberia, Peru, and Yugoslavia in the 1990s, anthropologist R. Brian Ferguson suggests that a conflict may transform itself from one where the future existence of the state (although challenged) is not in doubt, to a situation where the state fragments into smaller states, to the final crisis where the sovereignty of any national government is in doubt (2003: 3).

Since fragmentation can be taken as a sociological synonym for human divisiveness, and not just one of its consequences, the next section will try to explain why it acquires such force during civil wars. Consider the statement made by the British Prime Minister David Cameron at the NATO summit in September 2014. On the problem of Islamic extremism Cameron argued that only after the 'fracturing' of states through civil war did this extremism 'bubble to the surface'

(Cameron, 5 September 2014). In order to understand how the divisive traits in human beings—of which Islamic extremism is one form—'bubble to the surface', we need to understand the experience a society goes through when it becomes 'fractured', where this fracturing comes from, and what the fractures which result from this experience are based on. Since there is an analogy between this experiential approach to conflict and the way an individual personality can fragment under stress, the emphasis will be on how different sources of fragmentation can combine to devastating effect.

Human divisiveness as fragmentation

Fragmentation, and omens of fragmentation, have always been part of the experience of civil war. In Thucydides, it was fragmentation—not the acts of violence themselves—that threatened the unity of a *polis* whose primary purpose was the promotion of citizenship and education (Pouncey 1980: 149). The purpose of Hobbes' *Leviathan* was to prevent the fragmentation of Britain and Ireland into anarchy. The near-collapse of the Assad regime in Syria over the past three years has produced just exactly this situation. Since March 2011 no less than 6.5 million Syrians—50 per cent of the population—have been forced to leave their homes. Some put the figure much higher. In the 12 months before August 2014, 1 million of these had fled abroad, mainly to Jordan, Lebanon, Turkey, and Iraq. By August 2014 the number of those killed in the civil war was just under 200,000 (*Zaman* 20 August 2014). If the concept of fragmentation illuminates anything about civil war, the extent and rapidity of such a collapse must be explained.

The first question is where fragmentation comes from. For Hobbes fragmentation was a top-down process. Had the public not perceived a division of powers emerging between the Crown and Parliament, the division of England into rival armies, and the superimposition of religious differences onto political ones, would not have happened (1985 [1651]: 236). Fearful, competitive, and selfish human nature came into play only when central authority weakened. Hobbes' fear of unbridled political competition led him to juxtapose 'civil society' with the nightmarish 'state of nature'. His concepts for conflict ('contumely', 'civil warre', 'tumult', 'rebellion', 'sedition') can all be used by those 'above' to denounce challenges to their rule coming from 'below'.

In contrast to Hobbes' stress on state collapse as the source, the discipline of sociology can help us see fragmentation coming from below. Hobbes' top-down approach does not help us trace the way in which the disintegration of a state proceeds through that intricate, but always potentially destructive, latticework of personal relationships, kinships, local and regional loyalties, and ideological beliefs that structures any society (Regan 1999: 6). The fragments that result are neither random nor natural: they reflect pre-existing social relations. Consider Afghanistan, scene of continuous destruction and warfare since the 1980s. The consequences include over 1.5 million war-related deaths, many more wounded and traumatized, and the flight abroad of over a quarter of the population. One source of friction that has been exacerbated by the experience of Taliban rule is the divide between the Pashtuns and everyone else. Yet many Pashtuns hate the Taliban too, and the rivalry between two ancient Pashtun tribes, the Durrani and the Ghilazi, is another complicating factor. When one considers that the other ethnic groups reject the Taliban, and that the cleavages also reflect rivalries between cities (such as the Taliban stronghold Kandahar and Kabul) we can see just how many divisions have been reignited by the US-led invasion in 2001. Their cumulative effect has been to fragment the society from the very top down to each valley and village.

The next question is why the process of fragmentation is sometimes unstoppable, and why fragmentation can destroy not just states, but societies, so quickly. The ancient historian and classicist Peter Pouncey (1980: 145) notes that in Thucydides stasis took on a whirlpool character and, as people were sucked into the conflict and sought only to save themselves, this only fragmented the *polis* further. This spiral of descent can happen where the state is artificial in the sense that it is not grounded in strong social relations. For instance, since the collapse of the Gaddafi regime, Libya has become 'a land of regional, tribal, ethnic warlords' (Cockburn 2014). The prospect that another strongman will be needed to put an end to the assassinations, fragmentation, and racketeering is certainly Hobbesian. Oil revenues are a fraction of what they were, people are vulnerable to the arbitrary rule of rival militias, and no one has the authority to disarm them. The current divisions are not ideological; because of the absence of a cohesive Libyan identity, sectarian, ethnic, and regional divisions seem more important (ibid. 2014).

Fragmentation may also become unstoppable when it has many sources. The Greek conception of stasis was of a state of discord between different parts which produced so much division as to disrupt the healthy functioning of the whole. The medical term metastasis, which means the movement of a disease from one part of the body to another, has stasis as its root. The connection between the two concepts implies that the affliction of civil war is at its worst when all parts of the body politic become afflicted by internal divisions of different kinds. In *Syria: The Death of a Country*, *The Economist* (23 February 2013) depicted a land increasingly prey to feuding warlords, Islamists, and gangs—'a new Somalia rotting in the heart of the Levant' (ibid.: 13). The process of disintegration began with the emergence of cracks in the political system, and may end up destroying the social and geographical basis of the Syrian state. An early aspect of this was territorial. The regime was determined to consolidate its grip along a north–south axis from Damascus through Homs and Hama to Latakia, the port and region that were home to the Assad family and its Alawite sect. As more Alawites were recruited into the army, the Syrian conflict became increasingly sectarian. What has emerged is a hardened and increasingly sectarian underclass on each side. Disenfranchised, mainly Sunni rebels, and the regime's mainly poor Alawites, have come to bear the brunt of the fighting. In other words the Syrian body politic is being afflicted by fractures of many kinds.

The final question concerns the nature of the fragments that are produced by civil war. A sociological approach should be able to show that these are not simply a product of the randomness of civil war. In Syria, three possible outcomes are a partitioned national homeland, a divided and resentful population within an authoritarian state, or a situation of indefinite de facto multiple sovereignty. A restructuring of the Syrian state may produce fragments which appear as the remnants of a formerly unified society. Yet if separate political entities are not formed, the concept of fragmentation may just refer to the polarized social relationships within a divided Syria, with the fragments which result from the war remaining interrelated, if disconnected, parts of Syrian society as a whole. Either way the lines of division—Cameron's 'fractures'—will reflect pre-existing social relations.

If we want to explain the enduring associations of civil war with chaos and disaster—especially why the tendencies towards human divisiveness gain such momentum during civil wars—tracing the sources of fragmentation in this way is one approach. The advantage of this understanding of conflict is that, as with any illness, once you understand it, you are less likely to be affected by it. The same cannot be said of the tendency to blame everything on human nature, as if the sources of extreme human divisiveness need no specific explanation. Moreover, as with an individual whose mind has disintegrated, finding social and political explanations for these events may help us to see them as being other than random. In terms of their sociology, Afghanistan and Libya show that religious, tribal, and regional divisions can be easily exploited to break up a state; they are not, however, so malleable that they can be manipulated from above to reconstruct a more cohesive state.

Perhaps the central lesson is that these tragedies are usually the result of many processes combining; as with a nervous break-down, the sources of fragmentation are plural, not singular. For example, observers were quick to see in the rapidity of Syria's collapse over the past three years the fragility of the whole regional system of mandate states constructed by the British and the French at the end of World War I. Initially, Syria was a state simply hacked away from the carcass of the Ottoman Empire, and jammed between Turkey, Lebanon, Jordan, Iraq, and Palestine. That the whole regional state system around these states is fragmenting is a good example of how a process which seems unstoppable on the ground, and seems to come 'from below' (in the form of ethnic, territorial, and religious disputes), may actually have its origin in a structural change at higher levels of world politics. The Yugoslav wars also occurred at a time, immediately after 1989, when a structural transformation in the inter-state system was taking place. Without the collapse of communism after 1989, it is unlikely that these wars would have happened, or that the West would have been free to encourage the break-up of the Yugoslav state.

A similar combination of factors from 'above' and 'below' gives ethnic conflict its general potential to fragment states. On the one hand, the political salience of ethnic identity reflects structural changes in the international system ('from above') which date back to the French Revolution in 1789 and which gave rise to the nation state as the default political form. To these we can add that a taboo against secession no longer exists, as demonstrated by Catalonia, Timor Leste, Eritrea, Crimea, Scotland, and most recently South Sudan, where the south Sudanese diaspora managed to persuade the US administration to support independence. Hence there are fewer barriers to state formation than ever before. On the other hand, ethnic and secessionist conflicts come from below in the sense that they feed off material grievances and attachments to specific territories on the ground. When he compares the effects of secessionist ethnic nationalism to Russian *matrioshka* dolls, the political scientist John Coakley gives us a good image of the potential for fragmentation that this combination of 'above and below' brings (2012: 191). He asks us to visualize a doll representing the United Kingdom. We may open it to find it contains a smaller doll, called Ireland. Opening the Irish doll, we find another smaller doll Ulster, and opening the Ulster doll we find the Northern nationalist Catholic community.

Much of the recent literature suggests that more economic development, more democracy, or more equality will move societies away from the dangers of fragmentation. The 2003 World Bank report went so far as to suggest that the whole world may become bifurcated between poor and marginalized economies stuck in a conflict trap and those out of the danger zone. One can only make the observation that when people feel beyond civil conflict, they have ceased to learn from experience in the sense that one generation actually learns from another. The tendency to suppress the possibility of civil war, to remove self-doubt from conceptions of present political orders, will ultimately diminish the very qualities of political conviction and leadership that peace actually depends on. One could make a comparison between the dangers of fragmentation during civil war with the fragility of the institution of marriage. Every marriage is a law unto itself, and many break down for reasons outsiders find incomprehensible. The analogy with civil war lies in the fact that if each marriage carries within it the seeds of destruction, a failure to recognize or admit this fact will only increase the risk of a break-up (Madden 2013: 163).

If fragmentation is what people experience during the fighting, how can a person, community, or society restore its lost wholeness afterwards? The late anthropologist Helio Belki noted that all the parties in the 1992 election in Angola made much of the question of national identity and the search for a common culture (2003: 252–5). The attention paid to *Angolidade* (literally, 'Angolan-ness'), plus the belief in some quarters that those who had lived through the war against the Portuguese and the subsequent civil war had proven their national identity beyond doubt, led him to wonder whether this shared suffering would strengthen a common national identity. In Spain, where non-elite accounts of the civil war now challenge those of the state, the ghosts of the past return only as fragments, as during the digging up of the graves of those killed by the Francoist regime after its formal conclusion (Ní Bhéacháin 2010). Those who 'recover historical memory' by digging for these remains can never recover the whole of the past. They can be compared to archaeologists, who work like detectives, looking not for corpses and murders, but for skeletons, shards of pottery, and fragments of tools. They may never succeed in establishing the whole truth about a conflict, but may patiently piece together the fragments, and close the circle of missing history by coming to a fuller interpretation of the past. Yet each step may also be dangerous because the discovery of just one more fragment can undermine the whole explanation (Braudel 2001: 27).

The theme of fragmentation was present in Thucydides' account of the changes in language that 'stasis' brought to Corcyra and, as we saw in Chapter 2, the traditional fear of civil war—from ancient Rome to seventeenth-century England—was of a form of conflict that would turn things upside down. Another persistent fear has been that of boundaries (between social classes, between crime and politics, or between private and public conflict) collapsing. Andreï Makine's image of only the mad being at ease during the Russian civil war suggests something similar. Since the boundary that collapses in Makine (and also Goya) is that between reality and delusion, the analogy between civil war and the emotional and psychological fragmentation that appear as symptoms of schizophrenia is important. Freud once said that to know the mind we must observe its collapse; that is what we have been doing with respect to civil war. The logic of such an enquiry was articulated well by Brian Masters, a biographer of the mass murderer Dennis Nilsen, who said that through considering the personalities of those that have disintegrated, we can better understand those who did not (BBC Radio 4: 14 June 2014). Were there no effort to explain them, they would remain random, and hence appear more frightening.

The question of definition

There is a basic definitional problem in the study of civil war. Much of the political science literature assumes civil war to be a general phenomenon, and classifies diverse cases as ostensibly similar in order to have enough examples from which to generalize. When violent ethnic conflicts, peasant insurgencies, revolutions, and terrorist campaigns are all considered civil wars, the result is 'semantic bleaching', the universal and indiscriminate use of a concept such that it loses all meaning (Richter 1995: 56). It is generally agreed that there is no empirical criterion specifying a level of violence that allows us to distinguish civil war from other types of internal conflict (Sambanis 2004: 815). Nonetheless, those of us who believe that we are not seeing a lot of one form of conflict (called 'civil war'), and hold that civil war is in fact a very distinctive type of conflict, still face the challenge of defining what makes it distinctive.

The definitions used in quantitative studies are suitable for the task of estimating how much conflict and violence there is in this world and of showing—through correlations—how one aspect of social reality (such as ethnic diversity) is related to another (violent politics). Few believe however that they can illuminate what is actually going on in the social world (Rogers 2000: 386). A very specific problem was raised in Chapter 2 vis-à-vis Fearon and Laitin's statement that of the 127 civil wars they covered, three-quarters were actually insurgencies (2003: 75). We do need a definition which can link different cases. Yet we also need a criterion which will enable us to distinguish between conflicts which escalate to the point where they imperil the basis of the political community, and those that are simply armed conflicts within a state, such as most insurgencies. This is important since we cannot meaningfully talk about causes and consequences unless we recognize that most internal wars strengthen the state in some way. Civil wars, in contrast, always bring with them dangers of fragmentation. Why else have the events which accompanied the deposing of the Muslim Brotherhood's President Morsi in Egypt in the summer of 2013 not been considered a civil war? The empirical criterion of at least 1,000 deaths was easily exceeded. In contrast, few doubt that the more than 200,000 deaths, and the 6–9 million people displaced from their homes in Syria, form part of a civil war.

The difference suggests that we do possess an intuitive conception of the typical social experience that would make a conflict a civil war. Moreover, this experiential perspective can help us identify what it is about civil war that is so destructive. In Syria, the clearest expression of human divisiveness was the division of the state into two armed blocs. Yet what has made for a total conflict of the kind Thucydides described above, has been the fragmentation of these blocs, potentially into many entities. It is this reality, and indeed the apprehension of this reality, which makes Syria's a qualitatively different and more destructive conflict than Egypt's. There was never a mortal threat to the future existence of the Egyptian state, and the violence has actually allowed the prior state apparatus and the military to assert their authority. Part of the problem is that civil wars continue to be viewed in much of the literature through the prism of violence. Yet it is not violence alone or its intensity that makes one conflict a civil war, and another a mere insurgency or rebellion. We need to define what is actually happening when a country experiences civil war.

A defining aspect is that the stakes are higher in a genuine civil war. Fragment (Latin: *fragmentum*) means 'broken piece'. The verb 'to fragment' (Latin: *frangere*) means 'to fall to pieces', or simply 'to break'. Thus fragmentation suggests either a fragment that is the end result of the process, or the actual process of breaking into pieces. Neither was on the cards in Egypt as a consequence of the Arab Spring, a set of protests which removed a despot (Mubarek) but did not change the regime. In contrast, the Syrian state can now survive only as a fragment of the former entity: the Assad regime fighting from a fortified enclave and remaining the biggest militia in a land of many militias. In the second meaning of the term ('breaking into pieces'), in the summer of 2013 fears emerged that the process of breaking into many pieces was intensifying, exemplified by the emergence of splits within the Syrian opposition. The first killing of a major Free Syrian Army figure by a jihadist group took place in July 2013 in Latakia province. As splinters emerged within the Free Syrian Army, between Jabhat al Nusra and al-Qaeda, and then with the emergence of ISIS and of

Ahrar al-Sham, the fear arose that the process of breaking into pieces would continue well after the defeat of Assad. This fear of further fragmentation eventually influenced those contemplating military intervention.

The initially broad-based democratic struggle against Assad has long given way to many different wars taking place simultaneously. One possible outcome, which also results from the fragmentation of modern cities (Navez-Bouchanine 2002: 19–44, 45–103), is chaos. Urban chaos results from the detachment of different parts of the city, and the establishment of internal boundaries that break with the city, as planned and perceived as a unified entity (ibid.: 57). In Syria, the local administration now rests in the hands of paramilitary groups, and enclaves have been established by the Assad regime, the main Sunni opposition, the Kurds, and Islamist groups like ISIS and Jabhat al Nusra. What one could describe as a state of chaos is this situation of effective 'multiple sovereignties': enclaves in which groups have emerged as 'quasi state actors', or regions that are governed by separate de facto governments, with the potential to eventually form rival states.

Kalyvas (2006: 17) argues that civil wars have three objective characteristics: (1) at the outset the rivals are subject to a common authority, (2) there is a high level of military organization on both sides, and (3) there is a de facto territorial division between the two sides. These criteria are consistent with classical definitions (by Plato, Grotius, and Rousseau), which focused on the situation of divided sovereignty (which made a civil war necessary to restore order). This conception is expressed by Caesar's immediate reaction to the possibility that the rumours of Pompey's death in Egypt were not true: 'uselessly we have embroiled the nations in civil warfare, if in this world there is any other power than Caesar, if any land belongs to two' (Lucan, 1992: 206). Kalyvas equates a civil war situation with a polity beset specifically by territorial divisions—physical divisions which are insupportable to those, like Caesar, wanting to exercise authority (2006: 17). Yet these three criteria could cover many succession crises, palace coups, rebellions, and insurgencies that do not see this divisive logic work itself out to its ultimate conclusion. A de facto territorial division may be sustainable for long periods of time, and a palace coup may have few implications for the general population. The split polity thus helps define a civil war or revolutionary situation, but not an actual civil war.

To identify what is distinctive about civil war, a fourth criterion would be that in order for an internal military conflict to be a civil war, attitudes to political authority must become affected by the prospect of fragmentation. Fragmentation may be understood in the objective sense: 'the Syrian state is really disintegrating'. Yet the subjective fact that people anticipated the collapse of the Assad regime—and through their response furthered the process of fragmentation—is important too. The apprehension of disintegration, and not only in Syria, is so important that this subjective factor should be incorporated into the definition of what a civil war is. When people begin to apprehend the consequences of fragmentation and act accordingly, they lose that sense of shared fate which underpins any community. Hence these conflicts become potentially catastrophic. This fourth criterion is consistent with political scientist Roy Licklider's (1995) point that, in order for a conflict to be considered a civil war, the contending sides must, at least at the outset, face the prospect of having to live together in the future. At some stage during the process of state collapse in Yugoslavia, the conflict reached 'a tipping point' when the force for drastic change became unstoppable, and people gave up on the possibility of living together in the future. At that precise point people's anticipation of what was going to happen became a source of fragmentation in its own right.

That sense of shared fate can be understood psychologically. The self as an object can be divided into the material self, the social self, and the spiritual self. Each can be still further divided (James 2007: 291–402). The American psychologist William James (1890) elevated the personal self to a high position. Perhaps the personal self that is lost in civil war is a shared idea of the state or the willingness to coexist in the future. In psychology the loss of self is also often seen as a product of fragmentation: in the worst cases of psychotic disassociation, people can have more than one personal self, or the distinctiveness of these three selves may be lost. This is what is happening in Syria; the spatial, ideological, and sociological foundations of what was Syria are disintegrating. Licklider's fourth criterion is also compatible with the nationalism scholar Steven Grosby's stress on people's capacity to foresee the future differently as a source of human divisiveness, since rival visions of the future will emerge with these fears of fragmentation (Grosby 2005: 107). This fourth criterion is also an example of a 'structure of feeling' (Williams 1977), a concept which highlights the less tangible characteristics or 'feeling' of an era or point in time, the social experience that is 'in solution' and that has not yet crystallized into institutions or any explicit manifesto for the future. What makes a civil war situation a civil war is the addition of such a structure of feeling to an objective de facto territorial division; this then leads to the escalation of conflict to civil war proportions.

A criticism could be that this fourth criterion is subjective. One could invoke Thucydides. Scholars have noticed the parallels between his treatment of the effects of the plague in Athens, and those of stasis in Corcyra. No one doubts that the visible signs he reports were evidence of these changes. Both are analysed as objective states into which people have fallen. Since studying the symptoms of illness is scientific, one could argue that the same method should be applied to contemporary conflicts. However, as the contemporary historian John Lukacs (2012: 11–13) has suggested, the dichotomy between objective and subjective reality assumed by this criticism is no longer applicable, even in natural sciences like physics. The way this 'structure of feeling' converts an objective situation into a real civil war—as an apprehension of reality, rather than a reaction to it—is an example of the human mind intruding into, and complicating the structure of events, as it inevitably does (ibid.: 13). If we are forced to hang on to the core assumptions of mechanical explanations of social events—causes must precede the effects, and objective situations must be anterior to subjective response—then we will not have grasped how the conviction that 'Syria will be the next Somalia' becomes an enormously important social fact too.

The question of scientific method takes us back to an issue posed in the introduction to this book: was Thucydides' focus on the moral distemper occasioned by stasis scientific? Social science has probably gone as far as it can go within disciplinary boundaries in trying to *define* civil war. The arts and the humanities have better insights into the *experience* they generally bring. Were we to extract images and metaphors of experiences of civil war from the literature of the past, the idea of fragmentation would still be prominent. Sovereignty to Hobbes was the 'soul' of the Commonwealth (1985 [1651]: 272). He likened the process which led people to seek sources of protection other than from the state to the soul's departure from the body. This 'soul' can be the state, the idea of the state, the political community, the nation, or simply the willingness to live together. For William James, the psychologist, the analogy to the soul was the personal self. Once it goes, the body (and by implication the state) is rendered lifeless or irreparably fragmented. More recently, the analysis of the Bolshevik revolution put forward by the Russian historian Pitirim Soronkin in his *Sociology of Revolution* (c. 1925), shows how the marks of such wars are inflicted on the bodies of a changing society. His work stressed, above all, the biological and demographic damage to the tissue of Russian society, specific examples being the physical degradation of the population, widespread disease, mental disturbances, falling birth rates, rising mortality rates, and famine (Sztompka 2014: 450). The painting by Salvador Dalí, 'Soft Construction with Boiled Beans: Premonitions of Civil War', also uses a bodily image to show how Spain in the 1930s was destroyed not by one thing, but by many afflictions at once. This is often what happens to the human body during a terminal illness, and takes us back to Thucydides' depiction of the plague in Athens during the Peloponnesian wars. Dalí, in his intuition that the distinctive experience of civil war should be understood not by comparison to other forms of war, but with reference to the mortal nature of political systems, was certainly not alone.

Conclusion

The conclusions to each chapter in this book discussed three issues. The first was the continuing importance of the state to civil war studies. Were the state (and state formation) not central to the explanation of why the post-1945 context has been so explosive, political science might become redundant in this field. Causes always have contexts, and to know the former we must understand the latter (Gaddis 2002: 97). Of the many reasons why the world that emerged after World War II made for such an explosive situation, the formation of so many new states was *the* critical factor. The importance of the state is stressed in this conclusion because the understanding of civil war in some of the most prominent contemporary approaches has not sufficiently taken the importance of the state and political explanations into account. The economists' emphasis on civil war as 'development in reverse' means that factors such as decision-making, state power and legitimacy—which were traditionally held to explain the rise and fall of states during conflicts—do not feature much in their theories. Perspectives on civil conflict linked to a humanitarian agenda, such as Keen's (2008) definition of some civil wars as 'complex emergencies', similarly rule out the primacy of politics. And finally, the stress on environmental factors (such as rough terrain) in 'large-N' causal explanations of why these conflicts occur is another reason why political scientists (and explanations which stress the primacy of politics) have been left in a state of relative under-employment in recent years.

This was not how things began. Thucydides is lauded for being the first political scientist. In his history of the Peloponnesian wars, the category of politics included two factors: the internal political competition within a state or nation, and the relations between states in times of peace and war. Underlying conditions (environmental or sociological) *do* frame and influence the political choices people make in these realms, but they do not make these political factors any less decisive (Kagan 2009: 229–30). And no amount of globalization has made the political issue of who can speak with the authority of the state less important. Angola, for example, is one of the poorest countries in the world and the way its rich deposits of natural resources attract outside interests, complicates its state-building efforts. Not surprisingly, the Angolan civil war has been recruited into a story of greed versus grievance, of weak and shadow states, of ethnic conflict, and of outside intervention. Yet both sides in its civil wars relied on the idea of the state in order to mobilize people. Each claimed legitimacy as the successor to the independence movement, as the symbol of anti-colonial resistance, and as provider for and defender of the Angolan people (Pearce 2012). Interviews done by the political scientist Justin Pearce (ibid.) on the way in which both UNITA and the MPLA projected an image as 'states in wartime', showed that non-combatants also appraised the claims of the two sides in terms of these categories. Diamonds or not, there was a struggle over who could speak with the authority of the state.

The second issue discussed in the conclusion to each chapter of this book is the indiscriminate way in which the concept of civil war is used in much of the recent literature. Koselleck showed that after the European Enlightenment, the concept of crisis was increasingly used to diagnose a relatively permanent world situation. Today a semantically bleached conception of civil war is now being used to make the same diagnosis with respect to much of the developing world. In ancient Greek, to diagnose a situation as one of crisis suggested the existence of two radical and irreconcilable alternatives, one of which the actors had to immediately choose (Koselleck 2002: 237). Crucially, each alternative was said to involve the saving or destruction of the existing order (Richter 1995: 55–6). This conception of conflict made the ability to make hard decisions the supreme virtue of politics. A useful definition of civil war should also highlight the *drama* of such moments and, given the danger of fragmentation, the implications of such moments for the continuance of the existing social order. If not all armed conflicts have implications for the continuance of the existing social order, they should *not* be called civil wars.

The third issue we have repeatedly revisited in this book is the problem of human divisiveness The traditional fear of civil war assumed that wars brought out the worst in human nature. This is expressed in the naturalist explanation of civil war. The situationalist explanation, on the other hand, was that the creation of more than 130 new states since 1918 provided a tailor-made context for so many civil wars. Yet any attempt at establishing the historical foundations of the form of divisiveness represented by civil war will always run into the simple question: why have civil wars arisen in *every* regime form known to humankind (Grosby 2005: 103)? Perhaps the creation of so many states provided only an opportunity for something in human nature never far below the surface. This epilogue has attempted to find a middle ground between these two perspectives on violent conflict. Readers can judge for themselves whether my use of the concept of fragmentation has provided such a bridge. Thucydides blamed stasis both on human nature and on the evolving Greek system of city states. Yet he knew that what sets in during civil war is less open to contextual explanation. Concepts such as crisis, escalation, polarization, radicalization, and here fragmentation, have been developed precisely for this reason. However well historical and sociological contexts explain *why* a conflict situation emerges, we also need to account for *how* human divisiveness expresses itself in those situations, and especially why one people breaks into two (or more). No doubt the situationalists are right: the contexts which make for really deep divisions are exceptional, and can be explained in terms of things going badly wrong. Yet their consequences cannot be predicted *ex ante*. Moreover, civil war results in the killing of one's neighbours, perhaps one's family, an aspect of human divisiveness that, in truth, is not explained by either perspective.

EXTERNAL INVOLVEMENT AND PEACE AGREEMENTS 1989–2014

Peace process	Agreement	Lasting	External parties involved
Angola	Luena Memorandum of Understanding	From 04/04/2002	UN verification
Angola	Lusaka Protocol	15/11/1994–1/12/1998	UN verification; UN Peacekeeping Force
Bangladesh	Chittagong Hill Tracts Peace Accord (CHT)	From 02/12/1997	UN verification
Bosnia-Herzegovina	General Framework Agreement for Peace in Bosnia-Herzegovina	From 21/11/1995	UN verification; International Arbitration Commission on Land; UN Peacekeeping Force
Burundi	Arusha Peace and Reconciliation Agreement for Burundi	From 28/08/2000	UN verification; UN Peacekeeping Force; Regional Peacekeeping Force; donors support; provisions for review of the agreement by external parties
Cambodia	Framework for a Comprehensive Political Settlement of the Cambodia Conflict	From 23/10/1991	UN Transitional Authority; UN verification; UN Peacekeeping Force; donors support

(continued)

Continued

Peace process	Agreement	Lasting	External parties involved
Congo	Agreement on Ending Hostilities in the Republic of Congo	From 29/12/1999	UN verification
Côte d'Ivoire	Ouagadougou Political Agreement (OPA)	From 04/04/2007	UN Peacekeeping Force; regional peacekeeping force; provisions for review of the agreement by external parties
Croatia	Erdut Agreement	From 12/11/1995	UN Transitional Authority; UN verification; UN Peacekeeping Force
Djibouti	Agreement for the Reform and Civil Concord	From 12/05/2001	Donor support
Djibouti	Accord de paix et de la reconciliation nationale	26/12/1994–01/02/1998	None
El Salvador	Chapultepec Peace Agreement	16/01/1992	UN verification; donor support; provisions for review of the agreement by external parties
Guatemala	Accord for a Firm and Lasting Peace	29/12/1996	UN verification; donor support
Guinea-Bissau	Abuja Peace Agreement	01/11/1998	UN verification
India	Memorandum of Settlement (Bodo Accord)	20/02/1993–2005	None

Indonesia	MoU between the Government of the Republic of Indonesia and the Free Aceh Movement	15/08/2005	UN verification
Lebanon	Taif Accord	22/10/1989	None (apart from syria)
Liberia	Accra Peace Agreement	18/08/2003	UN verification; UN Peacekeeping Force; regional peacekeeping force; donor support
Macedonia	Ohrid Agreement	13/08/2001	UN verification; donor support
Mali	National Pact	11/02/1992	Donor support
Mozambique	General Peace Agreement for Mozambique	04/10/1992	UN verification; UN Peacekeeping Force; donor support
Nepal	Comprehensive Peace Agreement	21/11/2006	Donor support; provisions for review of agreement by external parties
Niger	Agreement between the Republic Niger Government and the ORA	15/04/1995	Donor support
Papua New Guinea	Bougainville Peace Agreement	30/08/2001	UN verification; regional peacekeeping force; donor support; provisions for review of the agreement by external parties
Philippines	Mindanao Final Agreement	02/09/1996	UN verification; donor support; provisions for review of the agreement by external parties

(*continued*)

APPENDIX 1

Continued

Peace process	Agreement	Lasting	External parties involved
Rwanda	Arusha Accord, 4 August 1993	04/08/1993	UN verification; UN Peacekeeping Force; donor support
Senegal	General Peace Agreement between the Government of the Republic of Senegal and MFDC	30/12/2004	None
Sierra Leone	Lomé Peace Agreement	07/07/1999	UN verification; UN Peacekeeping Force; regional peacekeeping force; donor support; provisions for review of the agreement by external parties
Sierra Leone	Abidjan Peace Agreement	30/11/1996 – 01/05/1997	UN verification; donor support; provisions for review of agreement by external parties
South Africa	Interim Constitution Accord	17/11/1993	UN verification
Sudan	Sudan Comprehensive Peace Agreement	09/01/2005	UN verification; UN Peacekeeping Force; donor support; provisions for review of agreement by external parties
Tajikistan	General Agreement on the Establishment of Peace and National Accord in Tajikistan	27/06/1997	UN verification; regional peacekeeping force; donor support
Timor Leste	Agreement between the Republic of Indonesia and the Portuguese	05/05/1999	UN Transitional Authority; UN verification; UN

242

	Republic on the question of Timor Leste		Peacekeeping Force; donor support
United Kingdom	Northern Ireland Good Friday Agreement	10/04/ 1998	UN verification; provisions for review of agreement by external parties

Source: The table is based on The Peace Accords Matrix, 2012, by the Kroc Institute for International Peace Studies, University of Notre Dame. The Matrix codes all comprehensive peace agreements and their components since 1989. It lists Peace Agreements defined as a written document produced through a process of negotiation.

APPROACHES TO PEACE AND THE CONTENT OF PEACE AGREEMENTS 1989–2014

Peace process	Agreement	Force and security	Political and administrative reforms/Social changes	Social and economic equality	Reconciliation
Angola	Luena Memorandum of Understanding	Case fire; demobilization; disarmament; withdrawal of troops; amnesty; reintegration of ex-combatants	Transnational government; political and administrative reform; decentralization; military and police reform; human rights; media reform		Dispute resolution committee
Angola	Lusaka Protocol	Case fire; demobilization; disarmament; amnesty; reintegration of ex-combatants	Transnational government; political and administrative reform; decentralization; military and police reform; human rights; media reform		

Bangladesh	Chittagong Hill Tracts Peace Accord (CHT)	demobilization; disarmament; withdrawal of troops; reintegration of ex-combatants; prisoner release; amnesty	Political reform; decentralization; indigenous minority rights; citizenship reform	Social and economic development plan	Dispute resolution committee
Bosnia-Herzegovina	General Framework Agreement for Peace in Bosnia-Herzegovina	Cease fire; withdrawal of troops; prisoner release; programmes targeting paramilitary groups; amnesty; guarantees for possibility of return for refugees	Transnational government; constitutional reform; legislature and executive reform; political reform; boundaries demarcation; territorial power-sharing; decentralization; human rights; citizenship reform; rights guarantee for cultural minorities	Social and economic development plan	
Burundi	Arusha Peace and Reconciliation Agreement for Burundi	Case fire; demobilization; disarmament; withdrawal of troops; reintegration of ex-combatants; prisoner release; programmes	Transnational government; constitutional reform; executive and judiciary reform; political and administrative reform; military and police	Social and economic development plan; usage of natural resources agreements	Official body established to investigate human rights abuses; dispute resolution committee

(continued)

Continued

Peace process	Agreement	Force and security	Political and administrative reforms/Social changes	Social and economic equality	Reconciliation
		targeting paramilitary groups; amnesty; guarantees for possibility of return for refugees	reform; human rights; women and children rights; education reform; media reform; minority rights		
Cambodia	Framework for a Comprehensive Political Settlement of the Cambodia Conflict	Case fire; demobilization; disarmament; withdrawal of troops; reintegration of ex-combatants; arms embargo; prisoner release; programmes targeting paramilitary groups; guarantees for possibility of return for refugees	Transnational government; constitution reform; judiciary reform; political reform; military reform; human rights	Social and economic development plan	
Congo	Agreement on Ending Hostilities in the Republic of Congo	Ceasefire; demobilization; disarmament; reintegration of ex-	Constitutional reform; political and administrative reform; military and police		

		combatants; prisoner release; programmes targeting paramilitary groups; amnesty; guarantees for possibility of return for refugees	reform; education reform	Dispute resolution committee
Côte d'Ivoire	Ouagadougou Political Agreement (OPA)	Ceasefire; demobilization; disarmament; reintegration of ex-combatants; amnesty; arms embargo	Transitional government; political and administrative reform; military and police reform; citizenship reform	
Croatia	Erdut Agreement	Disarmament; guarantees for possibility of return for refugees	Police reform; human rights; citizenship reform	Inter-ethnic/state mediation
Djibouti	Agreement for the Reform and Civil Concord	Ceasefire; demobilization; disarmament; reintegration of ex-combatants; prisoner release; guarantees for possibility of return for refugees	Political and administrative reform; decentralization; military reform; citizenship reform; education reform; media reform	Social and economic development plan — Reparations

(continued)

Continued

Peace process	Agreement	Force and security	Political and administrative reforms/Social changes	Social and economic equality	Reconciliation
Djibouti	Accord de paix et de la réconciliation nationale	Ceasefire; reintegration of ex-combatants; amnesty; guarantees for possibility of return for refugees	Political and reform; decentralization; military reform	Social and economic development plan	
El Salvador	Chapultepec Peace Agreement	Ceasefire; demobilization; disarmament; reintegration of ex-combatants; prisoner release; programmes targeting paramilitary groups; guarantees for possibility of return for refugees	Constitutional changes; jurisdiction reform; political and administrative reform; military and police reform; human rights; media reform	Social and economic development plan; usage of natural resources agreements	Official body established to investigate human rights abuses; dispute resolution committee
Guatemala	Accord for a Firm and Lasting Peace	Ceasefire; demobilization; disarmament; reintegration of ex-combatants;	Constitutional reform; executive, legislature, and jurisdiction reform; political and administrative reform;	Social and economic development plan; usage of natural	Inter-ethnic/state mediation; official body established to investigate human

				resources agreements	rights abuses; repatriations
		programmes targeting paramilitary groups; amnesty; guarantees for possibility of return for refugees	decentralization; military and police reform; human rights; indigenous minority rights; women rights; education reform; official language and symbol change; rights guarantee for cultural minorities; media reform		
Guinea-Bissau	Abuja Peace Agreement	Ceasefire; guarantees for possibility of return for refugees	Transitional government		
India	Memorandum of Settlement (Bodo Accord)	Demobilization; disarmament; reintegration of ex-combatants; amnesty	Decentralization; boundary demarcation; administration reform; jurisdiction reform; military and police reform; indigenous minority rights; education reform; official language and symbol change; rights	Social and economic development plan	Repatriations

(continued)

Continued

Peace process	Agreement	Force and security	Political and administrative reforms/Social changes	Social and economic equality	Reconciliation
			guarantee for cultural minorities; minority rights		
Indonesia	MoU between the Government of the Republic of Indonesia and the Free Aceh Movement	Ceasefire; demobilization; disarmament; reintegration of ex-combatants; prisoner release; amnesty	Boundary demarcation; political reform; decentralization; jurisdiction reform; military and police reform; human rights; citizenship reform; official language and symbol reform; rights guarantee for cultural minorities; media reform	Social and economic development plan; usage of natural resources agreements	Official body established to investigate human rights abuses; dispute resolution committee; repatriations; arbitration commission to address damage and loss
Lebanon	Taif Accord	Programmes targeting paramilitary groups;	Transnational government;	Social and economic	Dispute resolution committee

		guarantees for possibility of return for refugees; withdrawal of troops	executive, legislative, and jurisdiction reform; political and administrative reform; decentralization; military reform; education reform; media reform	development plan	
Liberia	Accra Peace Agreement	Ceasefire; demobilization; disarmament; reintegration of ex-combatants; prisoner release; programmes targeting paramilitary groups; amnesty; guarantees for possibility of return for refugees	Transnational government; constitutional changes; political and administrative reform; decentralization; military and police reform; human rights; women and children rights	Social and economic development plan	Official body established to investigate human rights abuses; dispute resolution committee
Macedonia	Ohrid Agreement	Ceasefire; disarmament; programmes targeting paramilitary groups; guarantees for	Legislature and jurisdiction reform; constitutional reform; boundary demarcation; political and administrative		

(continued)

Continued

Peace process	Agreement	Force and security	Political and administrative reforms/Social changes	Social and economic equality	Reconciliation
		possibility of return for refugees	reform; decentralization; military and police reform; indigenous minority rights; education reform; official language and symbol change; media reform		
Mali	National Pact	Ceasefire; demobilization; disarmament; guarantees for possibility of return for refugees; withdrawal of troops	Legislative reform; decentralization; administrative reform; military and police reform	Social and economic development plan	Official body established to investigate human rights abuses; dispute resolution committee; reparations
Mozambique	General Peace Agreement for Mozambique	Ceasefire; demobilization; disarmament;	Executive reform; constitutional reform; political reform;		Dispute resolution committee

		reintegration of ex-combatants; prisoner release; programmes targeting paramilitary groups; amnesty; guarantees for possibility of return for refugees; withdrawal of troops	territorial power-sharing; military and police reform; human rights; media reform		
Nepal	Comprehensive Peace Agreement	Ceasefire; demobilization; disarmament; reintegration of ex-combatants; prisoner release	Transnational government; executive and legislature reform; constitutional change; political reform; decentralization; military reform; human rights; indigenous minority rights; women and children rights; education reform; minority rights	Social and economic development plan; usage of natural resources agreements	Inter-ethnic/state mediation; official body established to investigate human rights abuses; dispute resolution committee; reparations
Niger	Agreement between the Republic of Niger	Ceasefire; demobilization; disarmament; reintegration of ex-	Decentralization; military reform; education reform; official language and	Social and economic development plan	Dispute resolution committee

(continued)

Continued

Peace process	Agreement	Force and security	Political and administrative reforms/Social changes	Social and economic equality	Reconciliation
	Government and the ORA	combatants; prisoner release; amnesty; guarantees for possibility of return for refugees	symbol change; cultural protections; media reform		
Papua New Guinea	Bougainville Peace Agreement	Ceasefire; disarmament; reintegration of ex-combatants; amnesty; withdrawal of troops	Executive reform; constitutional reform; boundary demarcation; political and administrative reform; decentralization; jurisdiction reform; police reform; human rights; right of self-determination for the region; independence referendum	Social and economic development plan; usage of natural resources agreements	Dispute resolution committee
Philippines	Mindanao Final Agreement	Ceasefire; reintegration of ex-combatants;	Transnational government; executive; legislation and jurisdiction reform; constitutional	Social and economic development plan; usage of natural	Inter-ethnic/state mediation

			reform; boundary demarcation; decentralization; military and police reform; human rights; indigenous minority rights; education reform; official language and symbol change; cultural protections	resources agreements	
Rwanda	Arusha Accord, 4 August 1993	Ceasefire; demobilization; disarmament; reintegration of ex-combatants; prisoner release; guarantees for possibility of return for refugees; withdrawal of troops	Transnational government; executive, legislation, and jurisdiction reform; constitutional reform; political and administrative reform; military and police reform; human rights; citizenship reform	Social and economic development plan	Inter-ethnic/state mediation; official body established to investigate human rights abuses
Senegal	General Peace Agreement between the Government of the	Ceasefire; demobilization; disarmament; reintegration of ex-combatants; amnesty;	Human rights	Social and economic development plan	

(continued)

Continued

Peace process	Agreement	Force and security	Political and administrative reforms/Social changes	Social and economic equality	Reconciliation
	Republic of Senegal and MFDC	guarantees for possibility of return for refugees			
Sierra Leone	Lomé Peace Agreement	Ceasefire; demobilization; disarmament; reintegration of ex-combatants; prisoner release; programmes targeting paramilitary groups; amnesty; guarantees for possibility of return for refugees	Transnational government; constitutional reform; political reform; military reform; human rights; women rights; education reform	Usage of natural resources agreements	Official body established to investigate human rights abuses; dispute resolution committee; reparations
Sierra Leone	Abidjan Peace Agreement	Ceasefire; demobilization; disarmament; reintegration of ex-combatants; prisoner release; programmes	Political and administrative reform; jurisdiction reform; military and police reform; human rights;	Social and economic development plan; usage of natural	Official body established to investigate human rights abuses; dispute resolution committee

targeting paramilitary groups; amnesty; withdrawal of troops | education reform; media reform | resources agreements

South Africa	Interim Constitution Accord	Ceasefire; demobilization; reintegration of ex-combatants; prisoner release; amnesty	Transnational government; executive, legislation, and jurisdiction reform; constitutional reform; political reform; decentralization; military and police reform; human rights; citizenship reform; children rights; education reform; cultural protections; official language and symbol change	Social and economic development plan	Official body established to investigate human rights abuses; dispute resolution committee
Sudan	Sudan Comprehensive Peace Agreement	Ceasefire; demobilization; disarmament; reintegration of ex-combatants; prisoner	Transnational government; executive, legislation, and jurisdiction reform; constitutional	Social and economic development plan; usage of natural	Inter-ethnic/state mediation; official body established to investigate human

(continued)

Continued

Peace process	Agreement	Force and security	Political and administrative reforms/Social changes	Social and economic equality	Reconciliation
		release; programmes targeting paramilitary groups; guarantees for possibility of return for refugees; arms embargo; withdrawal of troops	reform; political and administrative reform; decentralization; boundary demarcation; territorial power-sharing; military and police reform; human rights; right of self-determination; women and children rights; education reform; cultural reform; official language and symbol change; media reforms; minority rights; independence referendum	resources agreements	rights abuses; dispute resolution committee
Tajikistan	General Agreement on the	Ceasefire; demobilization;	Transnational government; executive		Dispute resolution committee

	Agreement				
	Peace and National Accord in Tajikistan	reintegration of ex-combatants; prisoner release; programmes targeting paramilitary groups; guarantees for possibility of return for refugees; amnesty	reform; constitutional reform; political reform; military and police reform; media reform		
Timor Leste	Agreement between the Republic of Indonesia and the Portuguese Republic on the question of Timor Leste	Disarmament; withdrawal of troops	Constitutional reform; police reform; right of self-determination; independence referendum		
United Kingdom	Northern Ireland Good Friday Agreement	Ceasefire; demobilization; disarmament; reintegration of ex-combatants; prisoner release; programmes targeting paramilitary groups	Transnational government; constitutional reform; political reform; decentralization; judiciary reform; police reform; human rights; right of self-determination;	Social and economic development plan	Inter-ethnic/state mediation; dispute resolution committee; reparations

(continued)

Continued

Peace process	Agreement	Force and security	Political and administrative reforms/Social changes	Social and economic equality	Reconciliation
			citizenship reform; women rights; education reform; official language and symbol change; minority rights; independence referendum		

Source: The table is based on The Peace Accords Matrix, 2012, by the Kroc Institute for International Peace Studies, University of Notre Dame. The Matrix codes all comprehensive peace agreements and their components since 1989.

BIBLIOGRAPHY

Abrams, Philip. 1988. 'Notes on the Difficulty of Studying the State'. *Journal of Historical Sociology*, 1(1), 58–98.

Abulafia, David. 2014. *The Great Sea: A Human History of the Mediterranean*. London: Penguin.

Ackroyd, Peter. 2013. *Three Brothers: A Novel*. London: Chatto and Windus.

Alapuro, Risto. 2002. 'Coping with the Civil War of 1918 in Twenty-first Century Finland'. In K. Christie and R. Cribb (eds.), *Historical Injustice and Democratic Transition in Eastern Asia and Northern Europe: Ghosts at the Table of Democracy*. London and New York: Routledge, pp. 169–84.

Alapuro, Risto. 2003. 'Vallankumous'. In Matti Hyvárinen et al. (eds.), *Suomen politittisen kullusinen kasitehistoria*. Tampere: VastePano, pp. 519–68.

Alapuro, Risto. 19 May 2010. 'Violence in the Finnish Civil War in Today's Perspective'. Paper presented at the seminar *History, Memory, Politics*, Helsinki Collegium for Advanced Studies.

Alapuro, Risto. 2014. 'The Legacy of the Civil War of 1918 in Finland'. In B. Kissane (ed.), *After Civil War: Division, Reconstruction and Reconciliation in Contemporary Europe, 1918–2011*. Philadelphia: Pennsylvania University Press, pp. 17–43.

Alter, Peter. 1994. *Nationalism*. 2nd edn. London: Edward Arnold.

Appian. 1996. *The Civil Wars*. Trans. John Carter. London: Penguin.

Armitage, David. 2009. 'Ideas of Civil War in Seventeenth Century England'. *Annals of the Japanese Association for the Study of Puritanism*, 4, 4–18.

Artik, Çiğdem. November 2014. 'I Too Have Kurdish Friends!' *Research Turkey*, 3(2), 6–9. London Centre for Policy Analysis and Research on Turkey.

Aurelius, Marcus. 2003. *Meditations*. Trans. Gregory Hays. New York: The Modern Library.

Barbal, Maria. 2010. *Stone in a Landslide*. London: Peirene Press.

Barker, Rodney. 2001. *Legitimating Identities: The Self-Presentation of Rulers and their Subjects*. Cambridge: Cambridge University Press.

Barkey, Henri and Graham E. Fuller. 1998. *Turkey's Kurdish Question*. Boston: Rowman and Littlefield.

Barresi, John and Raymond Martin. 2006. *The Rise and Fall of Soul and Self: An Intellectual History of Personal Identity*. New York: Columbia University Press.

Beiser, Frederick. 2005. *Hegel*. London: Routledge.

Belki, Helio. 2003. 'Angola and the Fragmentation of the Post-colonial African State'. In R. Brian Ferguson (ed.), *State, Identity and Violence: Political Disintegration in the Post-Cold War World*. New York: Routledge, pp. 243–61.

Bell, John P. 1971. *Crisis in Costa Rica: The 1948 Revolution*. Texas: University of Texas Press.

Bellow, Saul. 1993. *Something to Remember Me By: Three Tales*. London: Penguin Books.

Berdal, Matts and Spiros Economides (eds.). 2007. *UN Interventionism 1991–2004*. Cambridge: Cambridge University Press.

Berent, Moshe. 1998. 'Stasis, or the Greek Invention of Politics'. *History of Political Thought*, 19(3), 331–62.

Bermeo, Nancy. 2003. 'What the Democratization Literature Says or Doesn't Say about Post-war Democratization'. *Global Governance*, 9, 159–77.

Bertelsen, Bjorn E. 'War, Peace and Development in Mozambique: A Critical Assessment'. Paper presented to the 'Peace Building and Post-war Aid' workshop, CMI, Bergen, June 2005.

Boeschoten, Riki van. 2015. 'Enemies of the Nation—A Nation of Enemies: The Long Greek Civil War'. In B. Kissane (ed.), *After Civil War: Division, Reconstruction and Reconciliation in Contemporary Europe, 1918–2011*. Philadelphia: Pennsylvania University Press, pp. 93–121.

Boethius, Ancius. 1999. *The Consolation of Philosophy*. London: Penguin.

Bolsinger, Eckard. 2001. *The Autonomy of the Political: Carl Schmitt's and Lenin's Poltical Realism*. Westport: Greenwood Publishing Group.

Braudel, Fernand. 1995. *A History of Civilizations*. Trans. Richard Mayne. London: Penguin.

Braudel, Fernand. 2002. *The Mediterranean in the Ancient World*. Trans. Sián Reynolds. London: Penguin.

Breuilly, John. 1996. 'Approaches to Nationalism'. In Gopal Balakrishan and Benedict Anderson (eds.), *Mapping the Nation*. Verso, London, pp. 146–75.

Brodsky, Joseph. 1999. *On Grief and Reason and Other Essays*. London: Penguin.

Brown, Graham K. and Arnem Langer (eds.). 2012. *Elgar Handbook of Civil War and Fragile States*. Cheltenham: Elgar.

Brown, Michael (ed.). 1996. *The International Dimensions of Internal Conflict*. Cambridge, MA: MIT Press.

Brubaker, Rogers. 1996. *Nationalism Reframed: Nationhood and the National Question in the New Europe*. Cambridge: Cambridge University Press.

Brubaker, Rogers. 2004. *Ethnicity Without Groups*. Cambridge: Harvard University Press.

Brunner, Otto, Werner Conze, and Reinhart Koselleck. 1972. *Geschichtliche Grundbegriffe: Historiches Lexikon zur politisch-sozialer Sprache in Deutschland*. Band 5 Pro-Soz. Stuttgart: Klett-Cotta.

Buber, Martin. 1958. *I and Thou*. London and New York: Continuum.

Burke, Edmund. 1969 [1790]. *Reflections on the Revolution in France and on the Proceedings in Certain Societies in London Relevant to that Event*. Harmondsworth: Penguin.

Burrow, John. 2009. *A History of Histories: Epics, Chronicles, Romances and Enquiries from Herodotus & Thucydides to the Twentieth Century*. London: Penguin.

Cartledge, Paul. 2009. *Ancient Greek Political Thought in Practice*. Cambridge: Cambridge University Press.

Casanova, Julián. 2012. *A Short History of the Spanish Civil War*. London: I. B. Taurus.

Casanova, Julián. 2013. *España Partida en Dos*. Madrid: Allianza.

Casier, Marlies and Joost Jongerden. 2010. *Nationalisms and Politics in Turkey*. London: Routledge.

Cederman, Lars-Erik, Kristian Skrede Gledistch, and Holvard Buhaugh. 2013. *Inequality, Grievances and Civil War*. Cambridge: Cambridge University Press.

Centeno, Miguel Angel et al. 2013. 'Internal Wars and Latin American Nationalism'. In John A. Hall and Sinisa Malešević (eds.), *Nationalism and War*. Cambridge: Cambridge University Press, pp. 279–306.

The Chambers Dictionary. 2013. Ed. Catherine Schwarz. Edinburgh: Chambers Harrap.

Checkel, Jeffrey, T. 2011. 'The Social Dynamics of Civil War: Insights from Constructivist Theory'. *Simmons Papers in International Relations*, 11. Simon Fraser University.

Checkel, Jeffrey. T. 2013. *Transnational Dynamics of Civil War*. Cambridge: Cambridge University Press.

Clogg, Richard. 2013. *A Concise History of Greece*. 3rd edn. Cambridge: Cambridge University Press.

Coakley, John. 2012. *Nationalism, Ethnicity and the State: Making and Breaking Nations*. London: Sage.

Collier, Paul. 2010. *Wars, Guns and Votes: Democracy in Dangerous Places*, London: Vintage.

Collier, Paul et al. 2003. *Breaking the Conflict Trap: Civil War and Development Policy 2003*. Washington DC: World Bank/Oxford University Press.

Collier, Paul and Anke Hoeffer. 2000. *Greed and Grievance in Civil War*. Policy Research Paper (2355). Washington DC: The World Bank.

Collier, Paul, Anke Hoeffler, and Dominic Rohner. 2009. 'Beyond Greed and Grievance: Feasibility and Civil War'. *Oxford Economic Papers*, 61, 1–27.

Collier, Paul and Nicos Sambanis (eds.). 2005. *Understanding Civil Wars: Evidence and Analysis. II: Europe, Central Asia and Other Regions*. Washington DC: World Bank.

Conor, Walker. 1980. 'Nationalism and Political Illegitimacy'. *Canadian Review of Studies of Nationalism*, VII, 201–28.

Cramer, Christopher. 2006. *Civil War Is Not a Stupid Thing*. London: Hurst & Co.

Cressy, David. 2006. *England on Edge: Crisis and Revolution 1640–1642*. Oxford: Oxford University Press.

Debord, Guy. 1995. *The Society of the Spectacle*. New York: Zone Books.

Diamond, Jared. 2006. *Collapse: How Societies Choose to Fail or Succeed*. London: Penguin.

Diner, Dan. 2008. *Cataclysms: A History of the Twentieth Century from Europe's Edge*. Madison: University of Wisconsin.

Dostoyevsky, Fyodor. 1999 [1868–9]. *Notes from the Underground and The Gambler*. Trans. J. Kentish. Oxford, New York: Oxford University Press.

Doyle, Michael. 2006. *Making War Building Peace: UN Peace Operations*. Princeton: Princeton University Press, 2006.

Eastmond, Marita and Anders H. 2010. 'Beyond Reconciliation: Social Reconstruction after the Bosnian War'. *Focaol-Journal of Global and Historical Anthropology*, 57, 3–16.

Eckhardt, William. 1992. *Civilization, Empire and Wars: A Quantitative Study*. McFarland and Co. Inc.

Eckstein, Harry. 1964. 'Introduction: Toward the theoretical Study of Internal War'. In Harry Eckstein (ed.), *Internal War: Problems and Approaches*. London: Collier-Macmillan, pp. 1–33.

Eckstein, Harry. 1965. 'On the Etiology of Internal Wars'. *History and Theory*, 4(2), 133–63.

Elbadawi, Ibrahim and Nicholas Sambanis. 2000. '"Why Are There So Many Civil Wars in Africa?" Understanding and Predicting Civil War'. *Journal of African Economies*, 9(3), 244–69.

Elias, Norbert. 1969. *The Civilising Process. I: The History of Manners*. Oxford: Blackwell.

Elias, Norbert. 1982. *The Civilising Process. II: State Formation and Civilisation*. Oxford: Blackwell.

Eliot, T. S. 1974. *Collected Poems 1909–1962*. London: Faber and Faber.

Etzioni, Amitai. 2007. 'Reconstruction: An Agenda'. *Journal of Intervention and Statebuilding* (1), 27–45.

Evans, Martin and John Phillips. 2007. *Algeria: Anger of the Dispossessed*. New Haven and London. Yale University Press.

Fanon, Frantz. 2001. *The Wretched of the Earth*. London: Penguin.

Fearon, James. D. 2004. 'Why Do Some Civil Wars Last So Much Longer than Others?' *Journal of Peace Research*, 41(3), 275–301.

Fearon, James and David Laitin. 2003. 'Ethnicity, Insurgency and Civil War'. *American Political Science Review*, 97(1), 75–90.

Feldman, Arnold S. 1964. 'Violence and Volatility: The Likelihood of Revolution'. In Harry Eckstein (ed.), *Internal War: Problems and Approaches*. London: Collier-Macmillan, pp. 111–29.

Ferguson, R. Brian. 2003. 'Introduction: Violent Conflict and Control of the State'. In R. Brian Ferguson (ed.), *State, Identity and Violence: Political Disintegration in the Post-Cold War World*. New York: Routledge, pp. 1–59.

Field, Bonnie N. 2010. *Spain's Second Transition: The Socialist Government of Jose Luis Zapatero*. London: Routledge.

Filiu, Jean-Pierre. 2011. *The Arab Revolution: Ten Lessons from the Democratic Uprisings*. London: Hurst & Co.

Foner, Eric. 2002. *Reconstruction: America's Unfinished Revolution, 1863–1877*. New York: Harper Collins.

Forsberg, Tuomas. 2009. 'Forgiveness, Post Conflict Justice and the Finnish Civil War 1918: Reconciliation without Truth'. Paper Prepared for Presentation at the Annual Convention of the International Studies Association, New York.

Fuentes, Juan J. 2008. 'Guerra Civil'. In Javier Fernández Sebastián and Juan Francisco Fuentes (eds.), *Diccionario politico y social del siglo XX espanol*. Madrid: Alianza Editorial, pp. 609–17.

Fusi, Juan Pablo. 2012. *Historia Mínima de España*. Madrid: Turner.

Gadamer, Hans-Georg. 1996. *The Enigma of Health: The Art of Healing in a Scientific Age*. Trans. J. Gaiger and N. Walker. Stanford: Stanford University Press.

Gaddis, John Lewis. 2002. *The Landscapes of History: How Historians Map the Past*. Oxford and New York: Oxford University Press.

Gardner, Howard. 1976. *The Quest for Mind: Piaget, Levi-Strauss and the Structuralist Movement*. London: Quartet Books.

Gellner, Ernest. 1983. *Nations and Nationalism*. London: Basil Blackwell.

Ghani, Ashraf, Clare Lockhart, and Michael Carnahan. 2006. 'An Agenda for State Building in the Twentieth Century'. *Fletcher Forum of World Affairs*, 30(1), 101–23.

Ghobarah, Hazem Adam, Paul Huth, and Bruce Russett. 2003. 'Civil Wars Kill and Maim People: Long after the Shooting Stops'. *American Political Science Review*, 97(2), 189–202.

Girard, René. 1995. *Violence and the Sacred*. Athlone Press: London.

Goldstein, Slavko. 2013. *1941: The Year that Keeps Returning*. New York: New York Review of Books Collection.

Goldstone, Jack. 2008. 'Pathways to State Failure'. *Conflict Management and Peace*, 25(4), 285–96.

González Calleja, Eduardo. 2013. *Las Guerres Civiles: Perspectivas de Analysis desde las Ciencias Sociales*. Madrid: Catarata.

Graham, Helen. 2005. *The Spanish Civil War: A Very Short Introduction*. Oxford: Oxford University Press.

Gramsci, Antonio. 1975. *The Modern Prince and Other Writings*. New York: International Publishers.

Grosby, Stephen. 2005. *Nationalism: A Very Short Introduction*. Oxford: Oxford University Press.

Grossman, David. 2008. *Writing in the Dark: Essays on Literature and Politics*. New York: Farrar, Straus and Giroux.

Grotius, Hugo. 1724 [1613]. *Le Droit de la guerre et de la paix, 1583–1645*. Amsterdam: Chez Pierre de Coup.

Gunter, Michael. M. 2012. 'The Kurds'. *Oxford Bibliographies Online* (added 24 April). www.oxfordbibliographies.com.

Hall, John A. 2010. 'State Failure'. In Glenn Morgan et al. (eds.), *The Oxford Handbook of Comparative Institutional Analysis*. Oxford: Oxford University Press.

Hall, John. A. and Siniṣa Malešević (eds.). 2013. *Nationalism and War*. Cambridge: Cambridge University Press.

Hamberg, Stephen. 2013. 'Transnational Advocacy Networks, Rebel Groups, and Demobilization of Child Soldiers in Sudan'. In Jeffrey Checkel (ed.), *Transnational Dynamics of Civil War*. Cambridge: Cambridge University Press, pp. 149–73.

Hampson, Fen Osler. 1996. *Nurturing Peace: Why Peace Settlements Succeed or Fail*. Washington, DC: U.S. Institute of Peace.

Hardt, Michael and Antonio Negri. 2004. *Multitude: War and Democracy in the Age of Empire*. New York: Penguin.

Harpviken, Kristian Berg and Sarah Kenyon Lischer. 2013. 'Refugee Militancy in Exile and upon Return in Afghanistan and Rwanda'. In Jeffrey Checkel (ed.), *Transnational Dynamics of Civil War*. Cambridge: Cambridge University Press, pp. 89–120.

Heaney, Seamus. *The Cure of Troy: A Version of Sophocles Philoctetes*. London: Faber and Faber.

Hegre, Håvard et al. 2001. 'Toward a Democratic Civil Peace? Democracy, Political Change, and Civil War, 1816–1992'. *American Political Science Review*, 95(1), 22–48.

Hironaka, Anne. 2008. *Neverending Wars: The International Community, Weak States, and the Perpetuation of Civil Wars*. Cambridge, MA: Harvard University Press.

Hobbes, Thomas. 1985 [1651]. *The Leviathan*. Ed. C. B. McPherson. London: Penguin.

Hobsbawm, Eric. 1995. *The Age of Extremes: The Short Twentieth Century, 1914–1999*. London: Michael Joseph.

Hobsbawm, Eric. 2007. 'War and Peace in the Twentieth Century'. In Eric Hobsbawm, *Globalisation, Democracy and Terrorism*. London: Little Brown, pp. 15–31.

Holsti, Kalevi. 1996. *War, State and the State of War*. Cambridge: Cambridge University Press.

Hook, Laurie van. 2013. 'Yugoslavian Civil War 1991–1995'. *Oxford Bibliographies* (added 24 July). www.oxfordbibliographies.com.

Hughes, James. 2007. *Chechnya: From Nationalism to Jihad*. Philadelphia: University of Pennsylvania Press.

Hughes, Robert. 2004. *Barcelona: The Great Enchantress*. Washington DC: The National Geographic Society.

Hutchinson, John. 2005. *Nations as Zones of Conflict*. London: Sage.

Hyde, Edward: The Earl of Clarendon. 2009. *The History of the Rebellion: A New Selection*. Ed. Paul Seaward. New York: Oxford University Press.

James, William. 1890. *Principles of Psychology*. Vol. 1. New York: H. Holt and Company.

Jongerden, Joost. 2015. 'Under (Re)Construction: The State, the Production of Identity, and the Countryside in the Kurdistan Region in Turkey'. In B. Kissane (ed.), *After Civil War: Division, Reconstruction and Reconciliation in Contemporary Europe, 1918–2011*. Philadelphia: Pennsylvania University Press, pp. 150–87.

Juliá, Santos. 2010. *Hoy no es ayer: Ensayos sobre la España del siglo XX*. Madrid: Rbalibros).

Kagan, Donald. 2009. *Thucydides: The Reinvention of History*. New York: Penguin.

Kaldor, Mary. 1999. *New and Old Wars: Organised Violence in a Globalised Era*. Cambridge: Cambridge University Press.

Kalyvas, Stathis N. 1999. 'The Greek Civil War in Retrospect'. *Correspondence: An International Review of Culture and Society*, 4, 10–11.

Kalyvas, Stathis N. 2001. 'New and Old Wars: A Valid Distinction?' *World Politics*, 54(1), 99–118.

Kalyvas, Stathis N. 2006. *The Logic of Violence in Civil War*. Cambridge: Cambridge University Press.

Kamen, Henry. 2007. *The Disinherited: Exile and the Making of Spanish Culture 1492–1975*. Harper Collins: New York.

Kant, Emmanuel. 2007 [1795]. *Perpetual Peace: A Philosophical Essay*. Trans. M. Campbell Smith. Montana: Kessinger Publishers.

Kapuściński, Ryszard. 2001. *Another Day of Life*. London: Penguin.

Kapuściński, Ryszard. 2007. 'The Desert and the Sea'. In Ryszard Kapuściński, *Travels with Herodotus*. London: Allen Lane, pp. 221–9.

Kasfir, Nelson. 2004. 'Domestic Anarchy, Security Dilemmas, and Violent Predation'. In Robert Rotberg (ed.), *When States Fail: Causes and Consequences*. Princeton and Oxford: Princeton University Press, pp. 53–76.

Kaufmann, Erik. 2012. 'The Northern Ireland Peace Process in an Age of Austerity'. *The Political Quarterly*, 83(2), 203–9.

Keane, John. 2004. *Democracy and Violence*. Cambridge: Cambridge University Press.

Kedourie, Elie. 1960. *Nationalism*. London: Hutchinson.

Kedourie, Elie. 1994. 'Nationalism and Self-determination'. In John Hutchinson, and Anthony D. Smith (eds.), *Nationalism*. Oxford: Oxford University Press, pp. 49–55.

Keen, David. 2006. *Endless Wars? Hidden Functions of the War on Terror*. London: Pluto Press.

Keen, David. 2008. *Complex Emergencies*. Cambridge: Polity Press.

Keen, David. 2012. *Useful Enemies*. New Haven: Yale University Press.

Kelly, Angeline (ed.). 2000. *Liam O' Flaherty: The Collected Stories*. Vol. 1. Palgrave: MacMillan.

King, Charles. 2001. 'The Myth of Ethnic Warfare'. Foreign Affairs, 80(6), 165–70.

Kissane, Bill. 2005. *The Politics of the Irish Civil War*. Oxford: Oxford University Press.

Kissane, Bill (ed.). 2015. *After Civil War: Division, Reconstruction and Reconciliation in Contemporary Europe, 1918–2011*. Philadelphia, PA: Pennsylvania University Press.

Kissane, Bill and Nick Sitter. 2013. 'Ideas in Conflict: The Nationalism Literature and the Comparative Study of Civil War'. *Nationalism and Ethnic Politics*, 19(1), 38–53.

Kolakowski, Leszek. 2012. *Is God Happy? Selected Essays*. London: Penguin.

Koselleck, Reinhart. 1988. *Critique and Crisis: Enlightenment and Pathogenesis of Modern Society*. Cambridge, MA: MIT Press.

Koselleck, Rienhardt. 2002. *The Practice of Conceptual History: Timing History, Spacing Concepts*. Trans. Todd Presner, Kerstin Behnke, and Welge Jobst. Stanford: Stanford University Press.

Koselleck, Reinhart. 2004. *Futures Past: On the Semantics of Historical Time*. Trans. and Intro. Keith Tribe. New York: Columbia University Press.

Kostovicova, Denisa and Vesna Bojicic-Dzelilovic. 2015. 'Ethnicity Pays: The Political Economy of Postconflict Nationalism in Bosnia-Herzegovina'. In B. Kissane (ed.), *After Civil War: Division, Reconstruction and Reconciliation in Contemporary Europe, 1918–2011*. Philadelphia: Pennsylvania University Press, pp. 187–213.

Laing, Roland D. 2010. *The Divided Self*. London: Penguin.

Laitin, David. 2007. *Nations, States and Violence*. Oxford: Oxford University Press.

Lake, David A. 2010. 'Building Legitimate States after Civil War'. In Caroline Hartzell, and Matthew Hoddie (eds.), *Strengthening Peace in Post-Civil War States: Transforming Spectators into Stakeholders*. Chicago: University of Chicago Press, pp. 29–51.

Le Marchand, René. 2013. 'War and Nationalism: The View from Central Africa'. In John A. Hall and Sinisa Malešević (eds.), *Nationalism and War*. Cambridge: Cambridge University Press, pp. 306–21.

Le Seur, James. D. 2010. *Between Terror and Democracy: Algeria since 1989*. London and New York: Zed Books.

Lehrer, Jonah. 2012. *Proust Was a Neuroscientist*. Edinburgh and New York: Canongate Books.

Lemay-Hebert, Nicolas. 2009. 'Statebuilding without Nation-building? Legitimacy, State Failure and the Limits of the Institutionalist Approach'. *Journal of Intervention and Statebuilding*, 3(1), 21–45.

Levene, Mark. 1998. 'Creating a Modern "Zone of Genocide": The Impact of Nation- and State-formation in Eastern Anatolia, 1873–1923'. *History of Genocide Studies*, 12(3), 393–433.

Liapis, Vayos. 2014. '"The Painful Memory of Woe": Greek Tragedy and the Greek Civil War in the Work of George Seferis'. *Classical Receptions*, 6(1), 74–103.

Licklider, Roy. 1995. 'The Consequences of Negotiated Settlements of Civil Wars, 1945–1993'. *American Political Science Review*, 89(3), 681–90.

Long, William J. and Peter Brecke. 2003. *War and Reconciliation: Reason and Emotion in Conflict Resolution*. Cambridge, MA: MIT Press.

Loraux, Nicole. 2006. *The Divided City: On Memory and Forgetting in Ancient Athens*. Cambridge, MA: MIT Press.

Luard, Evan. 1972. 'Civil Conflicts in Modern International Relations'. In Evan Luard (ed.), *The International Regulation of Civil Wars*. London: Thames and Hudson.

Lucan, *Civil War*. 1992. Trans. Susan H. Braund. Oxford: Oxford University Press.

Lucas, Robert E. B. 2006. 'Migration and Economic Development in Africa: A Review of Evidence'. *Journal of African Economies*, 15(2), 337–95.

Lukacs, John R. 2012. *The Future of History*. New Haven. Yale University Press.

Lund, Michael S. 2005. 'Greed and Grievance Diverted: How Macedonia Avoided Civil War, 1990–2001'. In Paul Collier and Nicholas Sambanis (eds.), *Understanding Civil War: Evidence and Analysis*. Vol. II. Washington DC: World Bank, pp. 231–59.

Machava, Benedito and Anna Pitcher. 2013. 'Comparative Politics of Angola, Mozambique and Guinea-Bissau'. Oxford Bibliographies (added 25 June). www.oxfordbibliographies.com.

MacIntyre, Alasdair. 1971. *A Short History of Ethics*. London: Routledge and Kegan Paul.

McPherson, James. 1988. *Battle Cry of Freedom: The Civil War Era*. New York and Oxford: Oxford University Press.

Madden, Deirdre. 2013. *Time Present and Time Past*. London: Faber and Faber.

Maier, Charles. 1981. 'The Two Postwar Eras and the Conditions for Stability in Twentieth-century Western Europe'. *American Historical Review*, 86(2), 327–52.

Makine, Andreï. 1997. *Le Testament française*. London: Hodder and Stoughton.

Makine, Andreï. 2002. *Requiem for the East*. London: Sceptre.

Makine, Andreï. 2013. *Brief Loves that Live Forever*. London: Maclehose Press.

Mališević, Siniša. 2010. *The Sociology of War and Violence*. Cambridge: Cambridge University Press.

Malouf, David. 2011. *The Happy Life: The Search for Contentment in the Modern World*. London: Chatto and Windus.

Manicas, P. T. 1982. 'War, Stasis and Greek Political Thought'. *Comparative Studies in Society and History*, 24(4), 673–88.

Mann, Michael. 1995. 'The Autonomous Power of the State: Its Origins, Mechanisms and Results'. *Archives européennes de sociologie*, 25, 185–213.

Mann, Michael. 2005. *The Dark Side of Democracy: Explaining Ethnic Cleansing*. Cambridge: Cambridge University Press.

Mannheim, Karl. 1940. *Man and Society in an Age of Reconstruction*. London: Routledge.

Marx, Karl. 1971. *The Paris Commune, 1871*. London: Sidgwick and Johnson.

May, Larry. 2012. *After War Ends: A Philosophical Perspective*. Cambridge: Cambridge University Press.

Mazower, Mark. 1998. *Dark Continent: Europe's Twentieth Century*. London: Penguin.

Mazower, Mark. 2001. *The Balkans: From the End of Byzantium to the Present Day*. London: Phoenix Press.

Melander, Erik, Magnus Öberg, and Jonathan Hall. 2009. 'Are New Wars More Atrocious? Battle Severity, Civilians Killed, and Forced Migration before and after the End of the Cold War'. *European Journal of International Relations*, 15(3), 505–36.

Müller, Jan Werner. 2011. *Contesting Democracy: Political Ideas in the Twentieth Century*. Princeton: Princeton University Press.

Navez Bouchanine, Françoise. 2002. *La Fragmentation en question: des villes entre fragmentation spatiale et fragmentation sociale?* Paris: L'Harmattan.

Naylor, Phillip C. 2012. 'Algeria'. *Oxford Bibliographies* (added 25 October). www.oxfordbibliographies.com.

Newman, Edward. 2009. 'Conflict Research and the "Decline" in Civil War'. *Civil Wars*, 11(3), 255–78.

Newman, Edward. 2014. *Understanding Civil War: Continuity and Change in Intrastate Conflict*. London: Routledge.

Ní Bheacháin, Caoilfhionn. 2010. 'Seeing Ghosts: Gothic Discourses and State Formation'. *Éire-Ireland*, 47(3), 37–64.

Nolte, Ernst. 1987. *Der europäische Bürgerkrieg, 1917–1945: Nationalsozialismus und Boleshewismus*. Berlin: Propylaen Verlagi.

Ober, Josiah. 2007. 'Social Science History, Historical Thinking and the Amnesty 403 BC'. In Josiah Ober, *Athenian Legacies: Essays on the Politics of Coming Together*. Princeton: Princeton University Press, pp. 171–83.

O'Connor, Frank. 2004. *The Lonely Voice: A Study of the Short Story*. New York: Melville House.

Olson, Mancur. 1993. 'Democracy, Dictatorship and Development'. *American Political Science Review*, 87(3), 567–76.

Orend, Brian. 2008. 'War'. *The Stanford Encyclopedia of Philosophy*. Ed. Edward N. Zalta. Online: Fall 2008 edition. http://plato.stanford.edu/archives/fall2008/entries/war/.

Ortega y Gasset, José. 2007. *Obras Completas*. Vol. 3. Madrid: Alianza.

Oz, Amos. 2012. *How to Cure a Fanatic: Israel and Palestine: Right or Wrong*. London: Vintage Books.

Paris, Roland. 2004. *At War's End: Building Peace after Conflict*. Cambridge: Cambridge University Press.

Parsons, Talcot. 1964. 'The Place of Force in Social Processes'. In Harry Eckstein (ed.), *Internal War: Problems and Approaches*. London: Collier-Macmillan, pp. 33–70.

Payne, Stanley. 2008. *Spain: A Unique History*. Madison: University of Wisconsin Press.

Payne, Stanley. 2011. *Civil War in Europe, 1905–1949*. Cambridge: Cambridge University Press.

Paz, Octavio. 2005. *The Labyrinth of Solitude*. London: Penguin.

Pearce, Justin. 2012. 'Control, Politics and Identity in the Angolan Civil War'. *African Affairs*, 111(444), 442–65.

Peceny, Mark and William Stanley. 2001. 'Liberal Social Reconstruction and the Resolution of Civil Wars in Central America'. *International Organisation*, 55(1), 149–82.

Pinker, Stephen. 2011. *The Better Angels of Our Nature: The Decline of Violence in History and its Cause*. London: Allen Lane.

Plato. 2012. *Republic*. Trans. and Intro. Christopher Rowe. London: Penguin

Porter, Dennis. 2014. *Haunted Journeys: Desire and Transgression in European Travel Writing*. Princeton: Princeton University Press.

Posen, Barry R. 1993. 'The Security Dilemma and Ethnic Conflict'. *Survival*, 35(1), 27–47.

Pouncey, Peter. R. 1980. *The Necessities of War: A Study of Thucydides Pessimism*. New York: Cambridge University Press.

Pound, Ezra. 2005. *Early Writings; Poems and Prose*. London: Penguin.

Price, Jonathan. 2001. *Thucydides and Internal War*. Cambridge: Cambridge University Press.

Rampton, David. 2011. 'Deeper Hegemony': the Politics of Sinhala Nationalist Authenticity and the Failures of Power-Sharing in Sri Lanka. Commonwealth & Comparative Politics, 49(2), pp. 245–273.

Ranzato, Gabriele. 1994. *Guerre fratricide: le guerre civili in eta contemporanea*. Torino: Bollati Boringhieri.

Regan, John M. 1999. *The Irish Counter-Revolution 1921–36*. Dublin: Gill and MacMillan.

Regan, Patrick. 2009. *Sixteen Million One: Understanding Civil War*. London: Paradigm.

Reilly, Ben. 2008. 'Post War Elections: Uncertain Turning Points of Transition'. In Anna K. Jarstad and Timothy D. Sisk (eds.), *From War to Democracy: Dilemmas of Peacebuilding*. Cambridge: Cambridge University Press, pp. 157–82.

Reinisch, Jessica. 2006. 'Comparing Europe's Post War Reconstructions: First Balzan Workshop'. *History Workshop Journal*, 61, 299–304.

Richani, Nazih. 2002. *Systems of Violence: The Political Economy of War and Peace in Colombia*. Albany: State University of New York.

Richards, Michael. 2014. 'State, Nation, and Violence in Spanish Civil War Reconstruction'. In B. Kissane (ed.), *After Civil War: Division, Reconstruction and Reconciliation in Contemporary Europe, 1918–2011*. Philadelphia, PA: Pennsylvania University Press, pp. 70–93.

Richards, Paul. 2011. 'A Systematic Approach to Cultural Explanations of War: Tracing Causal Processes in Two West African Insurgencies'. *World Development*, 39(2), 212–20.

Richmond, Oliver. P. (ed.). 2010. *Palgrave Advances in Peacebuilding*. Basingstoke: Palgrave MacMillan.

Richmond, Oliver, P. 2011. *Post Liberal Peace*. London: Routledge.

Richter, Melvin. 1995. *The History of Social and Political Concepts: A Critical Introduction*. New York and Oxford: Oxford University Press.

Ringmar, Erik. 1996. *Identity, Interest and Action: A Cultural Explanation of Sweden's Intervention in the Thirty Years War*. Cambridge: Cambridge University Press.

Roberts, David. 2011. 'Post Conflict Peacebuilding: Liberal Irrelevance and the Locus of Legitimacy'. *International Peacebuilding*, 18(4), 410–24.

Rogers, Mary. 2000. 'Alfred Schutz'. In George Ritzer (ed.), *The Blackwell Companion to Major Social Theorists*. London: Blackwell, pp. 367–88.

Romilly, Jacqueline de. 1991. *The Rise and Fall of States According to Greek Authors*. Ann Arbour: University of Michigan Press.

Rotberg, Robert. 2004. *When States Fail: Causes and Consequences*. Princeton and Oxford: Princeton University Press.

Rummel, Rudolph. J. 1994. *Death by Government*. New Brunswick, NJ: Transaction Publishers.

Rummel, Rudolph. J. 1995. 'Democracy, Power, Genocide and Mass Murder'. *Journal of Conflict Resolution*, 39(1), 3–26.

Salehyan, Idean. 2009. *Rebels without Borders. Transnational Insurgencies in World Politics*. Ithaca New York: Cornell University Press.

Sambanis, Nicos. 2004. 'What Is Civil War? Conceptual and Empirical Complexities of an Operational Definition'. *Journal of Conflict Resolution*, 48(6), 814–58.

Schama, Simon. 2002. *A History of Britain, II: The British Wars 1603–1776*. London: BBC.

Schmitt, Carl. 1996. *The Concept of the Political*. Trans. and Intro. Geroge Schwab. Chicago and London: Chicago University Press.

Seferis, George. 1995. *Complete Poems*. Trans., ed., and Intro. Edmund Keeley and Phillip Sherrard. London: Anvil Press.

Seifert, Ruth. 2015. 'Nationalism and Beyond: Memory and Identity in Postwar Kosovo/a'. In B. Kissane (ed.), *After Civil War: Division, Reconstruction and Reconciliation in Contemporary Europe, 1918–2011*. Philadelphia: Pennsylvania University Press, pp. 213–45.

Sevander, Mayme and Laurie Hertzel. 2004. *They Took My Father: Finnish Americans in Stalinist Russia*. Minneapolis. University of Minnesota Press.

Siani-Davies, Peter and Stefanos Katsikas. 2009. 'National Reconciliation after Civil War: The Case of Greece'. *Journal of Peace Research*, 46, 559–74.

Sidel, John T. 2012. 'The Fate of Nationalism in the New States: Southeast Asia in Comparative Historical Perspective'. *Comparative Studies in Society and History*, 54(1), 114–44.

Sills, David. L. (ed.). 1968. *The International Encyclopaedia of the Social Sciences.* New York: MacMillan.

Singer, J. D. and M. Small. 1982. *Resort to Arms: International and Civil Wars, 1816–1980.* Beverly Hills, CA: Sage.

Smith, Roger. 2013. *Between Mind and Nature: A History of Psychology.* London: Reaktion Books.

Sorokin, Pitirim Aleksandroviich. c.1925. *Sociology of Revolution.* Philadelphia and London: J. B. Lippincott Company.

Stedman, Stephen J. 1997. 'Spoiler Problems in Peace Processes'. *International Security,* 22(2), 5–33.

Stern, Geoffrey. 1993. *Leaders and Leadership.* London: BBC.

Strauss, Scott. 2012. 'Retreating from the Brink: Theorizing Mass Violence and the Dynamics of Restraint'. *Perspectives on Politics,* 10(2), 343–62.

Sztompka, Piotr. 2014. 'Cultural Trauma: The Other Face of Social Change'. *European Journal of Social Theory,* 3(4), 449–66.

Tarrow, Sidney. 2007. 'Inside Insurgencies: Politics and Violence in an Age of Civil War'. *Perspectives on Politics,* 5(3), 587–600.

Tetsas, Abdelaziz. 2010. 'Political Repression, Democratization and Civil Conflict in Post-independence Algeria'. *Democratization,* 9(4), 106–21.

Thucydides. 1972. *The History of the Peloponnesian War.* Trans. Rex Warner. London: Penguin.

Tilly, Charles. 1973. 'Does Modernization Breed Revolution?' *Comparative Politics,* 5(3), 425–47.

Tilly, Charles. 1995. 'War Making as Organised Crime'. In Peter Evans Dietrich Rueschmeyer, and Theda Skocpol (eds.), *Bringing the State Back In.* Cambridge: Cambridge University Press, pp. 169–86.

Tilly, Charles. 2002. 'Violence, Terror and Politics as Usual'. *Boston Review.* new. bostonreview.net/BR27.3/tilly.html.

UCDP. *Conflict Encylopaedia.* www.pcr.uu.se/data.

Üngör, Uğur Ümit. 2011. *The Making of Modern Turkey: Nation and State in Eastern Anatolia, 1913–1950.* Oxford: Oxford University Press.

United Nation Development Programmes. 1994. *Human Development Report.* New York: Oxford University Press.

US Bureau of Political-Military Affairs. 2009. *U.S. Government Counter-insurgency Guide.* http://www.state.gov/t/pm//ppa/pmppt.

Vermes, Pamela. 1988. *Buber.* Weidenfeld and Nicolson.

Vernon, Richard. 2012. *Historical Redress: Must We Pay for the Past?* London: Continuum.

Vilar, Pierre. 2011. *Breve Historia de la Cataluña.* Barcelona: Edicions UAB.

Vincent, Mary. 2010. 'Breaking the Silence: Memory and Oblivion since the Spanish Civil War'. In Efrat Ben-Ze'ev, Ruth Gino, and J. M. Winter. (eds.), *Shadows of War: A Social History of Silence in the Twentieth Century.* Cambridge: Cambridge University Press, pp. 47–68.

Volpi, Frederic. 2003. *Islam and Democracy: The Failure of Dialogue in Algeria.* London: Pluto Press.

Vulliamy, Ed. and Helena Smith. 2014. 'Athens 1944: Britain's Dirty Secret'. *The Guardian,* 30 November.

Wallerstein, Peter. 2011. *Understanding Conflict Resolution: War, Peace and the Global System.* 3rd. edn. London: Sage.

Walter, Barbara F. 1999. 'Designing Transitions from Civil War'. In Barbara F. Walter and Jack Snyder (eds.), *Civil Wars, Insecurity and Intervention.* New York: Colombia University Press, pp. 73–116.

Walter, Barbara F. 2002. *Committing to Peace: The Successful Settlement of Civil Wars.* Princeton: Princeton University Press.

Walz, Kenneth. 1979. *Theory of International Politics.* New York: McGraw Hill.

Wantchekon, Leonard. 2004. 'The Paradox of Warlord Democracy: A Theoretical Investigation'. *American Political Science Review,* 98(1), 17–33.

Weingast, Barry. 1997. 'The Political Foundations of Democracy and the Rule of Law'. *American Political Science Review,* 91, 245–63.

Williams, Raymond. 1977. *Marxism and Literature.* Oxford: Oxford University Press.

Wimmer, Andreas. 2013. *Waves of War: Nationalism, State Formation, and Ethnic Exclusion in the Modern World.* Cambridge: Cambridge University Press.

Woodward, Susan L. 1999. 'Bosnia and Herzegovina: How Not to End Civil War'. In Barbara. F. Walter and Jack Snyder (eds.), *Civil Wars, Insecurity and Intervention.* New York: Columbia University Press, pp. 73–115.

World Bank Group. 2002. 'Total Loans by Major Purpose in Millions of US Dollars, since Fiscal 1990'. *Encyclopaedia of the Nations.* http://www.nationsencyclopaedia.com/United-Nations-Related-Agencies/The World Bank.

Yeğen, Mesut. 2011. *Son Kürt Isyani.* Istanbul: Iletişim

Yekelchyh, Serhy. 2007. *Ukraine: Birth of a Modern Nation.* Oxford: Oxford University.

Zartman, William. 1993. '"The Unfinished Agenda": Negotiating Internal Conflicts'. In Roy Licklider (ed.), *Stopping the Killing: How Civil Wars End.* New York: New York University Press, pp. 20–37.

Zartman, William. 1994. *Collapsed States: The Disintegration and Restoration of Legitimate Authority.* Boulder, CO: Lynne Rienner Publishers.

Zartman, William. 1995. *Elusive Peace: Negotiating an End to Civil Wars.* Washington, DC: Brookings Institute.

Zürcher, Christoph et al. 2013. *Costly Democracy: Peacebuilding and Democratization after War.* Stanford: Stanford University Press.

Periodicals and newspapers

Civil Wars.

The Economist.

The Guardian.
The Guardian Weekly.
The Independent.
The New Scientist.
Irish Times.
The Times.

Specific media sources

Aykol, Mustafa. 2013. 'Turkey's Post-revolutionary Civil War'. *Hürriyet Daily News*, 21 December.

Bayne, Tim. 2013. 'Thought'. *New Scientist* 219 (2935) (special issue), 21 September.

Cameron, David. 2014. Full Speech at NATO Summit in Newport. 5 September. uneditedpoltiics.com

Cockburn, Patrick. 2014. 'Three Years after Gaddafi, Libya Is Imploding into Chaos and Violence'. *Independent on Sunday*, 16 March.

Margona, Maria. 2014. 'Cyprus: Divided Memory: United Future?' BBC Radio 4. Broadcast 11 May.

Masters, Brian. 2014. 'Interview with Dr. Anthony Clare'. *In the Psychiatrists Chair*. BBC Radio 4, 14 June (repeat podcast).

Mehta, Suketu. 2013. 'In the Violent Favelas of Brazil'. *The New York Review of Books*, LX(13), August/September.

Mert, Nuray. 2013. 'The Kurdish Predicament and 'the Radical Line'. *Hürriyet Daily News*, December 12.

Moriarty, Gerry. 2012. 'Northern Ireland's Quiet Revolution'. *Irish Times*, 17 November.

Morris, Errol. 2003. *The Fog of War: Eleven Lessons from the Life of Robert J. McNamara*. Documentary released December 2003.

Ruthven, Malise. 2013. 'Syria Is Not Alone in its Descent into Sectarianism'. *The Independent*, 27 June.

Sands, Sarah. 2013. 'We Must Apply the Lessons of Iraq in Syria'. *Evening Standard*, 11 June.

Seferis, George. 2014. 'Nobel Banquet Speech'. 10 December 1963. Nobel Media AB. Nobelprize.org.

Tuckman, Jo. 2014. '"Flee or Die": Child Migrants Driven North to Seek Refuge'. *The Guardian Weekly*, 18 July.

'How to Stop Fighting, Sometimes'. *The Economist*, 9 November 2013.

Wood, Peter and Seán Rocks. 2006. 'Rumours from Monaghan'. *Documentary on One*. Dublin: Radio Telefís Éireann.

INDEX

Note: Page numbers in **bold** type refer to maps and those in *italic* type refer to tables.